Contents

KU-035-376

....

A small bit of small print
Edexcel publishes Sample Assessment Material and the Specification on its website. This is the official content and this book should be used in conjunction with it. The questions in Now try this have been written to help you practise every topic in the book. Remember: the real exam questions may not look like this.

Edexcel

REVISE EDEXCEL AS/A LEVEL
Business

REVISION
GUIDE AND WORKBOOK

Series Consultant: Harry Smith

Author: Andrew Redfern

Also available to support your revision:

Revise A Level Revision Planner   9781292191546

The **Revise A Level Revision Planner** helps you to plan and organise your time, step-by-step, throughout your A level revision. Use this book and wall chart to mastermind your revision.

For the full range of Pearson revision titles across KS2, KS3, GCSE, Functional Skills, AS/A Level and BTEC visit: www.pearsonschools.co.uk/revise

Published by Pearson Education Limited, 80 Strand, London, WC2R 0RL.

www.pearsonschoolsandfecolleges.co.uk

Copies of official specifications for all Pearson qualifications may be found on the website: qualifications.pearson.com

Text and illustrations © Pearson Education Ltd 2018
Typeset and illustrated by Kamae Design
Produced by Out of House Publishing
Cover illustration by Eoin Coveney

The right of Andrew Redfern to be identified as author of this work has been asserted by him in accordance with the Copyright, Designs and Patents Act 1988.

First published 2018

21 20 19
10 9 8 7 6 5 4 3 2

British Library Cataloguing in Publication Data
A catalogue record for this book is available from the British Library

ISBN 9781292213217

Copyright notice
All rights reserved. No part of this publication may be reproduced in any form or by any means (including photocopying or storing it in any medium by electronic means and whether or not transiently or incidentally to some other use of this publication) without the written permission of the copyright owner, except in accordance with the provisions of the Copyright, Designs and Patents Act 1988 or under the terms of a licence issued by the Copyright Licensing Agency, Barnard's Inn, 86 Fetter Lane, London EC4A 1EN (www.cla.co.uk). Applications for the copyright owner's written permission should be addressed to the publisher.

Printed in the United Kingdom by Bell & Bain

Acknowledgements
The author and publisher would like to thank the following individuals and organisations for their kind permission to reproduce copyright material.

Text
Page 20: Reproduced with the permission of Bdaily Ltd; Page 21: Reproduced with the permission of House Simple Ltd.; Page 37: Reproduced with the permission of NETGEAR & Virtual Graffiti, Inc.; Page 121: Reproduced with the permission of THE FINANCIAL TIMES LTD.; Page 122: Reproduced with the permission of Forbes Media LLC; Page 197: Originally published by the Globalization and Localization Association (www.gala-global.org).

Photographs
(Key: b-bottom; c-centre; l-left; r-right; t-top)

123RF: 17l, Alamy Stock Photo: Riddypix 21, Richard Donovan 25tl, View Pictures Ltd 25tr, Chris Dorney 25cl, Donka Zheleva 25cr, Robert Evans 31, MSP Travel Images 54, Greg Balfour Evans 115, Lain Masterton 118, Allesalltag 174, AGF Srl 197, Getty Images: Gavin Roberts/Future Music Magazine 25b, Shutterstock: DutchScenery 11, Stokkete 17r, Gena Melendrez 27, Andrew Taylor 42, Aleksandar Karanov 52l, Wavebreakmedia 52r, Dan Kosmayer 59, Bezikus 68, JoeClemson 82, Silentwings 90, Khvost 91t, Philip Date 91b, Vima 108, Adam Isfendiyar 121, Xiaorui 137, Prasit Rodphan 193, Rawpixel.com 204, 4045 206tl, Monkey Business Images 206tr, S-F 206b, Igor Kardasov 207r, Sean Pavone 207l, William G Carpenter 214.

All other images © Pearson Education

Notes from the publisher
1. While the publishers have made every attempt to ensure that advice on the qualification and its assessment is accurate, the official specification and associated assessment guidance materials are the only authoritative source of information and should always be referred to for definitive guidance.

Pearson examiners have not contributed to any sections in this resource relevant to examination papers for which they have responsibility.

2. Pearson has robust editorial processes, including answer and fact checks, to ensure the accuracy of the content in this publication, and every effort is made to ensure this publication is free of errors. We are, however, only human, and occasionally errors do occur. Pearson is not liable for any misunderstandings that arise as a result of errors in this publication, but it is our priority to ensure that the content is accurate. If you spot an error, please do contact us at resourcescorrections@pearson.com so we can make sure it is corrected.

The market

Historically, markets are places where buyers and sellers come together to trade goods. However, in modern markets trade can exist via telephone, mail order or the internet. Different types of market have different characteristics with regard to how the market operates and the relationship between buyers and sellers.

The difference between risk and uncertainty

All businesses face the challenge of risk and uncertainty.

 Risk exists because entrepreneurs commit resources (such as money) that could be lost. Many businesses fail, and new start-ups face this risk.

 Businesses also must deal with **uncertainty**. Uncertainty exists because businesses operate in an ever-changing environment and are subject to changing external factors such as legal, economic and social factors.

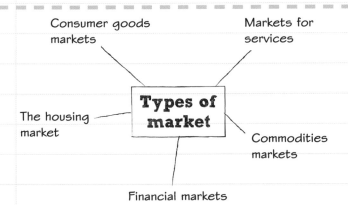

Consumer goods markets

Markets for services

Types of market

The housing market

Commodities markets

Financial markets

Marketing

Marketing involves a range of activities to support the process of communicating with customers with the goal of selling them products that meet their needs. Marketing involves:

- understanding customers' needs
- understanding the dynamics of the market (including competitors)
- developing successful products
- promoting the business and its products.

Mass and niche markets

- Targeting a large population of the market with a generic product
- Requires production on a large scale and investment in capacity
- Potential for high sales revenue
- May compete with many other businesses in the market
- Promotion will involve mass market techniques such as TV and newspapers
- Business will have to be competitive on price in order to succeed

Brand names are given to products to distinguish them from other products on the market. Brand names are used in particular by companies competing in the mass market.

Mass market

Niche market

Individual

- Targeting a small population of the market with a specialised product
- Production on a small scale (possibly bespoke)
- Low volumes but high profit margins
- Few competitors but limited number of potential customers
- Promotion through specialist mediums
- Direct marketing
- Business will have to compete on quality and customisation in order to succeed

In some industries technology has allowed businesses to profile individuals and customise their products so that they can target customers as individuals, such as online bespoke greeting cards.

Now try this

1 What is the purpose of marketing?
2 What is a niche market?

1

The dynamic nature of markets

Markets can have very different characteristics and over time change significantly. Businesses need to understand the changing nature of a dynamic market and must adapt in order to remain competitive.

Dynamic markets

Some markets stay relatively stable for a number of years, while others may be in a constant state of flux. One key characteristic of a market is its size. Opposite are some of the factors that contribute to this change. Overall, it is the needs and characteristics of customers that drive the dynamic changes in a market.

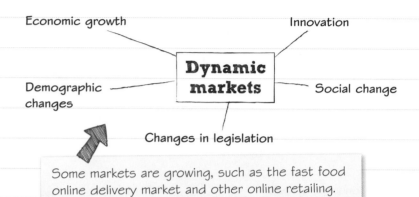

Some markets are growing, such as the fast food online delivery market and other online retailing. Others are in decline, such as the market for coal.

Market size and market share

The size of a market can be measured by **value** (total amount consumers spent on the product) or **volume** (total quantity sold by businesses).

Market share is the proportion of a particular market held by a business. Market share can be used as a measure of success. It is calculated as:

$$\frac{\text{Sales of a business}}{\text{Total sales in the market}} \times 100$$

Adapting in a dynamic market

The most successful businesses are those that can adapt and keep up with the changes in their market. Successful businesses adapt by:

1 Being flexible in the way they operate

2 Carrying out market research to have a better understanding of their customers

3 Investment in new technology, people and products

4 Continuous improvement – the ongoing desire to be better at what they do.

Competition

The level of competition in a market can vary. It has an impact on the way businesses operate and the experience of customers.

Businesses

- Can dominate the market
- Can afford inefficiencies
- Set high prices
- Little incentive to increase

- Incentive to innovate and get better
- Focus to improve efficiencies
- Competitive pricing

Low competition ◄──────────────────► High competition

- Limited choice
- High prices
- Poor service

- Lots of choice
- Good value for money
- Exciting new product development

Customers

Now try this

1 How can market size be expressed?
2 What are the benefits to customers of a highly competitive market?

Exam skills

The following exam-style questions explore the topics covered in Unit 1.1.1 and relate to the Round Round Records case study on page 11.

Worked example

What is meant by 'risk'? **(2 marks)**

Risk is the likelihood of a negative outcome happening and the chance of a business owner losing a resource they put in to the business. For example, the risk of losing capital invested in a business if it fails.

This type of question will only appear on the AS exam papers.

This question requires you to define a key term. The student has defined the term 'risk' and given a simple example in support.

Worked example

Explain how Round Round Records could adapt to the changing dynamics in the UK vinyl record market. **(4 marks)**

Round Round Records could adapt to the changing dynamics of the UK vinyl record market, such as the changing needs of customers and the size of the market, by carrying out market research. Carrying out market research would ensure that Rick understands his customers, such as the prices they are willing to pay and the types of records that are most popular. This would allow Round Round Records to ensure they are stocking products that are in high demand and setting prices at a point so the business is competitive. This may involve adapting to the trends in vinyl records or stocking the most popular artists.

The student has shown an understanding of the meaning of a dynamic market by giving specific examples. The student has also identified how Round Round Records could adapt (through market research) and applied their answer to the context of Round Round Records by analysing specific measures the business could take. To score all 4 marks the student should go on to develop a second strand to this answer.

Worked example

Although the UK market for vinyl records is growing, Rick still considers his business to operate in a niche market. Assess the importance of Round Round Records being a 'niche marketer' for the success of the business. **(10 marks)**

A niche market is a small segment of the market where customers have specialist needs. By operating in a niche market Round Round Records is able to avoid high levels of competition from other businesses that sell music, for example HMV and Amazon. As Round Round Records is a small business it is unable to compete on price with other larger companies, but it may be able to provide a specialist service for a small number of customers. This may allow the company to charge a higher price and maintain a loyal customer base because it is able to understand its customers better than a large business. However, as Round Round Records has a smaller number of potential customers, every sale is extremely important and it will have to rely on repeat purchasing for long-term success.

A student might approach this answer by discussing the benefits of operating in a niche market, but also consider the drawbacks. The student might also consider other factors that are similarly important to the success of Round Round Records.

This is a good opening paragraph to an answer. The student starts by defining what a niche market is. They have also identified a limitation of working in a niche market at the end of the paragraph. The student could now go on to discuss a second reason why working in a niche market is beneficial for Round Round Records.

Market research

Marketing research is the first stage of the marketing process and involves gathering and analysing qualitative and quantitative market data. Market research is the key indicator of customer needs, which drives decision-making across all business functions, not just marketing.

| Define problem/question | → | Develop market research plan | → | Collect data | → | Analyse data | → | Interpret and report findings |

The market research process

Questions market research will attempt to answer:

✓ Who are our potential customers?   ✓ Who are our competitors?

✓ What do our customers want?   ✓ What are customers willing to pay?

✓ How big is the market – is it growing? ✓ Is there a gap/opportunity in the market?

Primary market research

This is research collected first hand; it is:

👍 specific to the needs of the business

👍 more up to date and reliable

👍 better for two-way communication and follow-up questions

👍 often better if you want to collect qualitative data.

Sampling provides an insight into the market, but saves money as the whole population is not needed; a sample must be representative, unbiased and large enough to represent the whole market. Sampling can be:

👎 more time-consuming and therefore more costly

👎 difficult to conduct a large sample size.

Examples include questionnaires, consumer panels, interviews, focus groups and customer observations.

Secondary market research

This is research that already exists, conducted by another organisation; it is:

👍 easily accessible and a good starting point

👍 fast and less time-consuming

👍 often better if you want to collect quantitative data.

👎 Some data can be free but detailed reports can be expensive to purchase.

👎 It is not always up to date or specifically tailored to the business's needs.

Examples include market research reports, competitors, websites, government statistics and newspaper articles.

Product vs market orientation

| **Product orientated**
Focused on production efficiencies and the product itself (product features, profit margins and efficiency). | **VS** | **Market orientated**
Focused on consumer needs.
Understanding customers and developing products that meet their needs (customer attitudes, characteristics and how the product is used). |

Most successful businesses will tend to have a market orientation. This is because businesses can only succeed in a competitive market if they meet the needs of customers better than their rivals. However, some businesses still approach the market with product orientation if there is relatively little competition or information available to customers.

Now try this

1 Why is market research important for a business?
2 What is the best form of market research for a new business start-up?

The limitations of market research

There are a number of tools that a business might adopt to collect and analyse market research. However, the quality of the market research and the process of analysis can often be flawed.

Limitations

Market research can have several limitations.

👎 It is often biased.

👎 A small sample limits the reliability of the research.

👎 Causality can be hard to identify.

👎 Collecting it is very time-consuming.

Uses of market research

Product development

Cash-flow forecasting

Budgeting

Uses

Workforce forecast

Production forecast

Developing marketing activities – such as promotional campaigns

Sales forecasting

Sampling

Sampling involves selecting a representative group of people from the target population.

👍 It is quicker and easier than trying to collect research from everyone – this is often impossible!

👍 The bigger the sample size, the more representative it will be.

> If the sample size is not representative of the market then the market research will always be limited.

Correlation

Correlation helps businesses understand the relationship between two factors. If a business can understand the key factors determining demand for its products, then it can manipulate these to achieve greater sales. However, a strong correlation does not necessarily mean that one variable leads to another (correlation not causality).

ICT and market research

ICT can support the collection and analysis of market research data in a number of ways. Specific IT tools might include:

- collecting data through websites
- social media/networking
- analysing information in databases.

Technology and market research

Technology can make the collection of market research data much faster and more specific to individual customers. This data can also be processed more effectively so that trends, patterns and correlations can be uncovered and used to help make marketing decisions. For example, store and loyalty cards are an extremely effective way for businesses to collect data on their customers.

advantage card
More points. More treats.
633035 6000 1000 1932 7

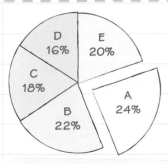

D 16%   E 20%

C 18%

B 22%   A 24%

The value of market segmentation

Market segmentation allows a business to:

👍 differentiate itself from its competitors

👍 develop and build its brand

👍 identify and satisfy the needs of a specific group of customers

👍 reach its customers with relevant marketing activities such as advertising

👍 focus the business activities

👍 build loyalty towards its brand and products.

> The process of dividing customers within a market into distinguishable groups based on their characteristics and needs to allow positioning of the business and customer targeting to take place.

Now try this

1 What are the limitations of market research?
2 What is the purpose of sampling?

Market positioning

A business will consider how it positions itself within a market in relation to its competitors. The process of positioning involves deciding on the nature and characteristics of the products and services it sells and who its target market is. One tool a business can use to carry out this process is a market map.

Market maps

This is a technique used to understand how products/businesses are viewed relative to competitors, based on two relevant characteristics.

👍 It helps businesses decide whether to set up in a market, asking the question: Is there a 'gap'/opportunity?

👍 It is a useful process for comparing similarities and differences between businesses – market positioning.

👍 It helps a business gain a better understanding of its competition.

👍 It is useful as a market research tool to gain an understanding of customer perceptions.

Positioning

Factors a business may consider when positioning a product or the business are:

1 The attributes of the product – such as features and quality

2 The origin of the product/business – such as its heritage

3 The classification of the product or business – e.g. a five-star hotel

Market mapping

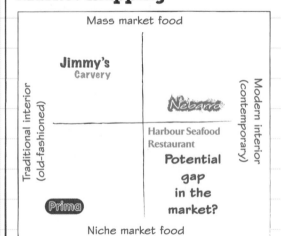

Market mapping is a technique used to understand how products/businesses are viewed relative to competitors based on two relevant characteristics. Market mapping:

✓ helps businesses decide whether to set up in a market – is there a 'gap'/opportunity?

✓ is a useful process for comparing similarities and differences between businesses – market positioning

✓ helps a business gain a better understanding of its competition

✓ is useful as a market research tool to gain an understanding of customer perceptions.

A limitation might be that it only considers two main variables – markets and customer perceptions are often very complex.

Head-to-head competition

There doesn't always have to be a gap in the market for a business to be successful. Businesses can target the same customers as other businesses and be successful if there is enough demand in the market (sufficient customers) or they are able to meet customer needs better than their competitors, for example by offering more choice or better customer service.

Limitations of market maps

Market maps are based on positioning against two variables. However, perceptions of customers, other businesses and society are often very complex and may not fit into this model. Furthermore, a market map is a planning tool and different stakeholders may have a different opinion of where the business is or should be positioned.

Now try this

1 How could a large supermarket chain use market mapping?
2 Why should a business be cautious when using market mapping?

Competitive advantage and differentiation

A competitive advantage is a set of unique features of a business and its products that are perceived by customers as significant and superior to the competition. Businesses that have a competitive advantage will often differentiate their products from those of their competitors.

Differentiation

Product differentiation is the process of making a product different from a competitor's products. Differentiation may also be applied to a business's brand. Differentiation may be achieved through:

- developing unique brand characteristics
- creating unique product features
- providing a unique/better customer experience
- building good relationships with customers
- offering a price that undercuts the competition.

Differentiation is closely linked to the concept of a unique selling point (USP). A USP is something that sets the business apart and makes it distinguishable from any other business.

Differentiation vs head-to-head competition

The process of differentiation means that a business does not need to position itself alongside rival firms. Therefore, they do not need to compete head on.

Head-to-head competition

| Business | Price > < Price | Competitor |

Differentiation

Quality / Customer service

Businesses that compete head on often compete on price if their products or services are very similar.

Competitive advantage

Competitive advantage exists where a business creates value for its customers that is greater than the costs of supplying those benefits and that is greater than that offered by competitors. A sustainable competitive advantage can only be achieved through three areas of practice:

1   **Innovation** – this is the ability of a business to create new and unique processes and products. These can sometimes be legally protected through a patent.

2   **Architecture** – this refers to the relationships within a business that create synergy and understanding between suppliers, customers and the employees of a business.

3   **Reputation** – brand values are hard to replicate and may take years to develop.

Each factor can lead to a **sustainable competitive advantage** because they are all unique, not easily copied and may take a long time to achieve. Competitive advantage gives a business a basis for competition and a way of adding value that other businesses cannot imitate – a reason for customers to choose the business over its rivals. However, over time each of the factors above can gradually erode, such as relationships in a business as the workforce changes over time or as a valuable patent expires.

Now try this

1 How might a business develop a unique selling point?
2 How can a business achieve a sustainable competitive advantage?

Adding value

Adding value is the basic purpose of all businesses. A business will start with raw materials, take them through a process and then sell them to customers at a price greater than the combined cost of the raw materials and the process involved in the transformation. Businesses will look to find new ways to add value to what they do.

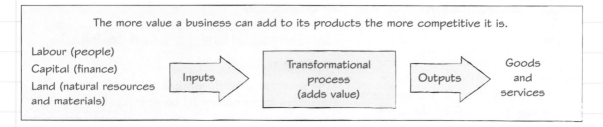

The more value a business can add to its products the more competitive it is.

Labour (people)
Capital (finance)
Land (natural resources and materials) → Inputs → Transformational process (adds value) → Outputs → Goods and services

Different ways of adding value

A business may add value in a number of ways:

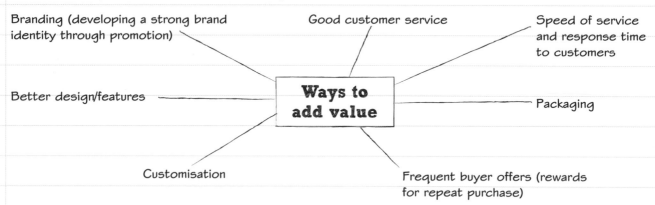

Branding (developing a strong brand identity through promotion)

Good customer service

Speed of service and response time to customers

Better design/features

Ways to add value

Packaging

Customisation

Frequent buyer offers (rewards for repeat purchase)

Relationship to profit

Adding value is closely linked to the concept of profit. The more value a business can add, the higher the price and the greater the profit margin. The challenge for any business is adding value without adding too many additional costs.

A business will be competitive where the value it adds to its products and services matches the price that it charges customers.

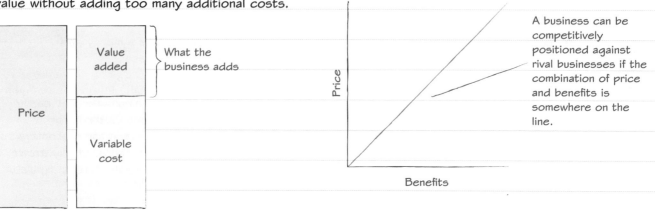

Price | Value added / Variable cost

What the business adds

Price (y-axis) / Benefits (x-axis)

A business can be competitively positioned against rival businesses if the combination of price and benefits is somewhere on the line.

Now try this

1 How might speed of service and response time to customers help a business add value?
2 What is the relationship between added value and price?

Exam skills

The following exam-style questions explore the topics covered in Units 1.1.2 and 1.1.3 and relate to the Round Round Records case study on page 11.

Worked example

Explain how Rick White could use IT to carry out market research. **(4 marks)**

Rick White could use IT to support his market research by analysing the number of searches for different bands and records on his website. This would allow him to gain an understanding of potential demand for different types of music. Rick can then use the market research to ensure he is stocking the most appropriate music. Therefore this will allow Rick order to maximise sales.

An 'Explain' question requires you to give a reason/method or point and then build your answer with linked strand development. Your answer should also be in context.

The student has linked their answer to the context by referring to Rick's website.

Worked example

Assess **two** factors that Rick White might consider when positioning Round Round Records. **(8 marks)**

... Rick may also position his business based on price. Price is an important factor for all businesses when positioning themselves in the market. If Rick decides on a high price then he must be able to justify this by ensuring his business provides sufficient benefits to the customer, such as through excellent customer service. Rick might choose to do this if he believed a rival business had set a relatively low price point for their records. This might mean that customers who are willing to pay a higher price for a better service would be attracted to Round Round Records instead of Rick's rivals.

This is the second paragraph of the student's answer. In the first paragraph they might have discussed how the type of music could be used to position Rick's business against the competition. For example, Round Round Records might specialise in rock music.

The final paragraph would need to explain how important these factors are and identify which of the two is the most relevant for Round Round Records.

Worked example

Access the importance of Round Round Records using market mapping to analyse the local record market. **(10 marks)**

... In conclusion, market mapping is a useful tool to help understand the perception customers have of a business and help a business position itself within a market. However, as Round Round Records sells records that are a standard product it might be difficult to identify suitable variables to base the market map on. There aren't any competitors locally for the business to be compared against either.

Ideally this answer should consider the limitations of market mapping as well as the benefits for Round Round Records.

This would be the conclusion to this question. The student has started by summarising both sides of the argument. The student could have also gone on to suggest other tools or market research techniques that might be as/more useful than market mapping. This would have been a recommendation and a good feature to include in their evaluations.

Had a go ☐   Nearly there ☐   Nailed it! ☐

Exam-style practice

The following questions refer to the content covered in Unit 1.1. For these questions refer to the Round Round Records case study on page 11.

1 a) What is meant by market share?   **(2 marks)**

   b) What is meant by competitive advantage?   **(2 marks)**

You need to show knowledge and understanding of the word in your definition.

2 Explain **one** factor that would suggest that the UK music industry is a dynamic market.   **(4 marks)**

Start by identifying a characteristic of a dynamic market and then use the context to link your answer to Round Round Records.

3 Explain **one** limitation of the market research that Rick White has carried out into the UK music industry.   **(4 marks)**

What sort of research has Rick carried out? What are its limitations and how might this compare to other approaches?

4 Assess the benefits of Rick White using a market map to analyse his competition.   **(10 marks)**

Analyse how Rick might benefit from using a market map.

Rick White is considering two options to improve the offer Round Round Records gives its customers. The two options are to modernise the interior of the record store or to provide a record player repair service.

5. Evaluate these **two** options and recommend which would be the most effective at adding value to his business.   **(20 marks)**

Remember to apply your answer to the case study. You should provide recommendations on the best option and justify why it will add more value than the other.

Case study

Round Round Records

Rick White had a passion for music and had played in bands since he was a teenager. Rick had always collected vinyl records which he bought from around the world. In 2014 Rick decided to set up his own record store, Round Round Records, specialising in vintage records and music memorabilia. Originally Rick decided to set his business up as a sole trader and invested £20 000 from the short-lived success of his band to rent premises and purchase stock. Before opening his store, Rick carried out some secondary market research into the UK music industry.

Figure 1: UK music industry data 2015
Key facts

- Music streaming – the rate of music streaming doubled in 2014, with 14.8 billion tracks streamed digitally.
- CD sales – the ongoing shift to digital from CD slowed in 2014, which may suggest LP or CD collecting is more resilient than expected.
- In 2015 the UK's first vinyl chart was launched following the growth of vinyl album and single sales.
- Vinyl record sales reached a 20-year high in 2015.

Figure 2: Vinyl record sales figures 2010–2014

Year	2010	2011	2012	2013	2014
Sales (000s)	234	337	388	780	1288
% share of UK Albums Market	0.2%	0.3%	0.4%	0.8%	1.5%

Source: Official Charts Company 2015

Although the UK music market continues to grow, a significant proportion of album sales are now bought digitally or streamed via music download sites. The vinyl market is certainly having a comeback with sales tripling over the past three years. However, it is still a niche market and accounts for a small segment of the overall market.

The store Rick rented was on the old high street in Derby, which suited the retro nature of his business. Rick anticipated his main customer to be men aged 35 plus, but found that the average age of his customers was early twenties, both men and women, and typically university students. Rick believed that customers visited the stores as much for the shopping experience and the opportunity to meet other enthusiasts, as to buy the records.

Rick knew that he would have to have an online presence if his business was going to succeed and set up a website with an online blog, stock inventory and e-commerce facility. Within weeks Rick found that his website was receiving a lot of hits, especially his vinyl record blog. By the end of 2015 his website accounted for 60 per cent of all sales.

With the changing trend in the market, Rick found that he was able to charge a premium price for his rare vinyl albums that many of his collectors wanted. The most expensive was a rare Led Zeppelin album that sold for £1000.

Demand

Demand is the amount of a product that consumers are willing and able to purchase at a given price. Demand is important because it affects the attractiveness of a market and the potential for sales.

Demand curves

Demand can be shown on a graph. Y = price, X = quantity demanded. The demand curve always slopes downward because the quantity demanded is lower at a higher price. In most markets, as price falls the quantity demanded will increase. A change in price up will result in the level of demand falling.

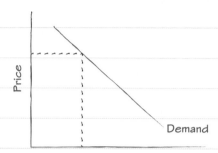

The lines on demand and supply graphs are referred to as curves even though they are drawn as straight lines for simplicity.

A demand curve – draw lines to show a point along the curve where price and quantity meet to determine a given amount of demand.

What factors increase or decrease demand

Common factors that can shift the demand curve to the left (decrease) or right (increase) include:

Price of substitute products – if a supermarket own-brand version of a branded item has a lower price this will affect demand of the branded item.

Seasonality – this is demand for goods at different times of the year, e.g. Christmas goods, garden goods in spring.

External shocks – these are factors beyond the control of a business, such as: arrival of a competitor in the market; government legislation; economic climate; social factors, e.g. increase in social media; environmental factors, e.g. concern for the environment.

Price of complementary products – sometimes products are bought together, such as burgers and tomato ketchup. If the price of burgers goes down then more ketchup might be bought.

Factors affecting demand

Demographics – the age of a population or its make up (more women than men) will influence the demand for certain goods.

Advertising and branding – if there is a successful advertising campaign the demand for some items might go up.

Changes in consumer incomes (normal goods) – if salaries go up then the demand for eating out or holidays will go up.

Fashion, tastes and preferences – these will increase sales in certain items, such as types of cars, clothing, types of foods.

Drawing shifts

Any of the factors above can create a shift in demand. For example, successful advertising will shift the demand curve to the right. Demand is higher at any given price point.

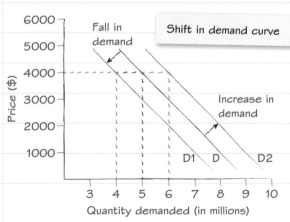

The diagram shows how you should draw an increase or decrease in the demand curve. This is also known as a shift.

Now try this

1 What will happen to demand as price falls?
2 Explain **one** factor that could shift the demand curve to the right.
3 What is an external shock?

Supply

Supply is the amount of a product that suppliers will offer to the market at a given price. The higher the price of a particular good or service the more that will be offered (supplied) to the market. Supply is directly influenced by how accessible and profitable a market is for suppliers (businesses).

Supply curves

As with demand, supply can be shown on a graph. The supply curve always slopes upwards because the quantity supplied will increase as the price rises. In most markets a change in price will alter the point of supply along the curve.

In some cases, supply will not change no matter what the price is. For example, the number of seats at a concert will not change.

A supply curve – draw lines to find a point along a curve where price and quantity meet to determine a given amount of supply.

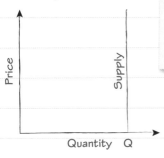

A graph showing how there is a fixed number of seats in a concert hall so regardless of price the supply will not change.

What factors increase or decrease supply?

Common factors that can shift the supply curve to the left (decrease) or right (increase) include:

Changes in the costs of production, such as wages, raw materials, energy, rent and machinery (left or right)

Introduction of new technology making production process more efficient (right)

Factors affecting supply

Indirect taxes (left or right)

External shocks such as world events/wars (left) and weather effects (left or right)

Government subsidies (support for suppliers) (right)

Drawing shifts

Any of the factors above can create a shift in supply: higher prices mean profit per item increases, so the incentive to firms to supply increases, therefore supply shifts right.

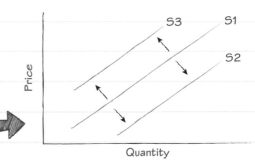

The diagram shows how you should draw an increase or decrease in the supply curve. This is also known as a shift.

Now try this

1 What will happen to quantity supplied if price rises?
2 Describe **one** factor that could shift the supply curve to the right.
3 When might supply not be affected by price?

Markets

The price in a market is set where the wishes of consumers are matched exactly with those of producers. This is known as the equilibrium (or market clearing price) and is where supply and demand meet.

Interaction of supply and demand

In the graph on the right, the price is set by the market at £2.30. At this price, supply meets demand and the market will clear. If the price increases, say to £5 there would be surplus (excess supply) because there would not be enough willing buyers at this price. If the price fell to £1 there would be a shortage (excess demand) as many buyers would be happy to purchase goods at this price, but not enough producers would be willing and able to supply at this price. Over time a market will always find its equilibrium price.

At prices below the equilibrium excess demand exists. At prices above the equilibrium excess supply exists.

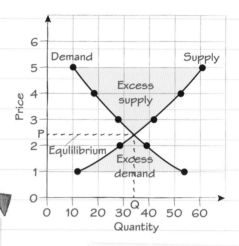

A supply and demand graph

Changes in demand

If demand increases (D1 to D2) then prices will rise (P1 to P2). This is because producers will react by putting up their prices. The opposite will happen if there is a fall in demand.

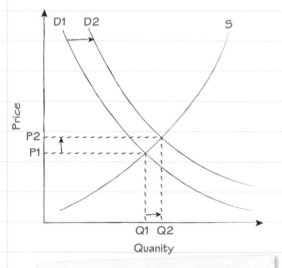

A graph showing a shift in demand to the right leading to an increase in price.

Changes in supply

If supply increases (S1 to S2) then prices will fall (P1 to P2). This is because there will be excess supply and producers will lower their price in order to sell all of their goods. The opposite will happen if there is a fall in supply.

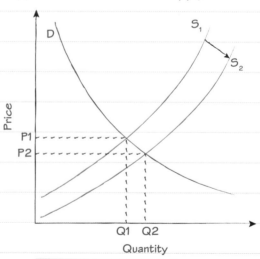

A graph showing a shift in supply to the right leading to a fall in price.

Now try this

1 What is meant by excess supply?
2 Why will all markets eventually find their equilibrium price?

Exam skills

The following exam-style questions explore the topics covered in Units 1.2.1, 1.2.2 and 1.2.3. The questions refer to the case study extracts on pages 20 and 21.

Worked example

With reference to Extract C, explain one factor that could have led to an increase in supply of houses in the UK. **(4 marks)**

One factor that may have led to the increase of house supply across the UK is the fact that there could be a relaxation in planning laws. This will encourage companies like Taylor Wimpey to put in more planning applications and purchase more land because it is less time-consuming and costly to do so. This will lead to the 3.7% rise in house supply because Taylor Wimpey will be able to build houses on plots that were previously not available when the planning permission was stricter.

The student has used the extract well to identify a reason for the increase in supply. They have explained this with linked strands of development.

Worked example

With reference to Extract B, construct a supply and demand diagram to illustrate the impact on house price of a fall in supply.

(4 marks)

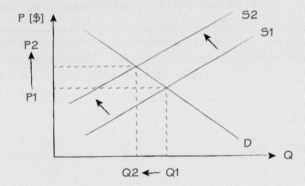

The student has clearly labelled the diagram and used P1 and P2 to show the direction of the change in price.

Worked example

Assess the impact on house prices in Battersea of Taylor Wimpey building 2000 new homes. **(10 marks)**

The introduction of 2000 new homes in Battersea will increase the supply of homes in the area. Increasing supply in a market will have the impact of lowering the price if demand remains at the same level. However, this will all depend on whether there was excess demand in the first place as there often is across the UK housing market.

Alternatively, 2000 new homes could actually increase the price of homes in the area. This is because the new homes will 'revamp' the surrounding area and make it a more desirable area for people to live.

The student has considered both perspectives and given an argument as to why house prices could fall or rise but it needs further development.

Price elasticity of demand

Price elasticity of demand is the responsiveness of quantity demanded to a change in price.

The impact of price elasticity of demand (PED)

For some goods a price change will result in a larger percentage change in the quantity demanded and for others a smaller percentage change in the quantity demanded. The graph opposite represents these two types of response. A steep demand curve represents a relatively price inelastic product (product A), whereas, a price elastic product will have a flat demand curve. For product B, quantity demanded is more responsive to any change in price.

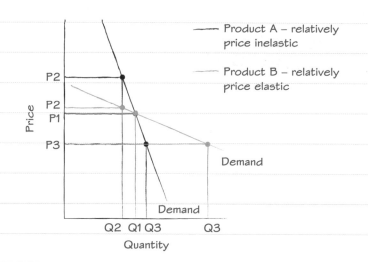

Calculating PED

$$\text{Price elasticity of demand} = \frac{\text{Percentage change in quantity demanded}}{\text{Percentage change in price}}$$

Above 1 demand is price elastic and below 1 demand is price inelastic.

Ignore the negative when calculating PED. Just focus on the decimal number. A change in price for a price inelastic product will have a smaller percentage change in the quantity demanded.

1 is the turning point where demand becomes price inelastic or elastic.

Interpreting PED

	Price elastic	Price inelastic
Price increase	Leads to a bigger percentage decrease in quantity demanded. Revenues fall.	Leads to a smaller percentage decrease in quantity demanded. Revenues rise.
Price decrease	Leads to a bigger percentage increase in quantity demanded. Revenues rise.	Leads to a smaller percentage increase in quantity demanded. Revenues fall.

PED scale

>1 ←————————————→ O
1

Highly price elastic   price elastic   Price inelastic

Impact on decision-making

Where demand is price inelastic a business may be able to raise prices to increase revenue, because there will be a smaller percentage change in the quantity demanded than the percentage change in revenue per unit.

Where a product is price elastic a business will have to think very carefully about any changes it makes to its pricing strategy. Lowering prices could significantly increase the quantity demanded, therefore boosting sales revenue, as long as competitors don't react.

Factors influencing PED

These include:

- number of substitutes/competitors
- relative effort/costs of switching to another product
- extent to which the product is considered a necessity
- perceived value of the brand
- time – the PED for a product will tend to fall over time as consumers find substitutes
- percentage of income spent on the product.

Now try this

1. What does a PED of 0.2 mean?
2. What impact will successful branding have on the PED of a product?

Income elasticity of demand

Income elasticity of demand is the responsiveness of demand to a change in incomes.

Elastic and inelastic demand

The amount of income that consumers have to spend is a key factor influencing the demand for a product. Income elasticity of demand (sometimes called YED) measures the responsiveness of demand to a change in incomes.

A family holiday has income elastic demand.

Necessity food items may have income inelastic demand.

Many goods have **income elastic demand**. This means that a percentage change in incomes would lead to a proportionate or greater percentage change in the quantity demanded. Goods that have income elastic demand include cars, TVs, holidays and clothing.

Most goods are **normal goods**. This is where an increase in incomes leads to an increase in the quantity demanded. Normal goods have a positive income elasticity of demand.

Some products have **income inelastic demand**. This is where a percentage change in incomes will lead to a proportionately lower change in the quantity demanded. These products might be considered necessities, such as some food types.

For **inferior goods**, an increase in incomes will lead to a fall in demand. The reverse is also true – a decrease in incomes will lead to an increase in demand. Inferior goods have a negative income elasticity of demand.

Calculating income elasticity of demand (YED)

$$\text{Income elasticity of demand} = \frac{\text{Percentage change in quantity demanded}}{\text{Percentage change in incomes}}$$

Value line

YED scale >1   1   0

For income elasticity greater than 1, demand is income elastic. For income elasticity less than 1, demand is inelastic.

Impact on decision-making

Businesses that sell goods with high income elasticity will be affected by the cyclical nature of the economy. In a recession, demand will fall significantly for products that have a high income elasticity of demand.

Businesses selling goods that have income inelastic demand are likely to find demand, and therefore sales, more stable during economic shifts.

Regardless of whether a business's goods are elastic or inelastic it should use economic factors to help plan for changes in production. For example, a supermarket stocking luxury products with a high YED may switch to value brands with a lower YED or even inferior goods.

Factors influencing income elasticity of demand

These include:

- whether the product is considered a necessity
- whether the product is considered a luxury
- the price relative to people's incomes (%). (The YED of a chocolate bar is relatively inelastic as it costs a small percentage of most people's income.)

Now try this

1 What is meant by a YED of +1.5?
2 How might a business selling products that have income inelastic demand respond to an economic recession?

Exam skills

The following questions use knowledge and skills covered in Units 1.2.4 and 1.2.5 and refer to the case studies on pages 20–21.

Worked example

Houses are considered a normal good that are relatively price elastic.

With reference to Extract B, explain one impact of house price changes between October 2015 and February 2017.   **(4 marks)**

Between 2015 and 2017 house prices have risen, but by a lesser extent than the previous year. This means that the rate of growth has slowed down, but as prices are rising demand might fall as consumers will be waiting to sell their house and some people may be waiting for house prices to fall. As a result fewer houses will be sold in the UK where there is plentiful supply.

Be careful when reading from graphs. Extract B shows a decrease between 2015 and 2017, but the Y axis shows that the graph is measuring percentage change. As the graph does not fall below 0 (negative growth) prices are still rising, but at a slower rate.

Worked example

Median disposable income for the poorest fifth of UK households rose by £700 (5.1%) between 2014/15 and 2015/16; in contrast the income of the richest fifth of households fell by £1000 (1.9%) over the same period.

https://www.ons.gov.uk/peoplepopulationandcommunity/
personalandhouseholdfinances/incomeandwealth/bulletins/
householddisposableincomeandinequality/financialyearending2016

Assess the impact of income changes in the UK on the demand for houses on the new Battersea development.   **(10 marks)**

An 'assess' question requires you to 'give a balanced assessment with wide ranging and well contextualised arguments leading to a supported judgement'.

As the demand for houses is income elastic we would expect to see the demand for houses rise on the Battersea development because a greater proportion of consumers will be willing and able to purchase the new properties. Furthermore, incomes have risen in the poorest fifth of the UK and the Battersea regeneration area is one of the capital's 'worst sink estates' and this would suggest that a significant proportion of this group will live in the area.

Wherever possible you should use quantitative and qualitative information. Look at Extracts A–C and see what quantitative information the student could have brought into their answer.

However, this will very much depend on the actual price of the new houses in Battersea. Many of this group may still not be able to afford these houses. An average income rise of £700 is not a lot and it may not be enough for some people to purchase their own home, unless they are given some sort of subsidy.

In conclusion, when consumers have rising incomes they will purchase more goods that are traditionally income elastic such as five-bedroom luxury houses. Furthermore, as incomes rise people become more confident in their spending and this is likely to encourage people to take out a mortgage to buy their own home providing interest rates are not too high.

Exam-style practice

The following exam-style questions refer to the content covered in Unit 1.2. For these questions refer to Extract A and Extract B in the case study on page 20.

1   Explain **one** factor that could lower demand in the UK housing market.   **(4 marks)**

A common misconception is that supply will affect demand. It does not – consider factors such as incomes and advertising.

2   Explain **one** way that a government subsidy for house builders could influence supply in the housing market.   **(4 marks)**

A government subsidy involves spending in a market to support buyers or sellers. The purpose of a subsidy is to create an incentive for suppliers to increase supply.

3   Assess the factors that may affect the price elasticity of a Taylor Wimpey Home.   **(10 marks)**

Remember to use information from the case study.

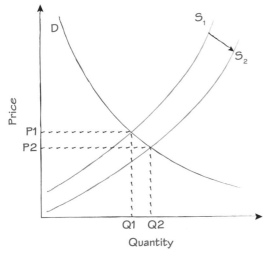

The supply and demand chart above represents changes in the UK housing market.

Start by interpreting what the supply and demand diagram shows. What does P1 to P2 represent?

4   Assess the impact that these changes would have on a firm like Taylor Wimpey.   **(12 marks)**

How might this affect the competitiveness of a firm such as Taylor Wimpey? How might it respond?

Case study

Extract A

Taylor Wimpey to deliver 2000 homes as part of massive Battersea regeneration

Housebuilder Taylor Wimpey has been revealed as the preferred bidder for a massive regeneration project in Battersea that will see a complete and utter revamp of some of the capital's worst sink estates.

The £1bn project focuses on a 32-acre site at Winstanley and York Road, which will create a new mixed-use neighbourhood on the site of the current council housing estates, delivering around 2000 new homes along with new retail, leisure and commercial space.

Extract B

Home Proud is one of the UK's largest house builders.

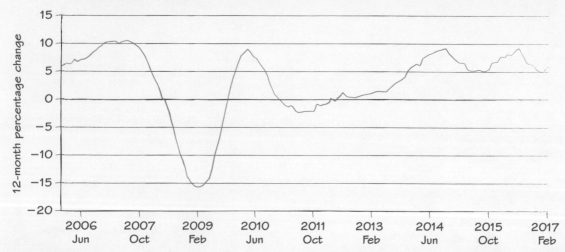

Annual house price rates of change, UK all dwellings from January 2006 to February 2017

Another sign of moderating house price growth in the UK, the Office for National Statistics says prices rose by 5.8 per cent in the year to February, below forecasts among economists for a rise of 6.1 per cent. That's a rise from the previous month's 5.3 per cent ascent, but that in itself represents a heavy downward revision; previously the ONS had estimated January's figure at 6.2 per cent. It is also below the average for 2016 of 7.3 per cent. The broad direction is still clear.

Case study

Extract C

UK property supply rose by 3.7% in March compared to February, the third month in a row that new listings have increased. Property listings rose in more than three-quarters (76%) of towns and cities in March. Two Scottish towns, Stirling and Dundee, saw the biggest hikes in supply, up 87.8% and 70.9% respectively.

One industry expert commented: "Although new listings were up in March, we'd have hoped to see more sellers, particularly in London, putting their homes on the market as we enter the Spring's peak property selling season.

We need a supply boost in April, because the demand from buyers remains strong and thanks to the continued competitive mortgage deals still on offer, they are more than committed to purchasing."

Product/service design

Businesses must consider the 'whole product' during development, along with the three factors that make up the design mix. All products must have a balance of **aesthetics** (design and appearance), **function** and **cost**. Amending any one of these features can have a detrimental impact on the other two. For example, improving the design could reduce the functionality of the product, or improving the functionality could increase costs.

The design mix

Refers to the design, style and appearance of a product. Aesthetics is about making products desirable.

Refers to the **benefits** that a product or service provides. It includes how well a product meets a need or solves the problem for which it was intended.

Encapsulates all production costs of a product. Specifically, the cost per unit.

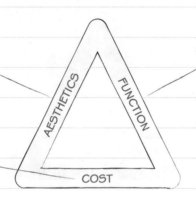

Designing products to meet social trends

Modern society is far more environmentally conscious than ever before and demands products that are sustainable with a limited impact on the environment. Businesses are more likely to succeed when developing products that address the issues of resource depletion. These could be:

- products designed for waste minimisation
- products designed for re-use
- products designed to be recycled (or produced from recycled materials)
- products sourced ethically (e.g. Fairtrade products).

Some businesses will use ethical sourcing to reflect social trends as more customers become aware of the need to protect the environment. Businesses will only use materials and services from suppliers who care and respect the environment. Ethical sourcing also involves paying workers a fair wage and making sure the working practices of the suppliers are ethical, such as not using child labour.

The challenges of product design

Product design involves carefully balancing the three elements of the design mix. Adapting any one of these features can have a detrimental impact on the other two. For example, anything that is aimed at reducing costs, in order to improve the profit margin, could have a detrimental effect on the functionality or design.

The benefits of adapting designs to changes in social trends

1 Reducing waste helps businesses cut costs.

2 Reflecting social trends through product design means they are more likely to sell large quantities.

3 Social trends can be used as a USP to differentiate products and services.

4 Attending to social trends means businesses are more likely to be seen as being socially responsible.

Now try this

1 What are the **three** elements of the design mix?

2 Identify **three** social trends that a business might consider when designing new products and services.

Exam skills

The following exam-style question relates to the content covered in Unit 1.3.1 and refers to the NETGEAR case study on page 37.

Worked example

In order to increase sales, NETGEAR is considering two options: improve the design of its product range or increase its promotional budget.

Evaluate these **two** options and recommend which option would help NETGEAR increase sales. **(20 marks)**

Product design is extremely important to the success of businesses such as NETGEAR because without excellent product design they would not have won the prestigious Red Dot Award in 2017. These, like most awards, help to promote the business and gain attention from all stakeholders, including potential customers. The additional publicity from these awards can lead to high sales volumes. Another reason why product design is important is that without products that do their job well and look appealing, no business would attract customers. The technology industry is very competitive and there are many brands of video recorder but because the product can recharge quickly and is wire-free and waterproof this means that it has features that give it a USP and this can lead to a competitive advantage over rival brands.

The student has given several points of analysis explaining why product design is important to the success of NETGEAR.

However, the design of the product will have little impact if NETGEAR does not communicate its products to its target market. NETGEAR products are already successful and this is highlighted by the Red Dot Award. It may be better for NETGEAR to ensure this success is successfully promoted to a wide range of customers.

The student has offered a counterbalance to their answer and discussed both options.

In conclusion, product design is extremely important for a business like NETGEAR which operates in a very competitive market where new products are launched regularly. If product design is not effective it will have products that are not competitive and will quickly lose market share to other brands. However, NETGEAR has recently innovated its products and in order to maximise the return on this investment it should now ensure sales are maximised before new product lines are developed. For this reason it would be better for NETGEAR to invest in a new promotion campaign to share the success of its products.

For evaluate questions it is important to offer a recommendation following a justified decision based on your analysis. The student has recommended that a promotion campaign would be a better option than further product development and clearly justified why.

Promotion

Promotion is the key method a business will use to communicate with its customers and potential customers. Successful promotion will create awareness, understanding and a desire for the product. There are two categories of promotion: above-the-line promotion and below-the-line promotion.

Above-the-line

Above-the-line promotion involves any form of advertising through the media, such as:

- ✓ television ✓ newspapers/magazines
- ✓ radio ✓ cinema
- ✓ posters/billboards
- ✓ internet (websites)
- ✓ direct marketing (emails, direct post).

The choice of medium will depend on the target market, the nature of the product, cost and the potential reach, i.e. how many people will be exposed to the advert.

Below-the-line

Below-the-line promotion includes all other forms of promotion that are not advertising. This may include:

- ✓ sales promotions (free gifts, coupons, loyalty cards and money-off deals)
- ✓ public relations (press conferences, press releases, sponsorship)
- ✓ merchandising and packaging
- ✓ direct selling/personal selling
- ✓ exhibitions and trade fairs.

Below-the-line forms of promotion can offer a two-way form of communication (through direct selling and trade fairs), encouraging customers to try new products (via sales promotions), and can be more believable than advertising (by using public relations).

The **target audience** – a business must choose the right method and channel to reach the right people, e.g. placing an advert in a magazine for a product that matches the demographic of the readership.

Promotion budget – the promotion budget will determine which methods are available and the geographical reach of the campaign.

Influences on promotion

Technology – technology can help a business narrow down its promotion so that it only reaches the right people. Subscription services also allow a business to target customers with personal messages and relevant information.

The **message** – a public apology might be posted on a company's website, but a sneak peek at a new product line might be shared via twitter. Sponsoring a sporting event might encourage an association with healthy living.

The reach and focus of advertising

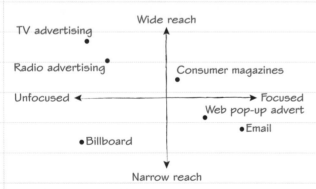

Wide reach

TV advertising •

Radio advertising •

Consumer magazines •

Unfocused ← → Focused

Web pop-up advert •

• Email

• Billboard

Narrow reach

The message – the purpose of an advert

Advertising can be used to give a different type of message. The message may depend on the nature of the product or stage of the product life cycle. An advert may be used to:

1. Inform customers   3. Remind customers

2. Persuade customers   4. Reassure customers

For more on the product life cycle see page 33.

Now try this

1 What is the purpose of promotion?

2 Identify **three** methods of promotion.

3 What promotional methods might be suitable for targeting children aged 5 to 8 years?

Branding

A brand is more than simply a logo or slogan. Although customers will remember and associate a business with its logo, slogan and imagery, a brand also represents the characteristics and personality of a business. For example, customers may associate a brand with characteristics such as sophistication, fun, value or premium quality. A strong brand can be achieved through investment in successful promotion.

Ways to build a brand

Developing a brand is about developing reputation and characteristics. Even without brand characteristics, a well-known brand gives consumers more trust. Brands can be developed through:

- exploiting a USP
- advertising
- sponsorship (associating characteristics and personality with the subject being sponsored, e.g. the values of the Olympic Games)
- using social media – more and more businesses are switching their attention to forms of social media.

Brands can take many forms including names, logos, phrases and symbols.

The importance of branding

Adds value to the product

Brands can be traded

Allows a premium price to be charged

Makes a product recognisable

Strong brands

Builds trust

Helps a business to position itself in the market relative to other competitors

Product might become the natural choice for the novice customer

Skullcandy is a US company making headphones. Products are popular for their cutting-edge design making for strong branding.

Types of brand

There are several types of brand. These are:

- **manufacturer's brands** – e.g. Kellogg's Corn Flakes
- **own-label brands** – brands associated with a retailer e.g. Sainsbury's crisps
- **generic brands** – products that do not have a particular brand association but simply use the name of the product e.g. carrots.

Each type of brand will be promoted in a very different way. Large amounts of money are invested in the promotion of manufacturer's brands.

Social trends

Businesses should maximise social trends to build their brands:

- Social media – attracting followers to social media sites is a key focus of marketing spending for many businesses.
- Viral marketing – the growth of social media and the sharing of images and videos is a huge opportunity for businesses to build brand awareness.
- Emotional branding – businesses often associate their brands with things that consumers have strong emotional connections to, for example, sports teams or good causes.

Now try this

1 What are the benefits of a strong brand?
2 Explain why a business might associate its brand with a celebrity through celebrity endorsement.

Had a look ☐   Nearly there ☐   Nailed it! ☐

Exam skills

The following exam-style questions explore the topics covered in Unit 1.3.2 and relate to the NETGEAR case study on page 37.

Worked example

Explain **one** reason why the Red Dot Awards will contribute towards NETGEAR building a strong brand. **(4 marks)**

The Red Dot Awards will contribute towards NETGEAR building a strong brand because many people will see the results of the awards as they will be published online and through other media such as industry magazines. As more people see this positive association with NETGEAR products they will start to trust the brand more than they would other technology products that have not won such awards. This results in a strong brand and means that people will be more willing to pay a premium for an Arlo product and will trust it over other similar products on the market.

The student has shown good understanding of how promotion can lead to brand development and the benefits of a strong brand for a manufacturer.

Worked example

Assess the possible factors that may lead to NETGEAR successfully promoting its new Arlo camera. **(12 marks)**

One factor that is important for NETGEAR to successfully promote its Arlo camera is the choice of medium. If NETGEAR chooses to use TV advertising then this will reach a far greater audience than most other channels. However, TV advertising is very expensive. NETGEAR may choose to use other media such as industry magazines or below-the-line promotion such as attending trade fairs or sponsoring a security event.

Other factors that are key to successful promotion include the message that the business sends out. If NETGEAR promotes the basic features of the Arlo camera, such as the long battery life and water-resistant camera, then some people may be interested. However, If NETGEAR promotes a sense of safety, peace of mind and a secure home for the family then this is likely to evoke people's emotions and they will be more likely to respond to the adverts...

The student has identified two factors that may contribute towards successful promotion. This will allow them to compare which is the most valuable in an evaluation.

The student has applied the concept of emotional branding by relating the context of the product and giving real examples, e.g. the value people place on a safe home.

To complete the answer the student now needs to make a judgement about the most important factor that may lead to successful promotion for NETGEAR. This must be a justified conclusion that draws on the analysis in the first two paragraphs.

Price

Price is a key factor in any product decision. Price will not only determine the demand for a product, it will also determine the contribution of a product and the overall profit margin for the business.

What influences price

Costs – what profit margin is the business hoping to achieve?

Other elements of the marketing mix – the 7Ps must complement one another

The price elasticity of demand – the potential for a business to change the price

Influences on price

Branding – the perceptions customers have of the brand and how much value they place on it

Competition – the level of competition and the price set by the market

Product life cycle – the stage of the life cycle the product is in

Price is very subjective. A price of £10 for a product might be appropriate one day and disastrous the next.

Pricing strategies

Expensive – high price

Dynamic pricing – applied to products where price can fluctuate with the level of demand, such as hotel rooms.

Price skimming – used to capitalise on 'first movers' (those people willing to pay a premium to be the first to own a product). The initial price is high so the profit in the market can be 'skimmed'. Suitable for established brands where anticipation for a new product is high. Particularly effective in technology markets.

Penetration pricing – applied to a new product attempting to enter the market. Initial price is low in order to penetrate the market by undercutting competitors. Over time price may increase as demand grows and reputation/popularity builds.

Cheap – low price

Queuing to purchase at the launch of a branded product.

Now try this

1 Why is the profit margin an important factor to consider when setting a price?
2 In what circumstance might a business decide to set a premium (high) price for a product?
3 What is penetration pricing?
4 Why is price subjective?

Pricing strategies

Types of pricing strategy

| Predatory pricing | Predatory pricing – also known as destroyer pricing, this is where the business sets a low price in order to price competitors out of the market. The business may make a loss for a period of time until the competitor fails. |

Competitive pricing – the business sets prices based on the nearest competitor. This is used in very competitive markets and helps avoid price wars.

Psychological pricing – the business bases the price below the next whole number to trick consumers into thinking the price is lower. So £9.99 psychologically appears cheaper than £10.

Price skimming – the business sets an initially high price for a new product when it is in high demand. The price will fall over time.

Cost-plus pricing – a business bases a price on the unit cost and then adds a percentage as a mark-up. This strategy is effective as it considers the profit margin the business is willing to accept.

Mark-up = unit cost X percentage mark-up

In reality, a business may adopt a number of strategies over time. For example, an initial mark-up will be calculated. This will then be compared with competitor pricing and the final price rounded to the nearest pence e.g. 99p.

Pricing and the product life cycle

A business will also adjust its pricing strategy according to the stage of the product life cycle that the product is in. For example, penetration pricing may be appropriate at launch, whereas, during decline, a loss leader strategy might be effective. See page 33 for more on the product life cycle.

Value for money

Businesses cannot make a profit unless they consider their costs alongside any pricing strategy. Customers do not care about the costs of the business. They simply want value for money. Businesses must understand the value customers place on their product and not simply the costs of production.

A business can charge a higher price for its produce if it has a unique selling point (USP) or can offer something different and innovative compared to a competitor. Customers value the particular USP and are prepared to pay over the odds for it.

Adapting to the market

Apart from the factors affecting the choice of price outlined on page 27, social trends such as the ones below will have a significant influence on how businesses adapt their pricing over time. Overall, the key is for a business to monitor the market and be ready to adapt.

Auction sites – Ebay and Gumtree allow customers to gain the best prices, but through a sense of urgency encourage people to bid so they don't miss out. Many businesses use these sites for selling alongside their own e-commerce sites.

Adapting price to reflect social trends

Personalised pricing – technology and online databases collect customer information and allow businesses to target them with a personal price.

Price comparison sites – Sites such as Uswitch (energy) or Trivago (hotels) make it easy for customers to compare prices and choose the best deal. Businesses have to remain competitive in a dynamic market.

Subscription pricing – a business charges customers a monthly fee to use a service. This is suitable for online services such as film rental sites.

Now try this

1 What is meant by cost-plus pricing?   2 How have online comparison sites changed the way people shop?

Exam skills

The following exam-style questions explore the topics covered in Unit 1.3.3 and relate to the Round Round Records case study on page 11.

Worked example

Explain why Round Round Records might use a price skimming strategy for newly launched records. **(4 marks)**

Price skimming is where a high price is initially set for a new product. When a new album is launched, perhaps by a popular artist, there will be high demand for it. As a result, Round Round Records could capitalise on the high demand by setting the price high to maximise the contribution made by the early sales of the album. Over time Round Round Records may reduce the price after the initial launch so that the price is in line with similar albums. This may help maintain demand and steady sales revenue.

The answer starts by explaining what price skimming is. This is always a good approach and demonstrates that the student understands the concepts in the question.

Worked example

Explain **one** factor that Rick White should consider when pricing his records via his e-commerce website. **(4 marks)**

One factor that Rick should consider when selling his records via his website is the impact that price comparison websites may have on his sales. Customers will be able to search and compare the price of his records against other popular online e-commerce sites in order to choose the cheapest option. As there is no way for Rick to differentiate the records he sells online, because his USP is the experience his customers gain from visiting his store, he will then have to compete on price and ensure he adopts a dynamic pricing strategy.

In this answer the student should identify a specific pricing strategy appropriate for selling records online. Note that a high price or a low price is not a valid pricing strategy. Although a price could be described as high or low, you will have to identify the specific strategy, e.g. price skimming.

The student has applied the case study well, and used information about the business and the nature of the product in order to answer the question.

Distribution (place)

Distribution refers to how the product gets to the customer. Many products use multi-channel methods to reach the customer. The key is to make distribution easy and convenient for the customer in order to maximise sales.

Parties in the distribution network

 Agents or brokers – agents link buyers and sellers together and operate in industries such as insurance. Agents have specialist knowledge and will often give both parties advice. Agents are common when businesses export.

 Retailers – retailers provide customers with a specialist service and give customers the opportunity to browse, enjoy the shopping experience and get advice and support from retail employees.

 Wholesalers – wholesalers take bulk quantities from manufacturers and distribute them across a network of retailers. They store, break down bulk and offer a distribution service for manufacturers.

 Direct selling – the main route to direct sell today is through online sales and e-commerce websites. However, direct channels also include telephone selling, door-to-door and online shopping channels.

Channels of distribution

The factors above will determine the mix of channels used to get the product from the business to the customer. Many modern products use multiple channels, such as direct, click and collect and in-store purchasing.

Each stage in the distribution network adds to the cost and/or adds value, therefore increasing the price of the product.

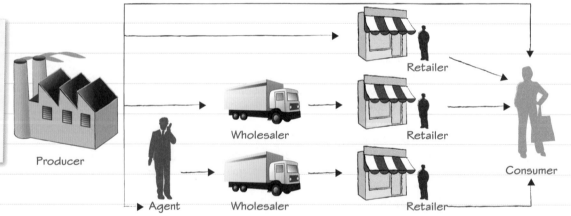

What influences distribution

Scope/scale – a product sold internationally may require distribution through an extensive network of wholesalers, agents and distribution companies. By contrast a local business may simply require one retail outlet.

Nature of the product – some products are not suitable for certain channels. For example, it can be difficult and costly to ship plants, flowers and other delicate objects.

Influences on distribution

Control over promotion and pricing – a business may opt to use its own website or retail chain if controlling these factors is important.

Expectations of customers – will customers expect to access the product via multi-channels or will one suffice?

Now try this

1 What is the role of a retailer in the distribution process?
2 What is the role of a wholesaler in the distribution process?

Online distribution

Social trends in distribution

There is a growth in direct ordering of products through the internet, with many manufacturers using courier businesses to deliver their products directly to customers. There is also a big increase in service providers selling on-demand services via websites and smartphone apps. Brands like Deliveroo, Uber and Urban Massage allow customers to have services delivered to their door.

Many companies that might have traditionally sold products are now selling on demand services via websites. An example of this is newspaper publishers who traditionally would have sold physical papers, now sell news as a service online.

A meal being delivered to a customer via an online service.

Digital marketing and e-commerce

Allows small businesses to target a global market

Allows businesses to gather customer information easily

The value of digital marketing and e-commerce

Builds relationships through a more personal service by tracking buying habits

Opportunities for personalisation and involving customers in the design of products

Targeting specific segments is much easier – even on an individual basis

The benefits of online distribution for businesses

Businesses operating online are known as E-tailers.

👍 E-tailers do not have to meet the costs of operating retail stores.

👍 Lower start-up costs make it easier for small businesses to launch.

👍 Transactions can take place in a secure online environment.

👍 Businesses can take sales 24/7.

👍 Businesses can offer goods to a much wider market.

The benefits of online distribution for customers

👍 Customers benefit from lower prices as E-tailers pass on lower costs.

👍 Customers can shop 24/7.

👍 Comparison between brands is much easier.

👍 There is usually a wider choice available from E-tailers.

👍 Customers can see reviews of products and services before making an informed choice.

Now try this

1 Why might a business opt to sell through a direct channel such as its own website?
2 Why has the internet led to a growth in on-demand services?

Exam skills

The following question explores the topics covered in Unit 1.3.4 and relates to the NETGEAR case study on page 37.

Worked example

> Explain **one** reason why NETGEAR may choose to distribute its products through retailers.　　　　**(4 marks)**
>
> NETGEAR may choose to sell its products, such as the Arlo camera, through retail stores as retailers provide customers with advice and allow them to experience a product before they buy it. This allows NETGEAR to focus its attention on developing innovative products as it is important to keep innovating in a fast-paced industry such as technology. As a result, NETGEAR does not need to deal with customer enquiries or returned orders.

One benefit of using retailers is explained. The student has then developed their answer by explaining how sole use of retail could benefit a business like NETGEAR.

The following question refers to the Round Round Record case study on page 11.

Worked example

> Assess the importance of direct distribution channels for Round Round Records.　　　　**(10 marks)**
>
> ... In conclusion, online channels such as Round Round Records' e-commerce site are extremely important if Rick wants to expand his business. This is because without online sales his market will always be limited. However, this will depend on Rick's ambitions and whether he wants to grow the sales of his business. If, on the other hand, Rick is happy to run his record store then the e-commerce site might increase sales and attract new customers, but it will not be as important as his retail store in building relationships with his loyal customer base and the enjoyment of running his business.

This is a model evaluation for the question.

The student has made a choice with their answer. They have also used the 'it depends' rule to consider factors that have not been exposed in the case study. This shows insight and useful counterbalance to the evaluation. The student has also identified what they believe to be the most important factor. This is often important as the analysis of a question may identify several key factors.

Product portfolio analysis

Product portfolio analysis (PPA) can be used to analyse and track the development of multiple products over time taking into account a number of factors such as growth, sales and market conditions.

The product life cycle

Price may be low to initiate sales. Heavy promotion to create awareness. Low number of product variations launched.

Price may increase with popularity. New varieties and distribution methods introduced. Business must keep up with demand growth.

The market is 'full' – all potential customers have the product and there are other better/cheaper alternatives. Price may be cut to maintain competitiveness.

Consider cutting price to maintain demand. Promotion slows as customers are aware of product. Introduction of new customers slows down – focus instead on retention and repeat purchase.

Further price cuts to maintain demand. Variety of products streamlined to the most popular. Business may consider discontinuing product if replacement can be introduced. An **extension strategy** may be used to re-launch the product to boost new growth. For example, slight modifications may be made to the design and packaging of a product to make it appear new or 'fresh'.

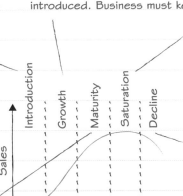

Life-cycle curve

Not all products have the same life-cycle curve. Fad products may grow and decline very quickly whereas some products will maintain maturity for a long time.

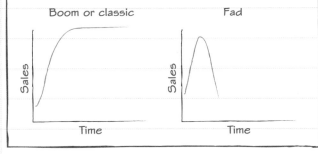

The value of PPA

👍 Useful analysis tool for a business with a wide product range.

👍 Useful for making decisions about where funds should be allocated.

👍 Can be used to predict future sales and therefore plan production/distribution.

👎 Products and markets are complicated and do not necessarily follow a pattern.

👎 Does not provide clear solutions for a business.

👎 As with all models, PPA simplifies what can be a complex issue.

The Boston Consulting Group Matrix

Possibly a leading brand in the market. Distribution must be effective to ensure product availability.

Fast-growing market but not yet an established product. Normally requires heavy investment to develop and ensure success. Usually lots of competition from rival brands.

Source: Adapted from The BCG Portfolio Matrix from the Product Portfolio Matrix, ©1970, The Boston Consulting Group.

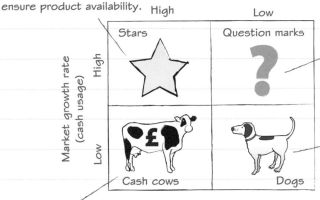

Invest to revitalise or discontinue the product.

Successful products in mature markets. Cash cows generate high revenue for a business that can be invested in other areas. Relatively little promotion is required.

Now try this

1 What are the important issues when a product is going through 'growth'?
2 What is the benefit of a 'cash cow'?
3 What are the limitations of product portfolio analysis?

Marketing strategies

A marketing strategy is a set of plans that aim to achieve a specific marketing objective. Typical marketing objectives might include: becoming market leader; building customer loyalty; improving brand recognition; or increasing market share. A business may use a number of strategies to achieve these aims.

Adapting the marketing mix for mass markets

A mass marketer might operate globally and have millions of potential customers.

Product	Products may be very generic; therefore it is key that the business finds some way to differentiate.
Price	Competitor pricing and managing costs are key to success as many products will have a similar price.
Promotion	Heavy advertising and promotion are used to build brand image through media with a wide reach.
Place	Multiple channels will be used to distribute and sell goods, including wholesale and retail outlets and the internet.

Adapting the marketing mix for niche markets

Customers in a niche market have very particular needs that a business will try to satisfy.

Product	Differences in the product will be quite significant. It is important for the business to communicate these differences and the benefits they bring.
Price	Niche marketers have more flexibility to offer premium pricing strategies due to the unique value they can add.
Promotion	Promotion tends to be targeted using specialist media and direct methods.
Place	Niche marketers are more likely to sell direct to customers or use a small number of carefully selected channels.

Inbound and outbound marketing strategies for B2C and B2B

Outbound marketing includes any strategy that involves pushing a message out to customers. This can include above-the-line and below-the-line methods.

Inbound marketing includes any technique that attracts potential customers to a website when they are looking for a particular service or product. Methods include: blogging, social media and search engine optimisation.

Hybrid strategies involve a combination of both. Outbound strategies are seen as more short term and inbound strategies take around six months to start generating real interest.

Marketing may differ between B2B (business to business) and B2C (business to customer). B2B marketing will require more information and detail on how a product/service could reduce costs or increase productivity; B2C marketing will involve emotive techniques to attract customers.

Customer loyalty

It is often easier to keep customers and encourage them to repeat purchase than it is to attract new customers.

Good communication – keeping customers informed of new products and developments

Customer incentives – e.g. reward schemes and money-off vouchers

Developing customer loyalty

Excellent customer service

Preferential treatment for returning customers

Now try this

1 How might the approach of a niche marketer differ from that of a mass marketer?
2 What is inbound marketing?

Exam skills

The following exam-style questions explore the topics covered in Unit 1.3.5 and relate to the NETGEAR case study on page 37.

Worked example

Explain **one** reason why NETGEAR might choose to use inbound marketing strategies. **(4 marks)**

NETGEAR may choose to use inbound marketing strategies in order to direct customers to its website. NETGEAR could use search engine optimisation or post links through social media in order to direct customers to its website. The benefits of doing this are that the website can contain lots of information, such as FAQs, videos and specifications of all NETGEAR's products. This means that customers will be able to access far more information about products such as the Arlo than if they visited a retailer's website. This may result in NETGEAR gaining more sales than simply using outbound marketing strategies.

The student has shown a good understanding of inbound marketing strategies. Throughout their answer they have given relevant examples and developed the consequences by suggesting how this might benefit NETGEAR.

Worked example

Assess the value of NETGEAR using product portfolio analysis to manage its range of products. **(12 marks)**

NETGEAR may use product portfolio analysis to make decisions about product launches, promotions and pricing strategies. Launching the Arlo Pro may mean that customers may not value the original product as much and sales may start to decline, pushing the product into the decline stage of the product life cycle or it being considered a 'dog'. As a result, NETGEAR may lower the price or adopt different forms of promotion to maintain high sales volumes. Using product portfolio analysis allows a business to manage a range of products and make decisions about the marketing mix and compare them to the products of its competitors...

This is an opening paragraph for the student's answer.

This first paragraph explores the benefits for a business such as NETGEAR of using product portfolio analysis. The student should now go on to discuss some of the limitations of product portfolio analysis before giving an evaluation on the value of models such as the Product Life Cycle and BCG Matrix.

The limitations of product portfolio analysis might be that it does not consider customer opinions of a product, but simply sales volumes and, in the case of the BCG Matrix, the growth in the market. Also, it does not consider factors such as profit margins, distribution and the relationship between products, e.g. whether or not a product complements another in the product range.

Had a go ☐   Nearly there ☐   Nailed it! ☐

Exam-style practice

These exam-style questions relate to concepts covered in Unit 1.3. Refer to the case study on NETGEAR on page 37.

1 Explain **one** reason why aesthetics in product design is important to a business such as NETGEAR. **(4 marks)**

> Aesthetics is one element of the design mix. Remember to apply your answer to the NETGEAR context. To do this you might specifically refer to the Arlo Pro Security Camera.

2 Assess the impact of NETGEAR using price skimming with its security camera system. **(10 marks)**

> Why might it be appropriate for NETGEAR to use a price skimming strategy that makes their products more expensive than similar products on the market for a short period of time? In your answer you should also consider the limitations of this decision.

3 Assess the importance of NETGEAR using a wider variety of methods to promote its products. **(12 marks)**

> The key word in this question is 'wider'. Promotion is important for a business, but is a wide range of techniques appropriate for a business such as NETGEAR? In your answer refer to specific techniques that would be appropriate.

NETGEAR aims to be the market leader in the home security market by 2022. To achieve this, NETGEAR could focus on developing high levels of customer loyalty or innovating its products.

4 Evaluate these **two** options and recommend which option would help NETGEAR achieve its objective. **(20 marks)**

> In your answer consider how important customer loyalty is for a business such as NETGEAR. To demonstrate counterbalance, you could discuss both options.
>
> For an 'evaluate' question it is important to give your own recommendations. For this answer, you might provide advice on which of the two options would be better at achieving NETGEAR's objectives of becoming market leader.

Case study

NETGEAR, the worldwide leader in smart home security and networking products for both home and small businesses, has been recognised for its dedication to the highest calibre in product design excellence. The company has been honoured with six new accolades in the 2017 Red Dot Awards, the internationally sought-after seal of quality in product design. One of these awards was for its Arlo Pro Security Camera.

"NETGEAR has a long history of emphasising form as well as function," said James Hathway, senior industrial designer for NETGEAR. "We invest effort into designing technologically superior products that are pleasing to the eye and touch, and that highlight elegance as well as performance. We're proud that the Red Dot Awards jury has recognised our work year after year."

The original Arlo camera, launched in 2015, was the world's first 100% wire-free, weatherproof, rechargeable HD home monitoring system. The 2017 Arlo Pro model adds rechargeable batteries, an alarm siren and two-way audio features.

Source: netgear.co.uk
and
https://www.virtualgraffiti.com/50508/netgear-products-win-six-reddot-awards-for-innovative-product-design-in-global-competition

Approaches to staffing

The owners/leaders within a business may see their workforce from one of two perspectives. They might see employees as assets or as a cost and this will determine the decisions they make around the management of the workforce.

Employees as assets

Where employees see staff as an asset they are more likely to:

- provide good remuneration packages
- give reasonable holiday and sick pay
- invest in the working conditions
- provide workers with job security
- see training as an important investment
- delegate responsibility
- take care in developing policies that motivate staff.

Employees as a cost

Where employees see staff as a cost they are more likely to:

- pay workers the minimum
- provide the minimum legal sick/holiday pay
- provide basic working conditions
- find ways to maximise output while minimising staff costs
- see training as an unnecessary cost and one of the first things to be cut when in financial difficulty
- centralise decision-making
- give little thought to employee motivation.

Flexible working

In order to adapt to the changing demands of the business environment a business may want to adopt a **flexible** approach to its workforce. This may involve approaches other than employing workers on a permanent fixed-term contract.

Multi-skilling employees so that they can carry out multiple roles

Part-time and temporary contracts

Approaches to flexible working

Outsourcing – getting other businesses (specialists) to complete a particular task or business function, e.g. payroll

Flexible hours and homeworking

The advantages and disadvantages of flexible working

👍 Allows a business to respond to short-term changes in demand.

👍 Specialist jobs can be done by experts who do not have to be permanently employed.

👍 Easier to manage staffing costs.

👎 Employees may not feel committed to the company if they don't have a permanent contract.

👎 Communication can be a problem.

👎 Outsourced work may be of a lower quality.

Dismissal and redundancy

Employees may be **dismissed** from work for failing to meet the required standard or through misconduct. Employees may also be dismissed unfairly and this might result in an industrial tribunal.

Redundancy applies where there is no work, not enough work or the position no longer applies. Sometimes employees will be offered voluntary redundancy where they will receive a pay-out.

Now try this

1 What are the benefits of multi-skilling a workforce?
2 Why might some organisations/managers view employees as a cost?

Employer–employee relations

Developing and improving good employer–employee relations through effective communication can lead to improved performance of an organisation and an enhanced reputation as an employer.

Employee representation

Employee representation involves collective representation of employees. There are three key ways that employees can find representation and have their voice heard.

Trades unions	Works councils	Employee committees
An organisation established to protect and improve the economic and working conditions of workers, for example the National Union of Teachers (NUT).	A forum within a business where workers and managers meet to discuss issues relating to conditions, pay and training.	A group of employees meeting together to focus on specific issues within the workforce. Unlike a works council, this may not be recognised or attended by managers.
• Focus on negotiations through collective bargaining. • Focus on pay and conditions. • Represent members at industrial tribunals and give workers advice on employment issues. • Prominent in public sector. • Decline of trades unions membership over past 20 years.	• Members elected from the workforce by the workforce. • Builds cooperation with managers. • Allows the workforce to be heard without trades union representation. • Involves employees in key business decisions.	• Informal groups set up by workers to focus on a certain aspect of work. • Typically focus on issues such as employee social events, safety and working conditions. • Employee committees may influence decisions made at works councils.

Bargaining methods

There are two ways employees can bargain with employers to determine wages/salaries, terms and working conditions.

 Collective bargaining is a negotiated process where trades unions and businesses discuss and agree on pay, working conditions and other conditions for the benefit of trades union members. The principle of collective bargaining is that workers have more power and influence when negotiating as one body.

 Individual bargaining may be more appropriate in small businesses. Individuals negotiate their own pay and conditions. This might mean that agreements will differ from one worker to the next.

Influences on employee representation

The nature of the work carried out by employees – low-skilled workers are less likely to have a significant input into decision-making.

The history of the business – what has happened in the past?

Employment legislation, for example the European Union Information and Consultation of Employees (ICE regulations), dictates that employees within EU countries must be consulted on certain aspects of work and employment.

Employee representation in decisions

The leadership and management style of the boss – autocratic managers may want to limit the input of employees.

The corporate objectives of the business and mission statement – a business in crisis may want to make quick decisions and avoid consultation with employees.

Now try this

1 What is a trades union?
2 How is a works council different from a trades union?
3 What drawback might there be to individual bargaining?

Exam skills

The following questions explore the topics covered in Unit 1.4.1 and relate to the Retro Homes case study on page 56.

Worked example

Explain **one** reason why Retro Homes may choose to employ its workers on a permanent contract basis.   **(4 marks)**

Retro Homes may choose to employ people on a permanent contract because it will provide workers with greater job security. This may lead to the workers committing to the organisation in the long term and this is likely to build a strong team spirit across the organisation. This is important when employees work closely together in a factory making furniture. Consequently, employee morale and worker productivity should rise resulting in productivity increasing and more sofas being produced.

This answer gives a benefit of permanent contracts and then goes on to develop several strands of explanation. The answer is also in the context of Retro Homes.

Worked example

Explain **one** way in which Retro Homes could improve communication with its employees.   **(4 marks)**

One way that Retro Homes could improve communication with employees is to encourage an employee committee. As the organisation is growing it is important that the workers at Retro Homes have representation. An employee committee will help employees raise any issues and ideas on how to improve the company...

This is the opening paragraph of an answer. There are a number of ways the student could have approached the question. They could have discussed email, intranets or the use of social media. However, it is always important to consider the nature of the business/ situation and analyse a method that is appropriate. For example, email would work well in an office environment, but probably not in a restaurant or furniture factory.

Worked example

Assess the extent to which Paul and Louise consider their employees an asset to the business.   **(12 marks)**

Paul and Louise may consider their employees an asset to the organisation as Louise has introduced an opportunity for all employees to share their ideas and opinions through fortnightly meetings. This suggests that Louise cares about her employees and the contribution they make to the organisation. The opportunity to contribute ideas and influence decision-making is an opportunity for employees to take responsibility, which may lead to higher levels of productivity and motivation...

This is a good opening paragraph for this question. The student has used information from the case study to provide evidence and made inferences as to how this might affect the workforce. The student should now go on to look at evidence that could be a counterbalance to this claim before giving an evaluation.

Recruitment and selection

Recruitment and selection involves the process of attracting, identifying and selecting the best workers for a role. The effectiveness of this process will help a business recruit people who can provide a strategic advantage for the company.

> Human resource flow refers to the movement of employees through an organisation. There are three specific areas of the flow that must be managed effectively for the business to achieve its human resource objectives.

The **recruitment process** is expensive but worth it if it attracts employees who will add value to the organisation. The costs involved will be advertising the post; and interviewing and training of new employee.

Alternatively firms may 'headhunt' the best employees – these are generally managers or people with specialist skills.

Training can improve employee skills adding value and competitiveness. For more on training see page 42.

Redeployment means moving employees to new roles, teams or functions within the organisation to maximise productivity, efficiency and capacity and meet employee needs relating to promotion and new skills.

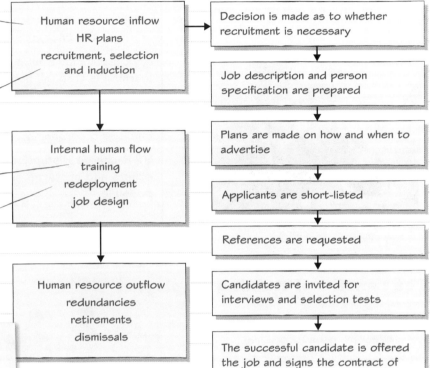

Human resource inflow
HR plans
recruitment, selection
and induction

Internal human flow
training
redeployment
job design

Human resource outflow
redundancies
retirements
dismissals

Decision is made as to whether recruitment is necessary

Job description and person specification are prepared

Plans are made on how and when to advertise

Applicants are short-listed

References are requested

Candidates are invited for interviews and selection tests

The successful candidate is offered the job and signs the contract of employment

A person specification provides details of the qualifications, experiences and characteristics of the desired employee. These may be broken down into 'desirable' and 'essential'. The person specification supports the selection process.

A job description states the title of a job and outlines the tasks, duties and responsibilities. Its main purpose is to show clearly what is expected of an employee.

Internal recruitment

This is when a role is filled by promoting employees from within the organisation. Some of the benefits:

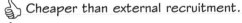 Cheaper than external recruitment.

👍 Managers know their employees so there is less risk – it is hard to foresee how an external recruit will perform.

👍 May require less training.

👍 Promotion opportunities are good for staff motivation and retention. For more on the costs of training see page 42.

External recruitment

This involves bringing new employees in from outside the organisation. Potential employees may be found using job adverts, employment agencies, government training schemes or through headhunting.

The main benefits:

👍 May attract a wider number of applicants.

👍 Brings in new skills and ideas.

👍 Helps increase the capacity within the business.

Now try this

1 Identify the steps in the recruitment process.
2 Why is recruitment a key aspect of human resource management?

Training

Training is the process of developing employees by improving their knowledge and skills so they can perform their duties better. Most managers would agree that a highly skilled workforce is important, but there is often a trade-off when businesses invest in employee training.

Induction training

Training is part of the recruitment and selection process as new employees need to be trained up so they can do their job effectively. This is called **induction**.

A new employee receiving training

On-the-job vs off-the job

Training

On-the-job

👍 Output may continue as learning is through actually doing the job.

👍 It may be easier and cheaper to organise.

👎 It can be disruptive for others and mistakes are possible.

Off-the-job

👍 Mistakes reduced because training is not on site.

👍 Safer.

👍 More motivating.

👎 Might be costly.

👎 May not always be relevant if not directly linked to the job.

The benefits of training employees

On-the-job (mentoring, job rotation, apprenticeships, graduate training)

Off-the-job (training centres, external courses)

Induction training (training new employees to learn the rules, systems and procedures in a new job)

Managers – better motivated workers

Owners – higher levels of productivity

Employees – reduces anxiety so more able to do their job and increases potential for promotion

Customers – better quality products and better customer service

When is training required?

Training may be required when:

- new employees join a company
- new technology/equipment is introduced
- there is new health and safety legislation
- there are new working practices.

Other types of training include **leadership development** training and ongoing **Continuous Professional Development** (CPD) – supporting the development of employees throughout their careers.

The costs of training

Training can be very costly for a business. Whether adopting on-the-job or off-the-job training, productivity will fall as employees will be away from the workplace, or producing goods and services at a slower pace (often with more mistakes). Training can be one of the first expenses a business cuts when it needs to save money, but investment in employee training is a long-term strategy. Another danger with training employees is that they may leave the organisation and the investment is then lost.

Now try this

Why might a business decide to adopt on-the-job training instead of off-the-job training?

Exam skills

The following exam-style question explores the topics covered in Unit 1.4.2 and relates to the Retro Homes case study on page 56.

Worked example

Retro Homes has identified two strategies to recruit new employees: to carry out the interview process itself or use a specialist recruitment company.

Evaluate these **two** options and recommend which Retro Homes should use to recruit the best employees for the tea room. **(20 marks)**

One approach that Retro Homes could have adopted in order to find the best employees is to use an interview process and additional assessment tasks. An interview would allow Paul and Louise to find out about each candidate and see how they respond to a series of questions linked to the job. Additional assessment tasks might also involve cooking or serving customers and this would allow them to find out if they had the skills and knowledge to do the job. However, the interview process and tasks are very time-consuming, especially considering they need 10 new employees and often interviews give limited indication of whether the candidate is the best person for the job.

The student has considered the benefits and limitations of each approach through their analysis in the first two paragraphs.

Another strategy might be to employ a specialist recruitment agency to find the employees for them. The benefits of this approach are that it can save Paul and Louise time and a specialist firm will have more expertise in the recruitment and selection process. However, a recruitment firm may charge a significant fee for each employee they find and Louise and Paul will not be able to use their own instinct when choosing the right candidates.

The answer is in context by effectively using data from the case study.

In conclusion, Retro Homes is a relatively small company to be using a specialist recruitment firm. Furthermore, carrying out the process itself may be more effective as it has a range of positions to fill and each decision may not be so vital. Louise based three positions on recommendation and she would have to pay a fee for these positions if she chose to use a recruitment firm. Overall, using an internal interview process is the best decision, but as Louise is filling 10 positions, it is important that she puts in place a comprehensive induction training programme to ensure all employees know their role and how to complete the tasks she requires. This would have helped reduce the 70% labour turnover she had in the first 18 months because employees would have felt more motivated and less anxious about the job.

A 20-mark evaluation question requires you to give a recommendation. The candidate has done this by suggesting that all employees receive induction training.

Hierarchies

All businesses are organised into a structure that dictates how workers relate to and work with one another. A business structure is known as a hierarchy, which can be drawn as an organisation chart, and explains the professional relationship, responsibilities and authority between employees.

Hierarchy structure

Authority refers to the powers in terms of **decision-making** that a worker has. The higher up the organisation chain, the greater the authority that employee has. Ultimate authority sits with the **Chief Executive Officer** (CEO) or the owner(s) of the company.

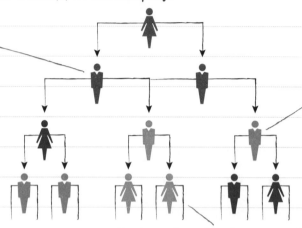

Employee B is the **line manager** of employee D.

Employee F is the **subordinate** of employee C.

Employees in an organisation structure may be grouped together into departments, branches or regions.

Employee J may be given responsibility for purchasing stock. However, the authority will sit with their line manager, E.

Roles within a business organisation

Roles

Directors – employed to run the business. The Managing Director may have ultimate authority but there will be a group of directors known as the board of directors who will take responsibility for various functions of the business e.g. Director of Finance.

Managers – take responsibility for managing and controlling an aspect of the business and make the day-to-day decisions. They may be responsible for a department and report to the directors.

Supervisors – monitor and regulate work of other employees. They may have delegated responsibility from a manager.

Team leaders – members of a team who take a leadership role to guide the work of the team and ensure employees are motivated and work effectively together.

Categories

Professionals – Staff with high levels of qualifications and experience. Posts involve a level of decision-making and responsibility e.g. doctors, architects, accountants.

....

Operatives – skilled workers who are involved in the production of a product or the delivery of a service. Operatives carry out the instructions of managers and supervisors.

....

General staff – roles carried out by workers with non-specific skills. These roles may require limited experience, skill or training e.g. receptionists, labourers.

Now try this

1 What does an organisation chart show?
2 What is the difference between a team leader and a supervisor?

Organisational design

Organisational design is a key factor when managing a business as it determines how a business responds to external factors, how people within the business relate to one another and how the company adapts to change.

Authority — Levels of hierarchy

Key factors in organisation design

Delegation — Span of control

Decision-making process (centralisation vs decentralisation – see below)

Organisation hierarchy

Chain of command
Refers to the levels in the hierarchy. Organisations with many levels are referred to as being 'tall' organisations. Organisations naturally increase the levels of the hierarchy as they grow.

Span of control
Refers to the number of employees that a manager is directly responsible for. An organisation with a wide span of control will encourage delegation and is referred to as having a 'flat' hierarchy.

Delegation

Delegation is the process of passing down authority through the organisation. Delegation can be used to lighten the workload of key personnel as the organisation grows and can be a key aspect of job design as it leads to job enrichment for junior members of staff. Delegation may not be suitable in certain situations where junior employees don't have the skills or in a crisis situation.

Centralisation

Centralisation refers to a decision-making process whereby the majority of decisions are led by senior managers.

👍 Works well where standardisation is required.

👍 Appropriate for situations where managers have the knowledge and workers are low skilled.

👍 Suited to authoritarian leadership styles.

👍 More suitable in times of crisis.

👍 Effective at cost minimisation and achieving economies of scale.

Decentralisation

Decentralisation refers to a decision-making process whereby the majority of decisions are delegated to managers in charge of regions, functions and product categories.

👍 Effective where local teams are best placed to make decisions to meet the customer needs.

👍 Appropriate where business is spread over a wide geographic area and local trends/needs are important.

👍 Effective at reducing workload of senior managers and promoting autonomy and the skills of subordinates.

👍 Allows for flexible working conditions and supports job enrichment.

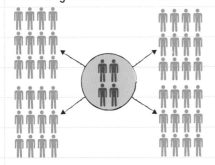

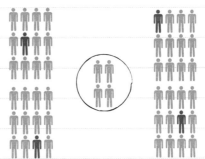

Now try this

1 What are the benefits of delegation?
2 When would centralisation be appropriate for a business?
3 What factors should a manager consider when thinking about organisation design?

Organisational structures

Types of organisation structure

Less delegation and empowerment

More opportunities for promotion

Communication takes longer

More control of employees

Organisation A

Less control and fewer opportunities for promotion

Faster - decision-making

Broader job roles

More flexible

Organisation B

A 'tall' organisation structure will generally have many levels in the chain of command and there may be a narrow span of control. Organisations tend to add levels to their hierarchy as they grow.

A 'flat' organisation structure is characterised by few levels in the chain of command. There will be few middle managers but the span of control for managers at the top of the structure could be wide.

Matrix structures

A matrix structure involves workers being organised by a project and business function. In a matrix structure teams are formed to carry out a specific project such as the development of a new product or opening of a new branch.

Matrix structures benefit through flexibility and the ability to bring specialists together for a common cause.

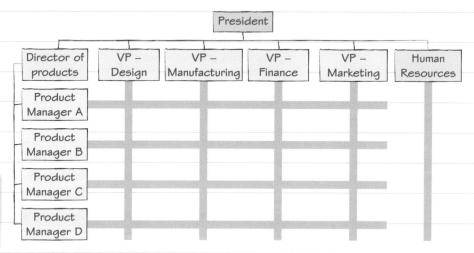

President

Director of products | VP – Design | VP – Manufacturing | VP – Finance | VP – Marketing | Human Resources

Product Manager A

Product Manager B

Product Manager C

Product Manager D

Impact of different structures on businesses

Tall structures

- 👍 Managers have tighter controls
- 👍 Clear promotional route
- 👎 Communication may be poor because of long chain of command
- 👎 Slow to make decisions because of long chain of command
- 👎 Tight control may be demotivating
- 👎 Expensive because lots of managers

Flat structures

- 👍 Communication good
- 👍 Decisions made quickly
- 👍 Workers more motivated because less controlled by managers
- 👎 Managers may lose control of workforce
- 👍 Can be cheaper because fewer managers

Matrix structures

- 👍 Motivational
- 👍 Flexible
- 👎 Can be expensive
- 👎 Can be difficult to coordinate

Now try this

1 When might a 'tall' organisation structure work best?
2 When might a 'flat' organisation structure work best?

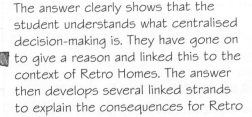
Exam skills

The following exam-style questions explore the topics covered in Unit 1.4.3 and relate to the Retro Homes case study on page 56.

Worked example

Explain **one** reason why Retro Homes might choose to centralise organisational decision-making.   **(4 marks)**

Centralised decision-making involves decisions being made by the managing directors of the business (Paul and Louise). Retro Homes may choose to centralise decision-making to ensure the three areas of the business are effectively co ordinated. This will ensure that communication between the showroom, delivery team and the factory are consistent and this will mean that there are fewer mistakes that the business makes. As a result, customer satisfaction will rise as they will receive their bespoke furniture on time and as they ordered it.

The answer clearly shows that the student understands what centralised decision-making is. They have gone on to give a reason and linked this to the context of Retro Homes. The answer then develops several linked strands to explain the consequences for Retro Homes.

Worked example

In 2014 Retro Homes Ltd had a flat organisation structure. Assess the impact on Retro Homes' organisation structure in 2014 on the effectiveness of managing employees.   **(10 marks)**

In 2014, the organisational structure at Retro Homes Ltd had a chain of command of three levels. This would mean that Paul and Louise would have close communication with all areas of the company. Indeed, Paul would be line managing both factory managers, the delivery team and the showroom team. This would allow good communication and allow him to keep close control of the running of each department. His management of the company through this structure has led to growth and profitability in recent years...

To complete this answer the student should now go on to consider some of the limitations of a flat organisation structure. For example, Paul has a wide span of control and as managing director he might find it difficult to line manage each function within the business. The structure may also not be suitable as the organisation grows.

Theories of motivation 1

Motivation refers to the willingness to work and achieve a given target or goal. Employee engagement involves the contribution an employee makes towards their work, including intellectual effort and positive emotions. Both of these factors are desirable in a workforce.

The scientific management school ⟵———— The extent to which employees are motivated by financial incentives or social interaction. ————⟶ The human relations school

Employees driven by financial incentives

Employees driven by the need to meet social needs

Frederick Taylor

👍 Focus on efficiency and improved competitiveness.

👍 People are motivated solely by money.

👍 Incentivise work with financial rewards.

👍 Improve efficiency through standardisation and the division of labour.

👍 Employees are given elementary training and clear instructions on how to complete a task.

👍 The application of Taylor's principles reduces the need for as many workers as productivity is raised.

Theory based on work study and improving productivity and efficiency of the workforce.

Elton Mayo

👍 Informal working groups are recognised as having a positive influence on productivity.

👍 Workers are not simply motivated by financial incentives.

👍 Social interactions outside of working hours are important.

👍 Efficiency can be achieved through teams and teamworking.

👍 Focus on the needs of the employees rather than the needs of the organisation.

Theory based on the fact that employees have social needs and these must be fulfilled through their work.

Abraham Maslow: Maslow's Hierarchy of Needs

Self-actualisation
morality, creativity, spontaneity, acceptance, experience, purpose, meaning and inner potential

Self-esteem
confidence, achievement, respect of others, the need to be a unique individual

Love and belonging
friendship, family, intimacy, sense of connection

Safety and security
health, employment, property, family and social stability

Physiological needs
breathing, food, water, shelter, clothing, sleep

- People are driven to achieve personal needs.
- Maslow identified five levels: people are motivated to achieve these in order, starting with physiological needs.
- Basic needs (physiological and security) refer to those linked to survival.
- Higher order needs (social, esteem, self-actualisation) refer to the needs people have within a social environment.
- A person cannot move up the hierarchy without first fulfilling the needs below.
- Businesses can motivate workers by giving them the opportunity to satisfy these needs at work.

The Neo-human relations school focuses on the psychological aspects of motivation and the fact that motivation comes from within an individual. The role of managers is to unlock this motivation.

Now try this

1 What are **two** principles of scientific management?
2 How does Elton Mayo's theory contradict Frederick Taylor's?
3 What are Maslow's five human needs?

Theories of motivation 2

Frederick Herzberg's theory identified that hygiene factors are important in so far as the satisfactory presence of them will not lead to the dissatisfaction of employees. However, hygiene factors do not motivate employees. Only those identified as motivators.

Frederick Herzberg's two-factor theory

Employee dissatisfaction

- Fulfillment
- Commitment
- Engagement

Employee satisfaction

Factors leading to dissatisfaction (hygiene factors):
- poor pay
- poor compensation
- poor work conditions
- lack of promotions
- poor benefits offering
- lack of job security.

When these factors are optimal, job dissatisfaction will be eliminated. However, these factors do not increase job satisfaction.

Factors leading to satisfaction:
- good leadership practices
- good manager relationship
- clear direction and support
- feedback and support
- personal growth
- advancement
- recognition.

When these factors are optimal, job satisfaction will be increased.

The value of motivation theory

Taylor	Mayo	Maslow	Herzberg
Although criticised as being against the well-being of the workforce, Taylor's focus on productivity and efficiency is still extremely important today.	Any job design and rewards package should consider the social dimension of work and ensure human interaction is designed to create the greatest benefit for the workers and the business.	Brings together other theories and encourages managers to provide the workforce with opportunities to fulfill their needs. It considers both financial and non-financial incentives of work.	Considers the dissatisfaction of the workforce and what employers must do to prevent this. Employers must secure the hygiene factors before they will be able to develop means of motivating employees.

Motivational theory

Motivational theory does not provide managers with the answers as to how they can motivate their employees. However, together they do provide a useful framework that managers can use to review and evaluate organisational policies, job design, pay, organisational structure and the way they communicate with employees.

 Exam focus **Motivation theory**

Unless specifically asked to explain a motivation theory it is not necessary to do so. However, when analysing workforce policies, it often useful to link your analysis to specific theories. For example, a good commission package on top of a basic salary might allow a worker to meet their physiological needs and prevent dissatisfaction as sufficient pay is a hygiene factor, but it may not help the worker achieve their higher order or social needs. (Motivation theories cross over and can be linked in your analysis.)

Now try this

1 Identify **three** hygiene factors.
2 What are the differences between Maslow's theory and Herzberg's theory?
3 How could a manager use motivational theory?

Financial methods of motivation

Financial methods are one way that a manager can motivate their workforce.

Benefits and drawbacks

Method	Benefits	Limitations
Commission A bonus paid based on achieving a sales target.	👍 Appropriate for sales jobs. 👍 Incentive to increase sales revenue for the business.	👎 Focus taken away from other areas of the job such as customer service. 👎 Little attention to aspects of the job that do not directly impact commission earned.
Piecework Payment based on the number of units of output produced.	👍 Appropriate for production jobs. 👍 Incentive to increase output (units).	👎 Employees may ignore factors such as quality.
Performance-related pay (PRP) A salary or bonus scheme linked to job-related targets. Targets and performance may be reviewed every 6 months or annually.	👍 Links pay to measurable targets specific to the nature of the job. 👍 Encourages review of employee performance.	👎 Can be expensive if a large proportion of the workforce achieve their targets; some areas of performance can also be very subjective. 👎 Difficult to ensure PRP is fair across the organisation.
Profit sharing/bonus schemes Distributing a percentage of net profit across the workforce.	👍 Reward linked to the overall success of the company.	👎 Depends on the profitability of the business.

What the experts say about financial methods of motivation

Financial reward will satisfy the basic needs and may boost self-esteem. It will not satisfy the higher order needs.

Maslow

Financial incentives are a hygiene factor and if satisfactory will only prevent dissatisfaction.

Herzberg

The rational man is driven by financial reward.

Taylor

Financial incentives are irrelevant if an employee's social needs are not met.

Mayo

Now try this

1 When might a business use commission?
2 What are the benefits of profit-sharing?
3 What are the limitations of financial rewards?

Non-financial methods of motivation

There are also non-financial ways for managers to motivate their employees.

Benefits and drawbacks

Method	Benefits	Limitations
Delegation, consultation and empowerment Giving employees autonomy, authority and the power to influence key business decisions.	👍 Employees feel involved, have the ability to make their own decisions and are able to influence the business.	👎 May slow down decision-making and consistency across the business. Some employees may not have the skills/experience to make important decisions/contribute their own ideas.
Team working Organising the workforce into teams in order to benefit from the social aspects of motivation.	👍 Meets employees' social needs and encourages a sense of belonging. Helps employees develop a connection to the organisation through their colleagues.	👎 Individual performance is harder to identify in a team situation. Ineffective workers may not be identified.
Flexible working Adopting flexible contracts and approaches that do not require employees to work in an office every day from 9am to 5pm.	👍 Employees can fit their work around their personal life. Employees have autonomy to decide how and when they work. Can help the business cut back on employment costs.	👎 Difficult to keep control of employees and ensure they are being productive. Difficult to build a team spirit if employees are not together all the time.
Job rotation/enrichment and enlargement Encouraging employees to work across a range of roles, develop understanding of different areas of the business and develop new skills.	👍 Employees are motivated through increased variety and personal development.	👎 Can be disruptive and reduce productivity in the short-term as employees develop their skills and learn new roles.

What the experts say about non-financial methods of motivation

Non-financial incentives are linked to achieving the higher order needs of love and belonging, self-esteem and self-actualisation.

Maslow

Non-financial incentives are the key to motivating the workforce.

Herzberg

Non-financial incentives reduce productivity and create inefficiencies within the workforce.

Taylor

Non-financial incentives help employees achieve their social needs.

Mayo

Now try this

1 Why might employee training motivate the workforce?
2 What are the drawbacks of team working?
3 Why is it important to help employees achieve their 'higher order' needs?

Choosing motivational methods

The most suitable methods of motivation will depend on a number of factors including the nature of the job, the industry and the individuals involved.

Methods of motivation

Costs – if profits are low a business will be unable to offer bonuses. Training and investment in job design may also have to be cut.

Attitudes – whether managers have a 'soft' or 'hard' approach to HRM will determine the methods used.

Financial and non-financial methods

Skill level of employees – a more skilled workforce may require more delegation and job enrichment.

Skill level of managers – the skill and training of managers will determine the variety and effectiveness of motivation methods. Managers trained in motivational theory may apply these concepts more effectively.

Nature of the organisation or work – creative industries may lean towards empowerment and enrichment in order to motivate their workforce. A competitive sales environment may only require an effective commission scheme.

 Exam focus **Understanding the workforce**

Employees will not be fully motivated by one thing alone. It is always important to have a balance of financial and non-financial methods. Always look for clues in the case study to identify what factors are important to the workforce.

Assessing methods of motivation

- Customer service
- Labour productivity
- Employee engagement
- Product quality
- Good relationships with managers

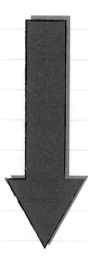

- Absenteeism
- Labour turnover
- Labour cost per unit
- Recruitment costs

Now try this

1 Identify **two** reasons why a manager might decide not to delegate decisions to their workforce.
2 Identify **three** benefits of a highly motivated workforce.
3 Why is the skill level of the workforce important when considering methods of motivation?

Exam skills

The following exam-style questions explore the topics covered in Units 1.4.4 and 1.4.5 and relate to the Retro Homes Ltd case study on page 56.

Worked example

Explain why Retro Homes might pay its workers a wage with overtime pay.   **(4 marks)**

Retro Homes may pay its workers a wage with overtime because the nature of the job is quantifiable and linked to the number of hours employees will work. Overtime will be appropriate because it will encourage employees to work for longer periods of time when the tea room or furniture showroom are busy. For example, they are likely to be busier at the weekends and leading up to Christmas as people order furniture.

The student has shown an understanding of both concepts and linked them to the nature of the work being carried out at Retro Homes. An example is used at the end of the answer to apply the context.

Worked example

With reference to relevant motivational theory, assess the possible benefits to Retro Homes of 'creating a team spirit within the company'.   **(10 marks)**

Achieving a team spirit will help employees achieve their 'love and belonging' needs as identified in the Hierarchy of Needs. This refers to employees' need to build social relationships with other colleagues in their working environment. If employees achieve this need they will feel motivated and this could lead to reduced absenteeism because they will enjoy their work. Furthermore, achieving these needs will improve employee engagement because they will care about their fellow workers and the overall success of the business.

You need to refer to motivational theories in this question. Any motivational theory will do, but you don't need to discuss them all!

The student has chosen to apply the theory of Maslow's Hierarchy of Needs. They have gone on to analyse how a team spirit could lead to greater levels of motivation. The student has shown limited application to the Retro Homes context.

Worked example

Assess the importance of a highly motivated workforce in helping Retro Homes increase profitability.   **(12 marks)**

... On the other hand, profitability cannot be achieved by motivation alone. If the fixed costs are too high then no matter how productive the workforce is, the business will find it difficult to break even and then generate a profit. Any business with high operating costs may find it difficult to manage cash flow and this could result in difficulties paying the workforce. If this should happen, motivation will quickly fall if employees are motivated by financial incentives as demonstrated by the scientific management theory of motivation...

In this answer the student must show an understanding of motivation and link it to the concept of profitability. They must also show an appreciation of the limitations of motivation.

This is part of the student's answer. This section of the answer shows that the student understands that motivation alone cannot create a profitable business. The first part of the answer will have explained the benefits of a highly motivated workforce, such as improved customer service and lower labour costs.

Management and leadership

Strong leaders drive businesses by setting a vision for the future and putting in place strategies to get there. Often, people make a clear distinction between the role of a manager and the role of a leader, although a leader may perform the role of a manager within a business. Leaders may also develop from within the business and may not hold managerial roles.

The difference between management and leadership

Managers	vs	Leaders
Build consistency	←→	Change the status quo
Implement strategy	←→	Devise strategy
Instruct	←→	Inspire
Control	←→	Empower
Think logically	←→	Think laterally
Reactive	←→	Proactive

In addition to the above, leaders are also considered to have traits such as vision, confidence, good communication, decisiveness and motivation.

An estate built in York by Joseph Rowntree for his factory workers. It is an example of paternalistic leadership (see table below).

Advantages and disadvantages of different leadership styles

Leadership style	Advantages	Disadvantages
Autocratic (authoritarian)	👍 Focused on getting the task done. 👍 High levels of control suitable for unskilled workforce. 👍 Speeds up decision-making process – important in times of crisis. 👍 Suitable for implementing a clear vision held by the leader.	👎 Can lead to low levels of motivation if employees do not feel respected or valued. 👎 No opportunity for employees to be involved in decision-making. 👎 No opportunity to collect opinions of the workforce that might be valuable. 👎 Employees might not feel as though they have a stake in the business.
Democratic	👍 Develops a team spirit. 👍 Opportunity for employees to 'buy in' to the task if they have a say. 👍 Allows a manager to collect ideas and opinions from the whole workforce.	👎 Decision-making can take a long time when done by committee. 👎 Employees may not see the 'bigger picture' and vote for decisions that benefit them.
Laissez-faire	👍 Allows employees autonomy to make their own decisions. 👍 Can lead to higher levels of creativity and motivation among workers.	👎 Lack of control over the workforce – deadlines and targets might be missed. 👎 Tasks may not be coordinated very well.
Paternalistic	👍 Attention given to employee welfare. 👍 Employees feel as though they are being looked after.	👎 Employees given no powers to make decisions. 👎 Low levels of motivation. 👎 Employees have no stake in the business. 👎 Leader may come across as unsure.

Now try this

1 Identify **three** traits you would expect to see in a successful leader.
2 What are the characteristics of a laissez-faire leader?

Exam-style practice

The following exam-style questions refer to the human resource function of a business. For these questions refer to the Retro Homes case study on page 56.

1 Explain **one** reason why Louise may have chosen to send her workers on a training course. **(4 marks)**

An external training course is off-the-job training.

2 Explain **one** suitable human resources objective that could be set by Louise. **(4 marks)**

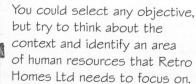
You could select any objective, but try to think about the context and identify an area of human resources that Retro Homes Ltd needs to focus on.

3 Calculate the change in labour costs as a percentage of revenue between Qtr 1 2014 and Qtr 4 2014. **(4 marks)**

Start with the formula and remember to show your workings.

4 Assess how Paul could improve the job design of his employees. **(10 marks)**

Note down the various aspects of job design and the benefits of effective job design before answering this question.

Paul and Louise have decided to introduce a number of fringe benefits for the employees at Retro Homes. These include 35% off all furniture and accessories and an extra two days paid holiday per year.

5 Assess how these fringe benefits could lead to a highly motivated workforce. **(12 marks)**

How might these measures motivate employees? Are there any aspects of human needs that are not being met?

Figure 1 below shows the new organisation chart for Retro Homes Ltd in January 2015.

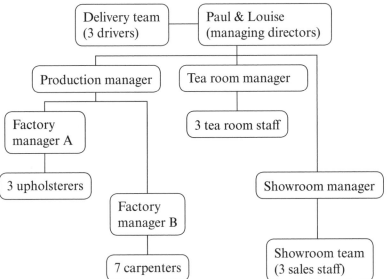

Figure 1. Retro Homes Ltd organisation chart as at January 2015

6 Assess the new organisational structure introduced by Paul and Louise in terms of its potential to improve performance at Retro Homes ltd. **(12 marks)**

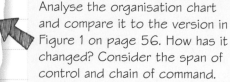
Analyse the organisation chart and compare it to the version in Figure 1 on page 56. How has it changed? Consider the span of control and chain of command. How might these affect factors such as communication, control and flexibility?

Case study

Paul had run Retro Homes, a successful furniture store, for four years. The company produced furniture at two local factories and distributed nationwide. Retro Homes also had a large three storey showroom in Chesterfield. Paul employed a team of 20 within the business who worked across three areas of the company. The organisation chart for Retro Homes is shown in Figure 1.

Figure 1: Retro Homes organisation chart as of December 2014

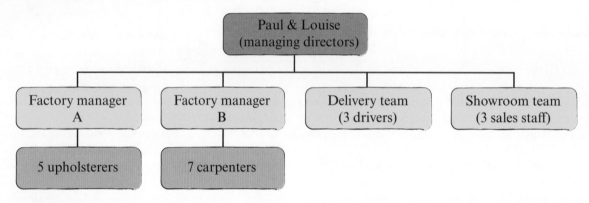

The showroom was always busy throughout the week and Paul's wife Louise saw the opportunity in 2014 to open a tea room on the ground floor of the showroom. The tea room was opened in January 2014 and soon became one of the most popular places to eat and drink in town. Louise managed the running of the tea room and the additional 10 employees. Despite its success, the tea room faced a number of human resource issues as key personnel left throughout the first 18 months of the tea room opening. Louise calculated that during this period there was a 70 per cent turnover of staff. Furthermore, despite being extremely popular, the tea room was not generating the profits that Paul and Louise had hoped for.

Figure 2: Cost for four six-month periods + tea room revenue

	Qtr 1 2014	Qtr 2 2014	Qtr 3 2014	Qtr 4 2014
Total labour costs (£)	12 000	27 000	29 000	35 000
Tea room revenue (£)	20 000	51 000	55 000	72 000

In 2015 Paul and Louise decided to restructure the business in order to employ a manager of the tea room and a manager of the showroom. Paul and Louise hoped that the restructuring would allow them to concentrate on growing the business.

In order to bring the two sides of the business together Louise introduced a fortnightly meeting between the workers of the tea room and furniture business. The intention was to encourage employees to share their ideas about moving the business forward and create a team spirit within the company.

The role of an entrepreneur

An entrepreneur is a person who is willing to take a risk in setting up and growing their own business. Entrepreneurs see business opportunities to make money and to meet the wants and needs of society. Entrepreneurs solve problems and create wealth in the economy.

Entrepreneurs

Entrepreneurs set up businesses and utilise the following skills and characteristics.

Innovate and invent – they create new ideas, products and services.

Take risks – entrepreneurs are often willing to risk their career and financial security to make their idea work.

What entrepreneurs do

Organise – they pull together resources such as **capital**, **technology** and **people** to set up a business.

Make decisions – entrepreneurs are **decisive** and make decisions.

Where ideas come from

New business ideas come from a whole variety of sources. An entrepreneur may decide to set up their own business for a number of reasons:

Business experience – some start a new business using the experience of their current job or profession.

Personal experience – a business may be based on a hobby or interest.

Lifestyle choice – some people may set up a business in order to be their own boss and work on their own terms.

Spotting a gap – some people see an opportunity in everyday life and decide that they can meet this need.

Skills – some people set up a business based on their interpersonal, artistic or technical abilities.

There is **risk and reward** in setting up a business. As many as one in three businesses fail within the first three years of opening. However, there are significant financial and personal rewards for an entrepreneur who creates a successful business.

Setting up a business

Entrepreneurs will go through the following process to set up a business.

The idea
The idea may come from a moment of inspiration or one of the processes listed above.

↓

Research
The entrepreneur will carry out research into the market, customer needs, competition, profitability and potential suppliers.

↓

Planning
The entrepreneur will usually draw up a detailed business plan

↓

Financing
Entrepreneurs will explore a variety of internal and external sources of finance. For more on business plans see Unit 2.1.4
To revise internal and external sources of finance, see Units 2.1.1 and 2.1.2.

↓

Location
For some businesses, location is a key strategic decision. For others, such as online retailers, it may be less critical but still important.

↓

Resources
Organising resources may include: suppliers, human resources, legal issues, utilities, manufacturing and marketing.

↓

The launch
The launch may involve an opening event to create good **public relations** (PR) or activities to create awareness of the new business.

Now try this

1 Why are entrepreneurs important?
2 What factors might lead to a person setting up their own business?

Running a business

An entrepreneur running a business will be involved in more areas than just the actual business activity. They must lead and coordinate all functions of the business. Often an entrepreneur will initially do these tasks themselves, but employ specialists as the business grows.

The functions of an entrepreneur

There are a wide range of **functions** that entrepreneurs must coordinate to run, expand and develop their businesses.

Financial management – raising capital, managing costs, profitability and cash flow

Administration – insurance, legal setup, tax and business records

Marketing – research, promotion and branding

Running, expanding and developing a business

Purchasing – liaising with suppliers, deliveries, logistics

Managing people – recruitment, training, motivation and leading people

Production – production of goods, storage, quality management and delivery

Intrapreneurship

Intrapreneurship refers to employees within a business who have the freedom and opportunity to develop their ideas and use their creativity to innovate. Intrapreneurial employees solve problems, create new and exciting products and keep big businesses moving forward. These employees add a huge amount of value and often give businesses a competitive advantage. It is important for businesses to motivate and give employees the opportunity to develop these traits.

Risk and uncertainty

Entrepreneurs deal with risk and uncertainty. Entrepreneurs can decide the level of risk they take but have less control over uncertainty such as legal and political change. Entrepreneurs can reduce risk and prepare for uncertainty by:

- carrying out detailed research
- producing detailed plans
- analysing external influences (for more on analysing external influences, see PESTLE in Unit 3.1.4)
- developing contingency plans (see Unit 3.6.3 for more on developing contingency plans).

Barriers to success

There are many rewards to setting up your own business, but many people face significant barriers that may stop them becoming entrepreneurs.

Lack of finance

Lack of entrepreneurial skills. See Unit 1.5.2 for more on entrepreneurial skills.

Competition from large, established businesses

Responsibility of becoming an employer

Aversion to risk

Legal barriers (red tape)

Lack of ideas – it is not easy to find a competitive and unique business idea

Now try this

1 Identify **three** functions of a business.
2 Why is intrapreneurship important to a business?
3 Why might a person choose not to set up their own business even if they have a good idea?

Characteristics and motives of entrepreneurs

Entrepreneurs often have a set of characteristics and skills that drive them and support them in setting up, developing and expanding a successful business.

Characteristics and skills of entrepreneurs

Characteristics

Self-confidence – entrepreneurs believe that they can succeed.

Self-determination – they have the drive to keep going when they come up against problems.

Self-starter – they are willing to work independently and make decisions.

Initiative – they are proactive and adapt to change.

Commitment – entrepreneurs commit to the project and put in time to make it work, often working night and day.

Skills

Organisation – there is lots to coordinate when setting up a business alone.

Financial management – cash flow management can be challenging for small businesses.

Managing and communicating with people.

Negotiating – negotiating deals and contracts with suppliers and customers.

Incentives for setting up your own business

Entrepreneurs may be motivated to start their own business for various reasons. These may include:

Financial motives

Profit maximisation
to generate as much wealth as possible

Profit satisfying
to generate enough income to live a comfortable lifestyle

Non-financial motives

Ethical stance
running a business to support their ethical principles e.g. climate change

Social enterprise
running a business for a social or environmental cause – not-for-profit

Independence and home working
entrepreneurs often want the control and flexibility of running their own business

Now try this

1 Explain **one** of the characteristics that might make an entrepreneur a success.
2 Identify **three** reasons why a person might want to set up their own business.

Exam skills

The following exam-style questions explore the topics covered in Unit 1.5.1 and 1.5.2 and relate to the case studies on page 71.

Worked example

Explain why Benedick Hope may have chosen to start his own business. **(4 marks)**

Many entrepreneurs open their own business because they have an interest in a certain aspect of the business they set up. Benedick may have chosen to start his own business because of his love for art. By setting up his own business he will have gained autonomy and be able to be his own boss. This means he can run the business how he wants to and do something that he loves while gaining an income from the business at the same time.

The student opens the answer by explaining one reason why entrepreneurs set up their own businesses. They have then drawn information from the source to identify why the owner might have set up his own business. They have then gone on to explain the benefits of this decision and how this links to Benedick's 'love for art'.

Worked example

Assess the importance of intrapreneurship to a business such as Well-Mate. **(10 marks)**

Intrapreneurship refers to employees within a business being given the freedom and opportunity to create new ideas and innovate. Intrapreneurship will be very important to a business such as Well-Mate because it operates in the technology industry and this industry is very fast paced with many new products being launched each year. Intrapreneurship will help the business develop new products and features of the app, such as the ability to aggregate new sets of information to make links between people's health and their lifestyle.

You won't be able to answer this question if you don't have a clear understanding of intrapreneurship. Ensure you understand all of the key concepts in the specification.

However, Well-Mate is a relatively new business and it has to be managed effectively. This will involve employees completing a specific role very well. Well-Mate has developed a successful product but it must now ensure it is marketed and distributed so that the business becomes profitable. This priority may be more important than employees coming up with new innovations.

The second paragraph offers counterbalance to the benefits of intrapreneurship. The student has suggested that Well-Mate may need to focus on other areas of the business.

In conclusion, intrapreneurship is important in very competitive markets and Well-Mate must keep innovating if other companies such as Apple and Google develop better products that are more competitive. It is important that Well-Mate promotes intrapreneurship but, at the moment, it is more important that Well-Mate focuses on marketing and distributing its current products to a wide market.

The evaluation brings in more context and weighs up the importance of intrapreneurship in relation to other aspects of running the business. An effective approach to evaluation is to justify why one approach or factor might be more important than another.

Business objectives

Objectives are medium to long-term plans that are established to coordinate the business and act as targets. Corporate objectives are those set by the owners or directors of the business. These will then influence the functional objectives set at departmental level.

Objectives

Businesses set objectives to:

- provide quantifiable steps to achieve aims
- clarify direction of the business
- measure success against targets
- motivate employees to achieve
- reward employees.

A good way to remember the appropriateness of an objective is to use the acronym SMART:

Specific

Measurable

Agreed

Realistic

Time-related

Potential profit is used as a measure by potential lenders.

Common business objectives

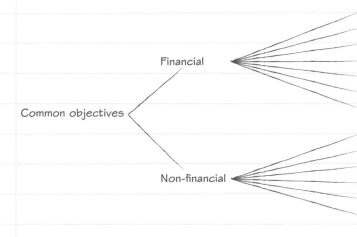

Common objectives
- Financial
  - Survival
  - Profitability
  - Growth
  - Market share
  - Shareholder value
  - Sales maximisation
  - Cost efficiency
- Non-financial
  - Personal satisfaction
  - Brand recognition
  - Sustainability
  - Customer satisfaction
  - Employee welfare
  - Social objectives

Some objectives are more appropriate for small businesses, e.g. survival and personal satisfaction of the owner.

It could be argued that achieving most of these objectives will impact the bottom line and overall aim of most businesses – profit.

Influences on business objectives

- **Size** – objectives may change as a business grows and becomes more successful. Most businesses when setting out will aim to survive.
- **Sector** – public sector organisations are driven by meeting customer needs, not profit.
- **Market** – some markets are more competitive than others and this will determine objectives e.g. targeting market share.
- **Ownership** – a Plc must satisfy shareholders, and so will set objectives around shareholder value.
- **Owner** – the owner may simply run the business for love of the job.

Importance of profit maximisation

Profit is one of the main incentives of running a business. The wealth created through profit allows the owners of a business to reinvest the money into new projects and stimulate economic activity. Profit is also important because it secures the long-term success of a business. Profits can be reinvested to help the business grow and keep up with the demands of the ever-changing business environment. Profit is what is left after all costs have been deducted from revenue.

Now try this

1 Why is it important for objectives to be SMART?
2 Are some objectives more important than others?

Exam skills

The following exam-style questions explore the topics covered in Unit 1.5.3 and relate to Extract A and Extract B in the case study on page 71.

Worked example

Explain **one** objective that the owner of Well-Mate might set for the company. **(4 marks)**

Well-Mate is a relatively new business that has recently launched a new product. An appropriate objective that the owner might set is to secure a certain percentage of the health app market. Setting a market share target such as 10% is appropriate because it will drive the business to increase sales and ensure brand awareness is spread. Once customers start buying the product they can then work on ensuring they are able to make a profit.

The student has made reference to the fact that Well-Mate is a relatively new brand. They have then explained why increasing market share would be an appropriate objective for a business like this. The answer has been developed with several linked strands of development.

The student could have opted for one of many business objectives, providing they could link it to the context of Well-Mate.

Worked example

In 2017, Benedick Hope set up his business with the objective of improving the appearance of the local area.

Explain why Benedick might have thought this was an important objective for his business. **(4 marks)**

Improving the appearance of the local area is a social objective. Benedick does not seem to be driven by profit maximisation. As Benedick has a passion for art this objective will allow him to share his love of art with the local community and bring people together. By improving the local area more people will be aware of Soul and are likely to visit the gallery, which will benefit all the artists who work there because they are likely to sell more artwork.

The introductory stem of this question adds further information to Extract A.

This answer is clearly rooted in the context of the business as the student has made several points linking the answer to Soul.

The answer has been explained and the student has developed their answer by identifying several consequences of achieving this objective – more visitors to the gallery and therefore more art sold.

Forms of business 1

A business can take a variety of legal forms. The legal form will often depend on the size of the business and businesses may change legal structure as they grow. A business will become a separate legal entity when it goes through a process of incorporation to become a limited company.

Business forms

Sole trader

- Easy to start up – no registration is needed
- Requires a wide range of skills and flexibility
- The owner can be their own boss but the hours are likely to be long
- The owner keeps all profits
- Unlimited liability

Sole traders owned by self-employed individuals

Partnerships

- Joint ownership of running a business
- A contract of relationship will be set up through a deed of partnership
- These are common in professions such as solicitors and veterinary surgeons
- Similar issues as faced by sole traders but with greater shared responsibility, risk and reward

Partnerships a business owned by two or more individuals

Private limited company

- Must go through the process of incorporation
- Limited liability
- Has a higher status than a sole trader
- Will have wider access to capital

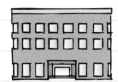

Private limited company owned by shareholders separate legal entity

Public limited company

- Can raise capital through selling shares to the public
- Size is measured by market capitalisation
- Has the ability to take over other businesses
- Can lose control of the business

Public limited company large publicly owned companies

Size – as businesses grow they gain more access to capital

Limited liability

This is where the liability of the owners is detached from the company. Shareholders can lose their investment in the event of financial difficulties, but their personal belongings are safe, unlike with unlimited liability where there is no distinction in law between the individual and the business. For more on limited liability see page 75.

Incorporation involves separation into two legal entities: the shareholders and the company. The company will be registered with Companies House and relevant legal documents produced, including a Memorandum of Association and Articles of Association.

Now try this

1 What are the benefits of being a sole trader?
2 Why would a business want to change from a private limited company to a public limited company?

Forms of business 2

Franchising

A franchise is a limited company that licenses the right for individuals or groups to set up an identical operation in a new region. Franchising allows a business to expand without the owners taking direct responsibility for each branch/store/division.

👍 Effective way to grow the business.

👍 Franchisor gets setup fee and royalty payments.

👎 Risk of franchisee damaging brand if not run effectively.

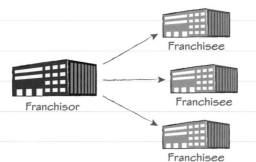

Franchisor

Franchisee

Franchisee

Franchisee

👍 Franchisees receive a 'business in a box' – plans, products, marketing and a recognised brand.

👍 Franchisees are provided with training and support from franchisor.

👎 Expensive setup fees and little freedom to change the business format.

👎 Royalty payments – a share of sales go back to the franchisor.

Private limited companies

Ltd – shares are traded privately

👍 Shareholders have limited liability.

👍 Easier to raise capital through internal shareholders (versus unincorporated businesses).

👍 Owners may pay less tax than if they operate as a sole trader (income tax vs corporation tax).

👎 Harder to set up than sole trader or partnership.

👎 Accounts published and publicly available.

👎 Cannot raise large amounts through selling shares publicly.

Public limited companies

Plc – shares are traded publicly

👍 Huge amounts of money can be made through stock market floatation.

👍 Finance easier to raise through issuing shares.

👍 Size makes it easier to gain economies of scale.

👎 Accounts openly available to the public.

👎 Greater external pressures from the media and pressure groups.

👎 Board of directors is accountable to external shareholders.

Social enterprises – not-for-profit organisations including cooperatives, mutual organisations and charities. These businesses may pay lower tax rates.

Lifestyle businesses – a business run in order to sustain a particular lifestyle for its owners. Often run by a single person and linked to an interest, skill or enthusiasm.

Other forms of business

Online businesses – could be run as any legal form, but providing products and/or services solely through the internet – e-commerce. Internet-based businesses are the fastest growing business sector.

Now try this

1 Why might someone choose to open a franchise instead of setting up their own business?
2 What are the dangers of a business being accountable to external shareholders?

Stock market flotation

A stock market flotation occurs when a company goes public and becomes a Plc. This means that the company's shares are offered on sale to the general public. As these shares can now be traded, it has a significant impact on how the company operates.

Going public

A business must go through a number of steps in order to be listed on a stock market. The process is both expensive and time-consuming.

| Issue a prospectus advertising the company to the public | → | The prospectus and information on the company are reviewed by lawyers | → | A minimum of £50000 share capital has to be provided up front | → | If successful a certificate to sell shares will be issued | → | The Initial Public Offering (IPO) goes live and the business can start trading on the stock market |

The value of shares can change when they are traded on a stock market.

Share price changes

Share prices are affected by the company's performance and the business environment in which it trades. A company's share price could fall even if it is performing well if there are fears for its future.

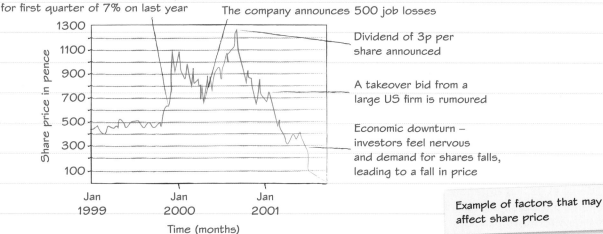

Company announces increase of profits for first quarter of 7% on last year

The company announces 500 job losses

Dividend of 3p per share announced

A takeover bid from a large US firm is rumoured

Economic downturn – investors feel nervous and demand for shares falls, leading to a fall in price

Example of factors that may affect share price

When share prices rise

👍 Managers may receive a bonus.

👍 The company finds it easier to raise capital.

👍 Consumers with shares feel more confident to spend.

👍 The business may receive positive publicity.

When share prices fall

👎 The company may become vulnerable to a takeover.

👎 Price fall gives an indication of poor performance.

👎 The company finds it harder to raise capital.

👎 Consumers with shares feel less confident to spend.

Now try this

1 Give **three** reasons why the share price of a company might change.
2 Why is share price important for a company?

Exam skills

The following exam-style questions explore the topics covered in Unit 1.5.4 and relate to Extract A and Extract B in the case study on page 71.

Worked example

Explain why the owners of Well-Mate may have wanted to set the company up as a private limited company. **(4 marks)**

The owners of Well-Mate may have established the business as a private limited company so that additional owners (shareholders) will be able to own and run the business together, each taking profit from the success of the company. With several people owning the company, risk is spread across a range of people who may also bring their own expertise in the healthcare industry into the company, such as technical expertise or financial management. These shareholders will also be investing in the company and this may make it easier for Well-Mate to raise the start-up capital it needs in order to develop the technology that runs the app.

The student could have looked at several benefits of operating a business as a private limited company, such as limited liability or the status of being incorporated.

The answer develops several benefits of operating as a Ltd. These are developed from the initial reason stated – additional shareholders.

Worked example

Benedick runs Soul as a sole trader. He is considering creating a partnership with Adam – a close friend and fellow artist. Assess the impact of Benedick Hope switching his company from a sole trader to a partnership. **(10 marks)**

A partnership operates in a similar way to a sole trader although there is a contract drawn up between the owners of a partnership known as a deed of partnership. The benefits of operating as a partnership are that Benedick will be able to share the responsibility of running the business with Adam. Adam may bring additional skills and experience to the business and the partnership will also alleviate the pressures of running a business for both partners. This could mean that Benedick has more time to focus on his passion for art.

However, a partnership has a few operating differences from a sole trader. Both Benedick and Adam will still have unlimited liability and will not have the status of some other business forms, such as a private limited company. Furthermore, by taking on a partner Benedick will have to distribute a proportion of the profits to Adam and there may be disputes between the partners if they have disagreement on how the gallery should be run.

In conclusion, the impact of becoming a partnership will depend on the reasons Benedick brought Adam on-board. If Benedick wanted to share the workload and benefit from Adam's skills then a partnership will be a suitable move provided that Benedick and Adam get along. Even though they are close friends it does not mean they will be successful business partners. Overall, Benedick wants to work closely with other local artists so a partnership is a good way to do this.

The student has opened their answer by defining what a partnership is and how this differs from a sole trader. It is good practice to demonstrate your understanding of the key concepts on longer 'assess and evaluate' answers.

To demonstrate counterbalance the student has compared a partnership with the benefits of becoming a private limited company.

The student has used the context well by referring to Benedick's love for art and his relationship with Adam. A judgement has been made on the impact of becoming a partnership.

Business choices

Businesses face endless choices. There are many ways that a business can deploy its resources and different directions the business can take. These decisions will lead to opportunity cost and trade-offs.

Opportunity cost

Opportunity cost is the benefit lost from the next best alternative.

Examples might include:

- the benefits lost from launching a new advertising campaign instead of investing in employee training
- the benefits lost from developing a new product instead of increasing production of an existing successful product
- the benefits lost from purchasing a new vehicle instead of upgrading IT facilities.

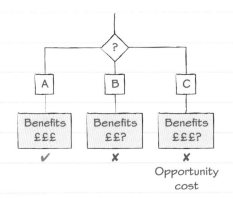

Non-monetary opportunity cost

Often opportunity cost cannot be calculated in financial terms. It is frequently not possible to calculate the monetary value of a decision if the choice has an impact on brand awareness, employee morale or goodwill.

Trade-offs

A trade-off will often involve the loss or compromise of another option or factor. For example, improving productivity in a factory may lower the quality of the products being made (e.g. increasing the number of defects). When making decisions, a business will consider the trade-offs it makes when taking strategic decisions, for example selling high volumes of low-quality products vs selling low volumes of high-quality products.

Choices

A business will consider a number of factors when making decisions.

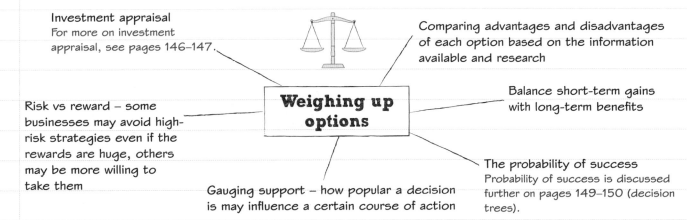

Investment appraisal
For more on investment appraisal, see pages 146–147.

Risk vs reward – some businesses may avoid high-risk strategies even if the rewards are huge, others may be more willing to take them

Weighing up options

Gauging support – how popular a decision is may influence a certain course of action

Comparing advantages and disadvantages of each option based on the information available and research

Balance short-term gains with long-term benefits

The probability of success
Probability of success is discussed further on pages 149–150 (decision trees).

Now try this

1 Give an example of opportunity cost.
2 Why might a business survey its stakeholders before making a key decision?

Entrepreneur to leader

Successful entrepreneurs will create and develop their business ideas and those that are successful will experience growth. Eventually the small start-up will stop being a small business and become a larger company with an organisation structure and a number of employees. At this point the entrepreneur has to become a leader of people.

The demands of becoming a leader

As an entrepreneur's business grows there will be increasing pressure for them to change their approach and become an effective leader of the organisation. This growth and move towards leadership may demand certain characteristics and approaches.

The need for strategic vision

The need to motivate and inspire others

Greater responsibility towards others

Non-monetary opportunity cost

Entrepreneurs will face a number of challenges when taking on the role of a leader for the first time.

Seeing themselves as a leader – entrepreneurs must accept the responsibility and adjust their mindset

Sharing ownership and control of their business

Difficulties of becoming a leader

Leaders need qualities such as confidence, compassion and interpersonal skills

Stress – larger businesses bring with them more responsibility

Overcoming difficulties

Entrepreneurs may adopt the following approaches to overcome the challenges of becoming a leader:

- Stress management – use approaches to reduce stress levels and find time to relax.
- Education – complete leadership development courses and qualifications.
- Mentor – gain advice and support from an experienced mentor.
- Delegate and trust – utilise qualified employees to lighten their load and take responsibility for aspects of running the business.

Preferring to stay small

Some entrepreneurs may prefer to remain as a small business in order to benefit from the advantages and avoid many of the difficulties outlined above. Many of the concepts in this unit are linked to Units 3.2.1 Growth, 3.2.3 Organic growth and 3.2.4 Reasons for staying small.

A restaurant owner may decide not to expand even though the restaurant is doing well.

Now try this

1 Why might an entrepreneur of a growing business find it difficult to delegate responsibility to others?
2 What might a leader of a large business be required to do that an entrepreneur running a small business would not?

Exam skills

The following exam-style questions explore the topics covered in Units 1.5.5 and 1.5.6 and relate to Extract A and Extract B in the case study on page 71.

Worked example

Explain **one** factor that Well-Mate may have taken into consideration when developing the new app. **(4 marks)**

One factor that the developers of Well-Mate may have considered before launching the app is the relative support for the product. The owners may have carried out market research into the app market to identify how many customers they thought would purchase and use the app to manage their health and lifestyle. If they found that many people spoke positively about the app they may have decided that it was a worthwhile risk and offered a better opportunity cost than developing other health-related products, which may not have had as significant an impact on well-being and didn't offer anything significantly different from competitors' products such as the I-Watch.

The student has identified a relevant factor that most businesses would consider when launching a new product.

The candidate has linked their answer to the context of the gadget/healthcare monitoring market.

Worked example

Assess the challenges Benedick may face as Soul grows and he makes the transition from entrepreneur to leader.
(10 marks)

Benedick may face a number of challenges as he takes on the role of a leader within Soul. Soul is becoming popular and more artists are getting involved. This means that Benedick may have to delegate areas of responsibility for running the gallery to other artists and may need to take on additional employees. Benedick is very much running the business to satisfy his own love of art and community and he may find it difficult to set a strategic direction and vision for the business.

The student has identified at least one challenge that entrepreneurs face as they become a leader.

Alternatively, Benedick may see this as a great opportunity to expand the influence of Soul and involve more local people in the initiative. Indeed, Benedick may thrive on the responsibility the gallery brings and be motivated by this level of responsibility. Benedick has already moved the business into new areas, such as the murals for local businesses, and this may show that he has the ambition to lead a larger organisation.

There are also good links to the case study and the unique context of Soul. The student has shown an appreciation of the nature of the business and made inferences about Benedick's motives.

Overall, the challenges Benedick faces will very much be down to his own ambitions. He is not driven by profit so it is unlikely that he will feel the pressure that some entrepreneurs do to make a profit and keep people in a job. Nevertheless, Benedick will be required to demonstrate the characteristics and skills of a good leader and taking part in a business leadership qualification may help him as the business grows.

The student has used a new factor to weigh-up their evaluation and make an informed judgement. Once again, the student has used the context for support.

Exam-style practice

The following questions refer to the content covered in Unit 1.5. For these questions refer to Extract A and Extract B on page 71.

1 Explain **one** entrepreneurial skill that may help Marley become a successful business owner.   **(4 marks)**

Make sure that you clearly link the entrepreneurial skill you choose to the context of Well-Mate Ltd.

2 Explain **one** reason why Benedick may prefer to run his business as a sole trader rather than a private limited company.   **(4 marks)**

Sole trader may offer more flexibility and simplicity than a private limited company. Why might this appeal to Benedick?

3 Assess how the growth of Soul may affect the business objectives set by Benedick.   **(10 marks)**

As businesses grow they will achieve more success. What sort of ambitions might Benedick have for his business?

In 2017 a large and well-known consumer technology brand made an offer to purchase Well-Mate from Marley for £800 000.

4 Assess the opportunity cost of Marley accepting this offer.
                                                                          (12 marks)

What will accepting the offer stop Marley from doing? Consider the relative benefits of the options forgone.

Case study

Extract A: Soul

Benedick Hope set up Soul in 2016. Soul is an artists' gallery set up over a three-storey building in Leeds. Benedick rented the property from a local charity and opened up the space free to local artists to display and sell their artwork. Benedick runs the business as a sole trader and asks for a small contribution from artists who use the gallery to create and store their art projects. In setting up Soul, Benedick's ambition was to bring local artists together to share their passion for art, support local social enterprise projects and offer a collective space where local people can explore, enjoy and buy local art.

The Ground Gallery has been designed to feel very much like a home. Locals can explore the various rooms filled with paintings, sculptures, murals and other exhibits. Benedick has recently started commissioning building murals for local businesses. Most recently, artists from Soul created a mural on the side of a local fruit and veg shop, which has since become famous in the area.

Extract B: Well-Mate Ltd

Marley Finders is the founder and 100 per cent shareholder of Well-Mate. Well-Mate is a smartphone app that aims to pull in information from over 1000 devices to help users better understand connected trends in their behaviour, health and well-being.

Well-Mate's core function is helping people monitor and improve health habits through data tracking. Such features are replicated by many other apps on the market, but Well-Mate differentiates itself by offering to aggregate the information collected by those separate gadgets and turning it all into one big data dashboard. It can be downloaded free to a phone and has the capacity to connect to over 1000 other devices. Well-Mate aims to pull data from health and fitness devices such as Fitbit, Runkeeper and Apple Watches. Information that the app may track and correlate might include a lack of sleep or high blood pressure with an overloaded email inbox. The aim of Well-Mate for Marley is helping people take responsibility for their own health instead of solely relying on healthcare services such as local doctors.

Well-Mate launched the app last year, but Marley still considers the product to be in the development stage with many other possibilities ahead. Marley currently employs two full-time app engineers.

Sources of finance 1

A business may require a range of financing options, which can be from internal or external sources. The availability will depend on a number of factors including the type of business. Managers will consider the availability, cost and risk associated with each source.

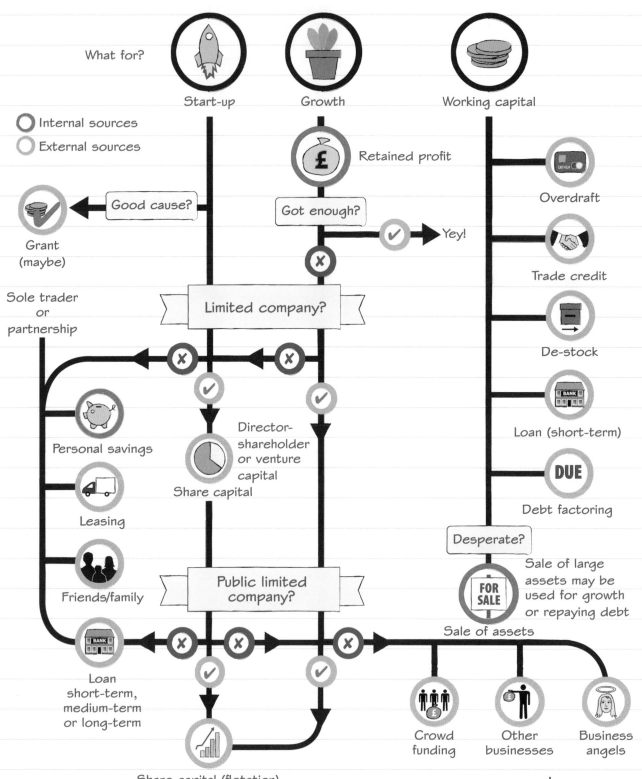

What for?

Start-up   Growth   Working capital

○ Internal sources
○ External sources

Retained profit

Good cause? ← Got enough?

Grant (maybe)

Yey!

Overdraft

Sole trader or partnership

Limited company?

Trade credit

De-stock

Personal savings

Director-shareholder or venture capital

Share capital

Loan (short-term)

Leasing

DUE

Debt factoring

Friends/family

Public limited company?

Desperate?

Sale of large assets may be used for growth or repaying debt

FOR SALE

Sale of assets

Loan short-term, medium-term or long-term

Crowd funding   Other businesses   Business angels

Share capital (flotation)

Different types of shares can be sold:
- ordinary shares
- preference shares
- debentures

Any form of borrowing will require a business plan

Sources of finance 2

Benefits and drawbacks

Internal sources		External sources	
Retained profit	👍 A free source of finance that does not incur interest. 👎 Shareholders may wish to receive it back in the form of a dividend.	**Overdrafts**	👍 Flexible way to fund working capital – acts as a buffer for day-to-day expenses. 👎 Bank may ask for repayment at any time and interest rates are high.
Sale of assets	👍 Frees up value in unwanted assets to be invested in other areas of the business. 👎 The business loses the benefit of the asset, e.g. no longer owning a delivery vehicle.	**Trade credit**	👍 Suitable for buying raw materials from suppliers as it gives the business opportunity to generate revenue before having to pay. 👎 Delays in payment can damage relationships with suppliers.
		Grants	👍 Government schemes might be available for some small businesses. 👎 Generally given for social, environmental or economic benefits.
		Leasing	👍 Assets can be acquired without large capital spending to acquire them. 👎 In the long-term a leased asset is more expensive than purchasing it outright.
Owner's capital (personal savings)	👍 A free source of finance that does not incur interest. 👎 Owners could lose their personal investment.	**Bank loans**	👍 Can be negotiated to meet business requirements. 👎 Business has to pay interest and may have to offer collateral to secure it.
		Venture capital	👍 Can bring expertise into the business. 👎 Owner may not want input from elsewhere into the running of the business.
		Share capital	👍 It can access very large amounts of capital and no interest. 👎 Only available to Ltd (people you know) and Plc (public).
		Crowd funding	👍 Cheap and easy to set up. 👎 Not suitable for raising large amounts of money.

Factors to consider in finance sourcing:

- Legal structure – some sources, such as share capital, are only available to companies.
- Cost – some sources have very high interest repayments.
- Risk – sources that require collateral can be high risk.
- Flexibility – some sources are highly adaptable to meet the business's precise needs.

Now try this

1 Give **three** short-term sources of finance.
2 Why is retained profit low risk?
3 What types of business can raise share capital?

Exam skills

The following exam-style questions explore the topics covered in Units 2.1.1 and 2.1.2. The questions refer to two extracts in the case studies on pages 90 and 91.

Worked example

The following exam-style question refers to Extract A.

Harmeet has decided that she wants to expand her cake business and has decided to invest £3000 of her personal savings.

Explain the benefits of Harmeet expanding her business using her own money. **(4 marks)**

The benefit of Harmeet expanding her cake business with personal finance is that this is a low risk method of finance. Although she might stand to lose the £3000 investment, she will not have to pay interest and is not subject to making regular repayments. This means that she will find it easier to manage her cash flow as the business gradually grows.

This is a good answer explaining the benefits of personal finance. However, the student could develop the benefits further and ensure the answer is rooted in the context of Harmeet's Cakes. They could do this by linking it to the type of business or giving specific examples pertinent to the case study. To complete the answer the student would need to develop a second strand of explanation in context of the case study.

Worked example

The following two exam-style questions refer to Extract B.

Assess why Jaume may find it difficult to secure a bank loan. **(10 marks)**

As Jaume is setting up a new business, he has no track record of success and the bank may find that this is a high risk venture. Furthermore, it is unclear whether Jaume has produced a business plan or financial planning documents and a bank will want to see these in order to be able to assess the level of risk....

It is OK to discuss things not mentioned in the case study. We don't know whether Jaume has produced a business plan, but the student has shown good understanding of the requirements of securing a bank loan.

In this answer the student might go on to analyse other reasons why Jaume might find it difficult to secure a bank loan, for example the fact that the bank might require collateral before it offers lending.

Worked example

Assess alternative sources of finance Jaume could use to finance his leavers' hoodie business other than using a bank loan. **(12 marks)**

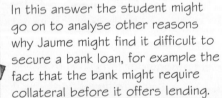

When answering questions on sources of finance, make sure the sources you suggest are appropriate for the situation, context and type of business.

As Jaume is starting a new creative business he could opt to raise finance through crowd funding. This would require Jaume to submit a proposal online through a crowd funding website and hope that his project attracts investors. The benefit is that this is easy to do and he would avoid paying high rates of interest. Nevertheless, Jaume still requires £7000 and it might be difficult to raise this amount through crowd funding if potential investors don't feel that a hoodie printing business is unique. In order for crowd funding to work, Jaume would have to submit a very convincing proposal to attract potential investors.

This is a good start to this question. The student has selected a relevant source of finance for a small business and analysed the issues in relation to Jaume's business. The second paragraph might go on to suggest a second source of finance and then evaluate which of the two is the most appropriate for Jaume.

Limited liability

Limited liability is where the liability of a company's shareholders is detached from the company. Shareholders can lose their investment in the event of financial difficulty, but their personal belongings are safe. Where a business has unlimited liability there is no distinction in law between the owner and the business.

Businesses with unlimited and limited liability

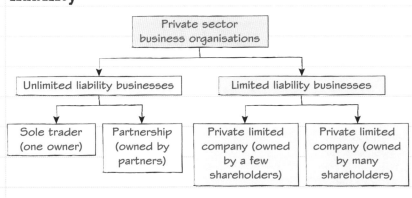

Implications of unlimited liability

Owners of unlimited businesses are exposed to the financial obligations of the business. If they are unable to pay business debts to banks and suppliers they could lose personal assets. The same obligations apply to any unlawful acts committed by the owners or employees. Unlimited liability companies sometimes find it easier to raise finance from lenders as the lenders can seek to regain any borrowings directly from the owners of the business.

Implications of limited liability

Businesses with limited liability are owned by shareholders. A shareholder is an individual or institution that owns a percentage of a company. As a limited liability company is a **separate legal entity** the personal assets of shareholders are protected. Limited liability companies may also find it easier to raise large amounts of capital through the sources available to them.

Shareholders gain from shares in two ways: through profits returned in the form of dividends and in the rise of the price of the shares held when they come to sell them.

The role of shareholders

The shareholders in a limited liability company have a significant impact on decision-making in a business.

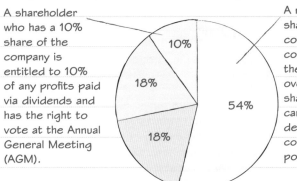

A shareholder who has a 10% share of the company is entitled to 10% of any profits paid via dividends and has the right to vote at the Annual General Meeting (AGM).

A majority shareholder controls the company as they have over a 50% share and can therefore decide company policy.

Finance appropriate for limited and unlimited liability businesses

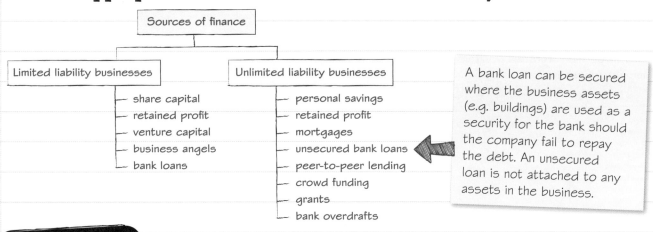

A bank loan can be secured where the business assets (e.g. buildings) are used as a security for the bank should the company fail to repay the debt. An unsecured loan is not attached to any assets in the business.

Now try this

1 What are the dangers of unlimited liability?
2 Why might a secured loan be a suitable source of finance for a limited company?

Exam skills

The following exam-style questions explore the topics covered in Unit 2.1.3 and relate to Extracts B and C in the case study on page 91.

Worked example

Explain why Jaume might decide to set up a company with limited liability. **(4 marks)**

Becoming a limited liability company may initially communicate a more professional image to schools. This might mean the school would trust his company and be more willing to purchase hoodies from him. Furthermore, Jaume's business requires a bank loan to fund the start-up costs. Limited liability would protect him and his personal belongings should the business fall into arrears when making these repayments because the company would be a separate legal entity. As a result, the maximum Jaume could stand to lose is the £5000 he invested himself through personal savings.

There are two strands of context in this answer and the student has demonstrated at least one benefit of Jaume setting up as a limited company.

Worked example

Explain the pressures Hands On Puzzles Plc may experience from its shareholders. **(4 marks)**

Hands On Puzzles Plc will have public shareholders as the company shares have been traded publicly. This means that some shareholders are external to the business and not directors in the company. Shareholders expect a financial return on their investment and Hands On Puzzles will have to ensure its new line of products is able to return a profit or at least generate high sales to please its shareholders. This is especially true since an additional £40 000 will be raised through the issue of new shares as it may be selling further equity in the company. As a new line of puzzles is being developed, shareholders will expect to see a return on this investment through positive sales figures and an impact on net profit.

In this answer the student has used specific financial information from the extract to support their explanation.

The student has shown an understanding of the pressures shareholders can place on a company and business decision-making.

The business plan

Research has shown that businesses are more likely to succeed when the entrepreneurs have created a detailed business plan.

The contents of a business plan

Any good business plan should contain at least the following information.

Factors of a business plan	Details
Executive summary	A one-page overview of the business outlining its purpose and the opportunity.
Business idea and opportunity	An outline of the business idea and concept so that all stakeholders can understand the owner's intentions.
Aims and objectives	Aims and objectives should be SMART (specific, measureable, achievable, realistic and time-related). The owner will measure their success against these targets.
Market research	Market research into the target market, the market and other competitors.
Financial forecasts	These will include forecasts on costs, revenue, profit and cash flow (cash flow forecast, budgets and break-even analysis).
Sources of finance	A plan on how the business will be financed and how any borrowings will be repaid.
Premises and equipment	The location of the business and its rationale. How this will be financed and any other equipment the business will need.
Personnel	An organisation chart outlining the personnel in the business, their areas of responsibility, skills and qualifications.
Buying and production	Details of how the product will be produced including details of suppliers.

Who uses a business plan?

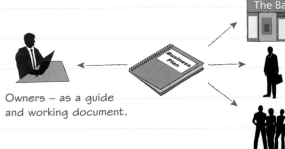

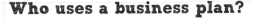

Owners – as a guide and working document.

The Bank — Lenders – e.g. banks will want to investigate the likely success and risk of lending to a new business.

Investors – to assess the risk and reward of investing in the business (e.g. Ltd or Plc).

Partners and employees – anyone wanting to work with/for the business.

Risk and planning

Owners can never be 100 per cent certain of their decisions and fortunes when starting a business, but the depth and detail of business planning reduces risk associated with unforeseen problems and poor decision-making and increases the likelihood of success.

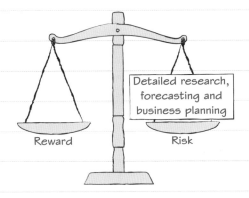

Reward   Detailed research, forecasting and business planning   Risk

Now try this

Explain how **two** stakeholder groups, other than the owner of the business, may use a business plan.

Cash-flow forecasts

A cash-flow forecast will predict the cash inflows (receipts) for a business and the cash outflows (expenditure). A cash-flow forecast should then determine the cash funds a business has at any one time. If a business knows what cash funds it needs, it can take measures to ensure that enough finance is available.

Constructing a cash-flow forecast

A cash-flow forecast is generally made up of three sections:

Generally a longer list of items than cash in.

Difference between monthly inflows and monthly outflows.

Net cash flow + opening balance. Closing balance is the available cash a business is forecast to have during that trading period.

		January	February	March
Cash in	Cash sales			
	Credit sales			
	Total inflow			
Cash out	Raw materials			
	Salaries			
	Other costs			
	Total outflows			
Net cash flow	Net cash flow			
	Opening balance			
	Closing balance			

Cash-flow forecast is calculated as:

(inflows − outflows = net cash flow) + opening balance = closing balance

Cash carried forward from previous trading period. For example, February's opening balance will be January's closing balance.

Interpreting cash-flow forecasts

When analysing cash-flow forecasts managers should consider the following questions:

> Are our monthly inflows greater than our monthly outflows?

> What are the forecast periods of high expenditure?

> Are inflows increasing over time?

> Is there a seasonal trend?

> Do we have enough cash reserves to cover unexpected costs?

In your exam you may be required to show your understanding of cash-flow forecasts by completing variables in a cash-flow table. In the cash-flow table opposite see how each of the missing figures is calculated.

Changing cash-flow variables

	Jan	Feb	Mar
CASH INFLOWS			
Investment	10000		
Credit Sales	2500	10000	10000
Total inflows	**12500**	**10000**	**10000**
CASH OUTFLOWS			
Project materials		3000	3000
Sub-contract labour	4000	4000	4000
Marketing	500	500	500
Legal and accounting	A	0	0
Equipment	2500	0	0
Sophie & Jack salaries	1000	1000	1000
Other costs	500	500	500
Total outflows	**9750**	**9000**	**9000**
NET CASH FLOW	**2750**	**1000**	B
Opening balance	0	2750	C
Closing balance	2750	3750	4750

A – Legal and accounting must be the difference between total cash outflows in Jan and sum of the known outflows = £1250

B – Total inflows March − Total outflows March

C – An opening balance is the previous period's closing balance. It can also be calculated by subtracting the net cash flow from the closing balance.

Now try this

1 What is the opening balance?
2 What might a cash-flow forecast be used for?
3 How is a cash-flow forecast calculated?
4 What is net cash flow?

Using cash-flow forecasts and improving cash flow

A key decision managers have to make is how they will improve the financial performance of the business. In particular, managers must know how to improve cash flow and profitability.

Improving cash flow

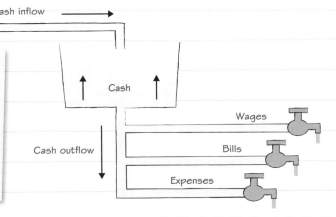

The causes of cash-flow problems include:

- overtrading
- allowing too much trade credit to customers
- poor credit control
- inaccurate cash-flow management
- unforeseen costs.

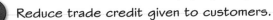

Speed up inflows

1 Incentivise early repayment by giving customers a discount for paying early.

2 Reduce trade credit given to customers.

3 Sell off stock at a discounted price to free up cash.

4 Inject fresh capital into the business.

A business should always plan to keep a minimum cash reserve in its bank account.

Slow down outflows

1 Delay payments to suppliers.

2 Increase trade credit agreements with suppliers.

3 Cut costs, such as finding cheaper alternatives or postponing spending in areas such as training or advertising.

The best way to ensure the business has a positive cash flow is to invest time and effort in researching and planning effective cash-flow forecasts.

The benefits of cash-flow forecasting

There are several reasons why a business should construct a cash-flow forecast:

1 To support an application for lending (perhaps as part of a business plan).

2 To support the budgeting process.

3 To identify any potential cash flow crisis.

A business must consider its payables and receivables in order to manage cash flow effectively. **Payables** – amount of time (days) taken for the business to pay creditors. **Receivables** – amount of time taken for debtors to pay the business.

The limitations of cash-flow forecasting

There are several limitations that have to be taken into consideration when producing and using cash-flow forecasts to support business planning and decision-making.

1 Some figures will be based on estimates.

2 Variables are constantly changing and cash-flow forecasts should be updated for them to be valid.

3 Cash-flow forecasts focus on one variable – cash. They do not consider other important variables, such as profitability or productivity.

Now try this

1 Identify **two** ways a business can increase cash inflows.
2 Identify **two** ways a business can reduce cash outflows.

Exam skills

The following exam-style questions explore the topics covered in Unit 2.1.4. The questions refer to Extract A in the case study on page 90.

Worked example

Using the data in the cash-flow forecast below, calculate:

A Total income for January
B Net cash flow for January
C Materials for February
D Closing balance for February
E Opening balance for March

(4 marks)

Harmeet's Cakes cash-flow forecast

	JAN	FEB	MAR	APR
INCOME				
Specialist cakes	400	500	900	1200
Parties	500	1600	1900	2200
TOTAL INCOME	A 900	2100	2800	3400
EXPENDITURE (Payments)				
Rent	400	400	400	400
Materials	450	C 600	800	900
Delivery costs	65	80	120	150
Advertising	200	40	40	40
TOTAL EXPENDITURE	1115	1120	1360	1490
NET CASHFLOW	B –215	980	1440	1910
OPENING BALANCE	100	–115	E 865	2305
CLOSING BALANCE	–115	D 865	2305	4215

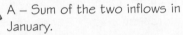

By knowing the calculations necessary to complete a cash-flow forecast the student was able to work out the five missing numbers.

A – Sum of the two inflows in January.

B – Total income – total expenditure for January.

C – The difference between total expenditure for February and the sum of the other three expenditures in February (400 + 80 + 40).

D – Net cash flow for February + opening balance for February.

E – The opening balance for March will be the same as the closing balance for February.

Worked example

Explain the potential benefits of Harmeet using the cash-flow forecast to support her application for a bank loan for her cake business.

(4 marks)

When applying for a business loan the bank would want to identify the level of understanding a business owner has of the market. Harmeet's cash-flow forecast shows that she understands the potential demand in the market and has a grasp of the costings. This is shown through her estimates for specialist cakes, parties and her business overheads such as materials for making her cakes. As a result, the lender may be more likely to grant the loan because having detailed financial information is vital if they are able to assess the level of risk and the likelihood that Harmeet will be able to pay back the loan. This is especially true in the case of Harmeet because she believes her business is seasonal. The bank will need to see that Harmeet can repay the loan even during the months when there might be a lull in sales, such as February–April.

The student has made several references to the case study and nature of the business (there are 2 marks for application on this question). They have also shown good understanding of how a cash-flow forecast can support business planning and support an application for finance.

Exam-style practice

The following exam-style questions refer to the content covered in Unit 2.1. For these questions refer to Extracts A to C in the case studies on pages 90 and 91.

1 What is meant by limited liability?   **(2 marks)**

> In the AS papers the exam will start with definition questions.

2 What is meant by crowd funding?   **(2 marks)**

> You can support your answers to a definition question with examples where appropriate.

The table below represents Harmeet's cash-flow forecast for the first four months of trading in 2016. Harmeet is concerned that she may find it difficult to manage her cash flow during the first few months of the year.

3 Assess how Harmeet could ensure she has a positive cash flow at the start of the year.   **(10 marks)**

> In your answer, you should draw on specific financial data from the cash-flow forecast. You should also attempt to make at least two suggestions for how Harmeet could maintain a positive cash flow and then justify which of the options is likely to be the most effective.

Harmeet's Cakes cash-flow forecast				
	JAN	FEB	MAR	APR
INCOME				
Specialist cakes	400	500	900	1200
Parties	500	1600	1900	2200
TOTAL INCOME	900	2100	2800	3400
EXPENDITURE (Payments)				
Rent	400	400	400	400
Materials	450	600	800	900
Delivery costs	65	80	120	150
Advertising	200	40	40	40
TOTAL EXPENDITURE	1115	1120	1360	1490
NET CASHFLOW	−215	980	1440	1910
OPENING BALANCE	100	−115	865	2305
CLOSING BALANCE	−115	865	2305	4215

4 Assess the likelihood of Hands On Puzzles Plc's business plan in helping it secure a £40 000 loan from the bank.   **(12 marks)**

> The question relates to two areas of the syllabus: sources of finance and business planning. In order to answer the question you should discuss the benefits of business planning, but also consider some of the limitations. Your evaluation should use the information available to justify how likely it is that Hands On Puzzles Plc will secure the loan and make recommendations for the content of an effective business plan. Try to be specific to the context of the business.

Sales forecasting

Sales forecasting involves a business using a range of techniques and information to predict future sales volumes and values. Sales forecasting is a key business process as the information will be used to make many other key decisions, such as purchasing raw materials, staffing, marketing and financing the business, for example, managing cash flow.

Approaches to sales forecasting

A business may use a range of information in order to accurately carry out a sales forecast. This may include:

- market research (e.g. market reports and customer surveys)
- backdata (e.g. time series analysis) economic forecasts.

> Time series analysis is predicting future sales based on past sales figures, taking into account the trend and seasonal fluctuations.

Economic variables

Economic variables combine to influence the level of demand and therefore sales in a market. Different markets respond differently to economic variables. Some of these economic variables include:

- economic growth (GDP)
- interest rates
- inflation
- unemployment
- exchange rates.

Consumer trends

Successful businesses will anticipate the needs of customers and adjust their products and operations accordingly to meet these needs. Businesses need to take into account the habits and behaviours of customers.

- Seasonal variations – sales fluctuate depending on the season or even day of the week.
- Fashions – fashions constantly change and can make it very difficult to carry out accurate sales forecasts.
- Long-term trends – fashions may change from season to season, but most consumer behaviours change over a longer period of time, e.g. the trend towards solar-powered energy.

Actions of competitors

A business is likely to adjust its sales forecasts based on the actions of its competitors. For example, if a big competitor were to launch a sales promotion, introduce a new and improved product line or open a new branch nearby, a business could rightly expect sales to fall. Similarly, the closure of a large competitor might lead to an increase in sales as the business picks up trade from the switching customers.

The failure of one business could lead to an increase in sales in another.

Limitations and problems

The process of conducting an accurate sales forecast is not easy and any forecast has its limitations.

Volatile customer tastes and preferences.

Fluctuations in economic variables – unforeseen external shocks such as changing commodity prices.

The data used – the quality of the data a business uses may vary considerably.

Subjective expert opinions – many forecasts will be supported by the opinions and experience of a manager within the business.

The problem with sales forecasting

Volatile markets – some markets are more volatile and unpredictable than others.

Now try this

1 How might a business conduct a sales forecast?
2 What are the limitations of sales forecasting?

Sales, revenue and costs

In order to calculate profit and make financial decisions a business must be able to accurately calculate sales volumes, sales revenue and all business costs, broken down into fixed costs and variable costs.

Sales volume and sales revenue

The **volume of sales** (expressed in units) is sometimes difficult for a business to calculate. For example, a restaurant will use the number of meals sold, whereas a car manufacturer will simply use the number of cars.

Revenue is the value of sales made during a trading period. It also includes products sold on credit as well as those sold for cash.

A business can increase revenue by increasing the price of their products and by stimulating more demand.

> Sales revenue = price × quantity sold
>
> Make sure you are clear on the difference between price and cost. Always look at this distinction from the business's point of view, not the customer.

Business costs

 Variable costs are those that change directly with the level of output or sales, e.g. materials.

 Fixed costs are those that do not change with the level of output or sales, e.g. rent.

Calculating fixed and variable costs can help when making decisions about profit margins, average costs and pricing decisions. A business can improve profit by reducing either of these costs while maintaining value in their products.

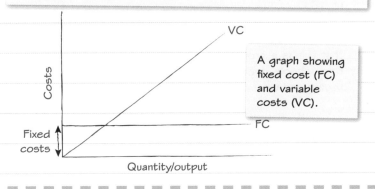

A graph showing fixed cost (FC) and variable costs (VC).

Short-run and long-run

The **short-run** refers to the immediate future. In the short-run it is true that variable costs are variable and fixed costs are fixed. However, in the **long-run** (long-term) all costs are variable. This is because fixed costs will eventually change over time. Some fixed costs may fall, for example utility costs, whereas others will rise, such as mortgage costs or employee salaries.

Measuring success

Revenue is an important measure for any business. Achieving high revenue demonstrates that the business has been able to produce a product or service that is desirable at the right price for consumers. However, the real test is whether the business has been able to turn revenue into profit. There is a saying in business: 'Revenue is vanity; profit is sanity'. When analysing sales information it is important to consider the **profit margin**. It is difficult to analyse the success of a business without being able to compare revenue and profit.

Average cost or unit cost

The average cost is the cost per unit of production. It is also referred to as the unit cost. This is an important measure for a business as the unit cost will determine the profit margin. The larger the output the lower the unit cost/average cost.

$$\text{Average cost} = \frac{\text{total cost}}{\text{output}}$$

Profit and loss

Understanding revenues and costs allows a business to work out its profit or loss. A business should be able to calculate its profit at any level of output/any level of sales.

> Profit = total revenue − total costs

Now try this

1 How is profit calculated?
2 What is the difference between variable costs and fixed costs?
3 How might a business increase its revenue?

Exam skills

The following exam-style questions explore the topics covered in Units 2.2.1 and 2.2.2. The questions refer to extracts A, B and C in the case studies on pages 90 and 91.

Worked example

The following exam-style question refers to Extract B.

1 Explain how Jaume may have worked out that the leavers' hoodies market is growing. **(4 marks)**

This question is also linked to Unit 1.1.2 Market research.

Jaume may have worked out that the hoodies market is growing by conducting his own primary market research or from his own experience and intuition. Jaume will not have been able to use back data to carry out a sales forecast as his is a new business and he will have no prior data on which to base this forecast. The more sources of information that Jaume can collect the more accurate will be his prediction that this is a growing market. For example, Jaume could also ring schools directly to find out the number of students buying and wearing leavers' hoodies.

2 Using the information from Figure 3 on page 91, calculate the total costs for Jaume's Hoodies should he produce 12 000 units. **(4 marks)**

Always start by writing out the relevant formula.

Total costs = fixed costs + total variable costs

FC = £20 000 + £15 000 = £35 000

VC = £13 × 12 000 = £156 000

Total costs = £191 000

When using variable costs, remember to use the relevant figure. Use total variable costs when working out total costs and variable costs per unit when working out the break-even point.

Worked example

The following exam-style question refers to Extract C.

Assess the value of Hands On Puzzles Plc conducting a sales forecast. **(10 marks)**

The student has started their answer by showing understanding of the uses of a sales forecast. They have also applied their answer to the Hands On Puzzles Plc case study.

A sales forecast is an extremely important piece of information for Hands On Puzzles. This is because without an accurate sales forecast they will not be able to make decisions on the production quantities, the equipment or the employees they require to produce the new bamboo puzzle line. Without this information they will not know how much money they need to borrow from the bank or raise through additional share capital. Furthermore, without a detailed sales forecast based on reliable sources it is unlikely that any potential lender will be willing to agree the loan of £40 000....

This is a partial answer. The student should now go on to explain some of the limitations of sales forecasting or other business decision-making tools/research that might be arguably more important than a sales forecast. They should then finish their answer with a justified conclusion.

Break-even 1

The break-even output is the point at which a business's revenue generated through the sales of its products will cover the total costs. At break-even the business is making neither a profit nor a loss. Break-even analysis can be used to help a business make important decisions about costs, prices and expected profit.

The uses of break-even analysis

👍 Decide whether a business idea is profitable and viable.

👍 Identify the level of output and sales necessary to generate a profit (and therefore the scale of the business).

👍 Assess changes in the level of production.

👍 Assess the effects of costing and pricing decisions.

$$\text{Break-even point} = \frac{\text{fixed costs}}{\text{contribution per unit}}$$

Contribution

Contribution is the difference between the variable costs of one unit and its selling price.

Contribution = selling price – variable cost per unit

Total contribution is total output × contribution per unit.

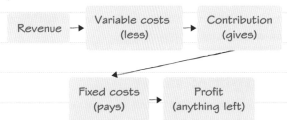

Understanding break-even

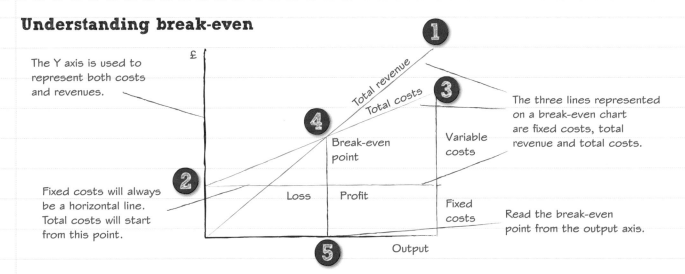

The Y axis is used to represent both costs and revenues.

Fixed costs will always be a horizontal line. Total costs will start from this point.

The three lines represented on a break-even chart are fixed costs, total revenue and total costs.

Read the break-even point from the output axis.

1 Plot total revenue line (price × quantity sold) at each level of output. You only need two points on a graph to draw a line. You know total revenue will start at 0 so you only need to calculate revenue at one other output level to draw your line.

2 Plot fixed costs line. As fixed costs will not change at any level of output, you know this will be a horizontal line.

3 Plot total costs line. Add variable cost at each level of output to the fixed costs. As your total costs line at 0 will start at the same point as fixed costs you only need to calculate one other point to get your line.

4 Where total costs meet total revenue is where break-even is identified. Label this.

5 If the current level of output is below break-even the business will make a loss. If it is above break-even it will generate a profit.

Now try this

1 How is the break-even point calculated?

2 What three pieces of information are included on a break-even chart?

3 Give **three** reasons why a business might use break-even analysis.

Break-even 2

Changing variables and break-even analysis

Analysing and manipulating break-even charts can help a business make decisions on whether to accept prices on orders different from those normally charged or the impact on profitability of a change in costs and output levels.

For example:

A Raising the price by £2 will increase revenue at each level of output and lower the break-even point.

B Using a cheaper supplier might lower variable costs by £1. This would move the total costs line down and lower the break-even point.

C An increase in rent of £200 per month would raise the fixed costs line, which in turn would increase total costs. The break-even point would rise.

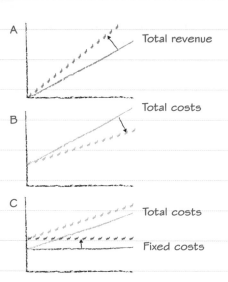

The margin of safety

This is the difference between the break-even point and the current level of output. The size of the margin of safety will determine the risk of the business – the margin of safety should be as high as possible.

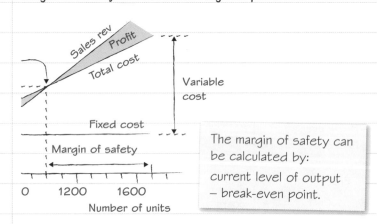

The margin of safety can be calculated by:

current level of output – break-even point.

Exam focus   **Break-even analysis**

When analysing financial information, break-even analysis can be used to evaluate the potential of a business to make a profit based on its output. For example, a business with a high break-even point will have to produce and sell a lot before it starts to make a profit. A small margin of safety could also suggest any negative impact on output or demand could lead to the business making a loss. As you will see below, break-even has its limitations and this should also be taken into consideration when analysing break-even data.

The value of break-even analysis

Benefits

👍 Can be used to analyse the impact of varying customers, prices and costs on a business's profit.

👍 It is simple and easy to use.

👍 The break-even point is a useful guideline to help businesses make decisions.

Limitations

👎 Break-even analysis simplifies what can be a very complex process – most businesses sell multiple products, which makes break-even more difficult.

👎 Costs are rarely constant – break-even analysis presumes that costs stay the same over various levels of output.

👎 Break-even focuses on output – it presumes that the business will sell all of its output at the same price.

Now try this

1 Identify **two** ways a business could lower its break-even point.
2 What is the margin of safety?
3 Give **two** limitations of break-even analysis.

Budgets

A budget is a financial plan for the future. An effective budget should drive many of the decisions taken across the functional areas of a business, for example the number of products to be made, how to promote the product and the number of workers to employ. Budgets can also be used to motivate the workforce when used in target setting.

Types of budget

Setting budgets helps a business achieve its financial and wider objectives. A business looking to grow will increase its revenue budgets. This in turn will inform the expenditure budgets, which will then determine the business's budgeted profits.

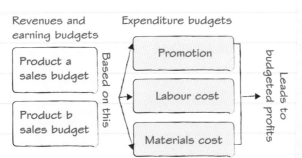

The purpose of budgets is to ensure efficiency in spending. Setting budgets allows large businesses to be coordinated and can be a way of motivating employees who are allocated a budget – a budget is a financial target and employees might be rewarded for meeting this target.

Historical and zero-based budgeting

Where prior data is available, budgets will be based on information gleaned from **historical budgets** and adjusted based on future events, estimations and professional judgement.

Where historical data is not available, a **zero-based budget** approach might be adopted. With zero-based budgeting, the opportunity cost of all spending decisions is considered. Any spending has to be justified by the budget-holder to ensure all spending is good value for money. Zero-budgeting can be efficient at minimising unnecessary costs but it is also time-consuming and can become a barrier to decision-making.

The problems with budgets

👎 A budget is only as accurate as the data on which it is based.

👎 Past trends can be a poor indicator of what is likely to happen in the future. Therefore, it can be very difficult to forecast sales.

👎 New decisions taken by governments and public bodies can affect budgets, e.g. interest rate changes and employment legislation.

👎 Unexpected changes in process, e.g. commodity prices, can impact budgets.

👎 When a budget is unrealistic it loses all value as a motivational tool.

Variance analysis

Variance analysis compares the forecast data to the actual figures. It can be used to analyse the accuracy of the budgeting process and to help make decisions about budget adjustments.

Which adverse variances are due to poor forecasting?

How effectively has the business budgeted revenue?

What are the key areas that have led to the budget being inaccurate?

Example of a variance analysis

Which adverse variances are due to unexpected factors?

Budget	2015 budget	2015 actual	Variance
Staff salaries and training	1.5 m	2 m	0.5 m adverse
Revenue	6 m	7 m	1 m favourable
Maintenance	2.3 m	4 m	1.7 m adverse
Marketing	0.5 m	0.5 m	0
Overheads	7 m	6.5 m	0.5 m favourable

How effectively has the business budgeted expenditure?

Now try this

1 Give **two** examples of an expenditure budget.
2 What is an adverse variance?
3 Give **two** reasons why it is difficult to forecast accurate budgets.

Exam skills

The following exam-style questions explore the topics covered in Units 2.2.3 and 2.2.4. The questions refer to Extracts A, B and C in the case studies on pages 90 and 91.

Worked example

What is meant by break-even point?   **(2 marks)**

The level of output where total cost (fixed costs plus variable costs) is the same as total revenue.

Worked example

The following exam-style question refers to Extract A.

Using the information in Figure 2 on page 90, calculate the budget variance for Harmeet's Cakes (1–5) for 2016 Qtr 1. For each variance identify whether it is favourable or adverse.   **(4 marks)**

	2016 quarter 1 forecast	2016 quarter 1 actual	Variance
Income budget			
Income from parties	6300	5850	
Income from specialist cakes	2700	2900	1 200 favourable
Total income	**9000**	**8750**	2 250 adverse
Expenditure budget			
Fixed costs	6000	6500	3 500 adverse
Cost of specialist cakes	1575	1575	
Other variable costs	675	575	4 100 favourable
Total expenditure	**8250**	**8650**	5 400 adverse

The key to calculating variance is to first identify the type of budget. In 1 the variance is favourable by 200 because the business exceeded its sales budget for specialist cakes. On the other hand, 3 is adverse because this is an expenditure budget and fixed costs are £500 higher than forecast.

Worked example

The following exam-style question refers to Extract B.

Using the information in Figure 3 on page 91, calculate the break-even point for Jaume's Hoodies for its first year of trading.   **(4 marks)**

Break-even = fixed costs / price – variable costs per unit

= £35 000 / (21.20 – 13)

= 4269 hoodies to break even

Fixed costs are calculated by adding the rent on premises and other overheads. Selling price – variable cost per unit is known as the contribution per unit.

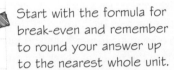
Exam-style practice

The following exam-style questions explore the topics covered in Unit 2.2. The questions refer to extracts A, B and C in the case studies on pages 90 and 91.

The following two exam-style questions refer to Extract A.

Harmeet estimated that her average monthly fixed costs for 2016 would be £900. The average price she planned to sell her cakes for was £45 with variable costs per cake being £16.

1　On average, how many cakes would Harmeet have to sell each month in order to break even?　**(4 marks)**

> Start with the formula for break-even and remember to round your answer up to the nearest whole unit.

2　Using Figure 1 on page 90, calculate the percentage growth in forecasted sales of Harmeet's Cakes between Qtr 1 and Qtr 4.　**(4 marks)**

> Start by working out the actual increase between Qtr 1 and Qtr 4.

The following two exam-style questions refer to Extract B.

3　Explain how Jaume could increase revenue for his business.　**(4 marks)**

> This is a very open question. Try to choose a method that you can easily apply to the context of Extract B.

4　Assess the value of cash-flow forecasting for a business like Jaume's Hoodies.　**(10 marks)**

> Consider the nature of Jaume's product and the stage that his business is at.

The following three exam-style questions refer to Extract C.

5　Explain how Hands On Puzzles Plc could lower the average cost of its new sustainable bamboo puzzles.　**(4 marks)**

> There are two types of cost that Hands On Puzzles Plc could reduce in order to have an impact on average costs – fixed costs and variable costs.

6　Assess the value of Hands On Puzzles Plc using break-even analysis to support the planning for its new range of puzzles.　**(12 marks)**

> There are a number of generic limitations of break-even analysis. Think how you could apply these limitations to Extract C.

Hands On Puzzles Plc is considering raising finance through issuing new shares or borrowing the capital through a long-term loan.

7　Evaluate these **two** options and recommend which is the best option for Hands On Puzzles Plc.　**(20 marks)**

> In your answer consider at least one other source of finance that would be appropriate for the context of Hands On Puzzles Plc. Your conclusion should also include a recommendation for the business.

Case study

Extract A – Harmeet's Cakes

Harmeet was a skilled baker of confectionery goods. For the past two years, she had been a part-time confectionery chef in a local cake store. As she felt that she knew the market well, she decided to open her own catering business making one-off specialised cakes for special occasions and baking for parties such as birthdays and weddings. She had built up a loyal customer base and had gained an insight into the types of cakes that worked best for different occasions.

Harmeet knew that her business would have highest demand during the summer, when people tended to have weddings, and over the Christmas period. However, she also knew that the market was becoming more competitive and that demand would fall sharply if the economy was weak. Harmeet constructed a forecast for demand (see Figure 1).

Figure 1: Forecast demand for Harmeet's Cakes

	2016 Qtr 1	2016 Qtr 2	2016 Qtr 3	2016 Qtr 4
Number of parties	45	45	60	75

Figure 2: Harmeet's budget forecast

	2016 Qtr 1	2016 Qtr 2	2016 Qtr 3	2016 Qtr 4
Income budget				
Income from parties	6300	6300	8400	10500
Income from specialist cakes	2700	2700	3600	4500
Total income	**9000**	**9000**	**12000**	**15000**
Expenditure budget				
Fixed costs	6000	3000	3000	3000
Variable cost of specialist cakes	1575	1575	2100	2625
Other variable costs	675	675	900	1125
Total expenditure	**8250**	**5250**	**6000**	**6750**

Case study

Extract B – Jaume's hoodies

Jaume planned to open a business selling hoodies to school leavers. Jaume had noticed that this was a growing market and that most schools in the region purchased hoodies for students leaving in Year 11 and Year 13. Jaume calculated his business start-up costs for the first three months of trading to be £12 000. Jaume had managed to invest £5000 of his own savings and considered raising the remaining funds through a bank loan.

Jaume had limited funds available but was able to use his skills in website design to create a website to promote his business and, once the business started trading, to allow online purchasing in the electronic market.

Figure 3: Jaume's financial information

Decision	Options chosen
Selling price	£21.20 per hoodie
Expected sales	9000 units per annum
Variable costs	Purchase high-quality hoodies at £13 each
Rent premises	£20 000 per annum
Other fixed costs	£15 000 per annum

Extract C – Hands On Puzzles Plc

Hands On Puzzles Plc is a large manufacturer of wooden puzzles and brain teasers based in China. The company manufactures around two million puzzles each year, which it exports all around the world. Its main markets are the USA and Western Europe. The company is looking to invest in a new line of traditional wooden toys for children. The toys will be made from locally supplied bamboo, an ecologically sustainable resource. The company is looking to finance the new product line through the issue of new shares and a £40 000 loan. The board of directors intends to produce a detailed business plan to support the application for finance.

As part of the business plan, Hands on Puzzles Plc has produced sales forecasts for the first four years once the new product line has been launched.

Figure 4: Hands On Puzzles Plc sales forecasts

	2018	2019	2020	2021
Sales of sustainable bamboo puzzles	40 000 units	100 000 units	175 000 units	200 000 units

Calculation of profit

We have already seen that profit is calculated by subtracting total costs from total revenue. However, accountants and managers calculate profit in a number of ways. Each method demonstrates something slightly different about the performance of the business.

Types of profit

There are three types of profit a business will calculate and use to measure performance.

1 **Gross profit** is the difference between revenue and the cost of sales (the direct costs of the business). It shows the profit made on the trading activity before any other costs are taken into account.

Gross profit = Revenue – Cost of sales

2 **Operating profit** takes into account the other operating expenses on top of gross profit.

Operating profit =
Gross profit – Other operating expenses

3 **Profit for the year** is the 'actual' profit the business has made (taking into account interest).

Profit for the year = Operating profit +/– Interest

Profit margins

The value of profit alone has limited value in determining the performance of a business. Managers will often calculate a **profit margin**. This is a ratio expressed as a percentage. It compares the profit figure to sales revenue – in other words, the proportion of sales revenue that has been converted into profit.

Gross profit margin

Gross profit margin is a useful indicator for analysing how a business has performed in terms of its direct trading activity. It helps a business answer the question 'Have our products been successful?'. However, gross profit has its limitations as it does not take into account indirect costs.

It is calculated using:

$$\text{Gross profit margin} = \frac{\text{Gross profit}}{\text{Revenue}} \times 100\%$$

Operating profit margin

Operating profit takes into account the performance of a business more fully, as the calculation takes into account direct and indirect costs. It is a useful tool when used alongside the gross profit margin.

It is calculated using:

$$\text{Operating profit margin} = \frac{\text{Operating profit}}{\text{Revenue}} \times 100\%$$

Profit for the year margin

This ratio takes into account all revenues and costs incurred by the business. It is a good measure of how effectively the business performed over the financial year. This ratio may be used to identify the potential to pay a dividend to shareholders.

It is calculated using:

$$\text{Profit for the year (net profit) margin} = \frac{\text{Profit for the year (net profit)}}{\text{Revenue}} \times 100\%$$

Now try this

1 What is profit for the year?
2 Why are financial ratios important?

The statement of comprehensive income

A business will produce a range of financial information to support its stakeholders in decision-making. Two key documents that all companies are required to produce are the **statement of comprehensive income** and the **balance sheet**.

The statement

The statement of comprehensive income at its most basic will communicate the revenue generated by a business and then its profit at various levels following a series of expenses and exceptional incomes.

Cost of sales
The direct costs associated with the production and sale of the product or service.

Administration/rent/salaries
Other operating expenses are deducted from gross profit.

Operating profit
The profit left after other indirect operating costs (overheads) have been deducted.

Statement of comprehensive income April 2016–March 2017	£m
Revenue	300
Cost of sales	(45)
Gross profit	255
Administration	(10)
Rent	(30)
Salaries	(25)
Operating profit	190
Interest	(25)
Profit for the year (net profit)	165

Gross profit
The profit after direct costs have been deducted. Gives a broad indication of the success of a business's trading activity.

Interest
The interest paid on loans. This is deducted after other expenses because it is a non-operating expense

Net profit
The bottom line – what a business has left to reinvest or return to shareholders/owners after tax has been deducted.

The statement of comprehensive income can be used to calculate profitability ratios such as gross profit margin, operating profit margin and return on capital employed (ROCE).

What we can find out from a statement of comprehensive income:

- ✓ Changes in sales revenue
- ✓ Changes in the direct costs of sales
- ✓ How well a business is managing its operating costs
- ✓ The profitability of a business
- ✓ Unusual incomes/expenses during the year

Now try this

1 What does a statement of comprehensive income show?
2 What is the difference between gross profit and operating profit?
3 What are other operating expenses?

Improving profitability

Profitability can be improved through measures taken by each functional area of the business.

Ways to increase revenue

1 Increase prices.

2 Reduce process (dependent on price elasticity of demand).

3 Create awareness and desire through marketing.

4 Add value to the product – increase benefits and features.

Improving profit

Profit is the difference between total revenue and total costs. Therefore, there are two general ways that a business can improve its profits. These are increased revenue or/and decrease costs.

Why businesses are unprofitable

There are a number of reasons why a business might be unprofitable:

👎 No demand for the product.

👎 Selling at the wrong price.

👎 Low contribution per unit.

👎 Poor management of costs.

👎 Expansion of the business – profit retained and not available for return to shareholders.

Revenue

Profit

Costs

Ways to reduce costs

1 Reduce production costs.

2 Improve efficiency.

3 Use capacity more fully.

4 Eliminate unprofitable processes – such as unprofitable product lines.

5 Reduce variable costs – negotiate better deals with suppliers.

6 Lower overheads – move to a cheaper location.

Cash vs profit

All businesses plan to be profitable. Profit is an absolute position when all costs have been deducted from revenue. However, cash flow is an ongoing concern. In order to reach a position of profit, a business must manage cash flow so that it can pay expenses and running costs. The problem with managing cash is that business expenses are often incurred before revenue is generated or received. A business cannot be profitable unless it can effectively manage its cash flow. This is a question of timing and can be crucial to business success.

The difference between cash and profit

	Cash flow statement		Statement of comprehensive income
	Cash inflows		Revenue earned
−	Cash outflows	−	Expenses incurred
=	Net cash flow (+/−)	=	Net profit (loss)

Now try this

1 Identify **three** costs a business could reduce in order to improve profit.

2 Why is price an important factor in a business's profitability?

3 Identify **three** problems a business might face when trying to improve profitability.

Exam skills

The following exam-style questions explore the topics covered in Unit 2.3.1. The questions refer to the Sartorial Ltd case study on page 101.

Worked example

Using the extracts from the statement of comprehensive income of Sartorial Ltd, calculate the operating profit margin for the two years 2016–2017. You are advised to show your workings. **(4 marks)**

$2016 = \dfrac{412}{1240} \times 100 = 33.22\%$

$2017 = \dfrac{195}{1390} \times 100 = 14.02\%$

 The student has clearly laid out their calculations and expressed the answer correctly as a percentage.

Worked example

Using the data in Figure 1 and Figure 2 on page 101, assess whether Sartorial Ltd is in a position to become the market leader within the next five years. **(12 marks)**

The statement of comprehensive income of Sartorial Ltd indicates that revenue has increased from £1.24m in 2016 to £1.39m in 2017. This increased revenue will be because of increasing the number of bespoke suits they sold or maximising the value on each suit sold. Revenue is a key indication that consumers are buying the products and this shows potential for future growth. Furthermore, growth in sales revenue indicates a potential growth in market share if similar businesses have not grown at the same rate. This will therefore support Sartorial in moving towards the position of market leader in the next five years.

 The student has presented a clear argument using the financial information presented in the statement. The second paragraph goes on to discuss some of the other factors beyond finance that the business must consider.

However, to become market leader Sartorial may have to invest heavily in further expansion in order to reach a wider range of potential customers. The business seems to have significant reserves, but it will need to be in a strong cash position if it is going to expand successfully. Furthermore, customer service and quality are key if it is going to differentiate itself from other bespoke suit retailers in the market. It has set ambitious operations targets, but there is little evidence at the moment to suggest it will be able to achieve these targets, such as zero defects.

Overall, Sartorial seems to be in a strong financial position and becoming market leader is a realistic ambition, but becoming market leader in the next five years will depend on how the business is able to maintain its level of quality and customer experience as it grows. It is extremely important that Sartorial is able to upscale its production facility in the Czech Republic if it is going to meet the demand necessary to dominate the market.

 The conclusion identifies several key issues and provides a recommendation for how Sartorial should achieve its aim.

Statement of financial position (balance sheet)

The balance sheet

A balance sheet is a financial document that records the assets and liabilities of a business. A balance sheet gives a snapshot of the value and financial strength of a business.

Non current assets
Also known as fixed assets, non-current assets are used to operate the business and include land and machinery (tangible or fixed assets) and brands and patents (intangible).

Current assets
Assets that the business expects to use or sell within the year. These can be converted into cash to pay off liabilities.

Net current assets
Current assets – current liabilities = the working capital a business has available.

Net assets
Total assets – total liabilities = the value of a business.

Balance sheet as at 31st March 2015		£m
Non-current assets		70
Intangible non-current assets	10	
Tangible non-current assets	60	
Current assets		55
Inventories	30	
Debtors	25	
Current liabilities		(35)
Creditors	(30)	
Interest	(5)	
Net current assets		20
Non-current liabilities		(50)
Long-term loan	50	
Net assets		40
Total equity		40
Share capital	30	
Reserves	10	

Current liabilities
Payments due within 1 year.

Non-current liabilities
Debts that a business does not expect to pay within a year.

Total equity
Will always balance with net assets – it represents how a business has been financed.

A balance sheet can be used to calculate financial ratios such as liquidity ratios, gearing ratios and efficiency ratios.

What we can find out from a balance sheet:

☑ The value of a business (equity)

☑ The current assets a business holds

☑ Short-term liabilities the business will need to pay within the year

☑ The liquidity of a business

☑ The long-term debts of a business

☑ How a business has been financed

Now try this

1 What does a balance sheet show?

2 What is a current asset?

3 What are net assets?

Liquidity

Liquidity refers to the ability of a business to pay its debts and liabilities in cash when they fall due. The concept of liquidity is closely linked to cash-flow management. Cash is the most liquid asset (cash is a current asset) that a business has and any business would quickly fail if it ran out of cash.

Current ratio

The current ratio is a key liquidity ratio. It compares current assets with current liabilities. In doing so it assesses whether a business has sufficient working capital to pay its short-term debts.

It is calculated by:

$$\frac{\text{Current assets}}{\text{Current liabilities}}$$

The current ratio is expressed as a ratio, e.g. 2 : 1. This suggests that the business has £2 of current assets for every £1 of current liabilities. If the ratio is less than 1 e.g. 0.5 : 1 then the business might struggle to pay its short-term debts.

The acid test ratio

The acid test ratio is considered a more severe measure of liquidity. This is because it does not take into account the inventories (stock) of a business. This is because for many businesses there is no guarantee that inventories can be quickly turned into cash.

It is calculated by:

$$\frac{\text{Current assets} - \text{Inventories}}{\text{Current liabilities}}$$

The acid test ratio is expressed in the same way as the current ratio. It is a more useful ratio for businesses that sell goods and hold large quantities of inventory, such as a retailer.

Working capital

Working capital is the money within a business that is needed to pay for the day-to-day running costs. This includes paying bills, wages and purchasing stock. Working capital can be calculated from the information contained in a balance sheet. Working capital is slightly different from cash as it takes into account other current assets. However, other current assets such as stocks and debtors cannot easily be used to pay expenses. This is why cash is the most important asset when assessing the liquidity of a business.

Working capital = Current assets − Current liabilities

Ways to improve liquidity

- Negotiate additional short-term loans
- Use an overdraft facility
- Encourage cash sales
- Delay payments
- Encourage early settlement of debts
- Take out credit agreements with suppliers
- Sell off current assets (stock)

Now try this

1 What is liquidity?
2 What does a current ratio of 0.8 : 1 suggest about a business?

Business failure

Businesses may fail for a number of reasons. Some of these reasons are due to poor management of the business. However, there may be unforeseen circumstances and external forces that are hard for the owners to plan for.

Internal and external factors of business failure

Poor planning can lead to important factors not being addressed. Poor planning may be the root cause of other issues, such as cash-flow problems or poor marketing through a lack of understanding of customer needs.

External

Competition

Internal

Poor planning

Economic conditions

Cash flow

Legislation

Marketing

Lack of skills

Market conditions

If owners/managers do not fully understand the needs of customers, perhaps through poor market research, they are unlikely to develop products and services that will be successful or they can fail to target customers through the right marketing strategies – getting the marketing mix wrong.

A lack of skills may include technical skills, such as financial management, or leadership capacity.

Allowing too much trade credit to customers

Poor credit control – not chasing debts and ensuring customers pay on time

Overtrading

Causes of cash-flow problems

Unforeseen costs – not accounted for in cash-flow forecasting

Inaccurate cash-flow management – poor research or lack of any cash-flow management

External factors for failure

External factors for business failure are often hard to predict and can be beyond the control of the business.

- Competition – a new competitor or an overcrowded market can lead to a shortage of demand and falling sales.

- Legislation – new legislation can often mean increased costs as a business adjusts its products and processes to comply.

- Market conditions – for example, changes in commodity prices or consumer tastes.

- Economic factors – see page 113 for an overview of the business cycle and how economic factors impact business.

Now try this

1 What deficit in skills might lead to business failure?
2 Explain how ineffective marketing could lead to the failure of a business.

Exam skills

The following exam-style questions explore the topics covered in Units 2.3.2 and 2.3.3. The questions refer to the Sartorial Ltd case study on page 101.

Worked example

Using the extracts from the statement of financial position of Sartorial Ltd, calculate the liquidity of the company. **(4 marks)**

$$\text{Current ratio} = \frac{\text{current assets}}{\text{current liabilities}}$$

$$\text{Current ratio} = \frac{252}{219} = 1.15$$

The student has not been told which ratio to use. You may be asked to analyse profitability, liquidity or efficiency using financial information. If so, you will need to choose the most appropriate ratio to use given the information available to you.

Worked example

Explain why it is important for a business like Sartorial Ltd to manage its working capital effectively. **(4 marks)**

Working capital is the finance a business has at hand to pay the day-to-day running costs such as wages and overheads. Working capital is very important for Sartorial because it has a six-week lead time on its suits. During this period the business must have sufficient cash available to pay for the production and shipping of the suit to the UK before it receives the final payment from the customer. For example, a customer could purchase a suit using a credit agreement. If Sartorial is not able to manage its working capital it may have liquidity issues and this could cause the business to fail if it cannot pay its short-term debts.

The student starts by defining the concept in the question. This is an appropriate way to start your answers on an 'explain' question.

Worked example

Explain how changing market conditions could lead to the failure of Sartorial Ltd. **(4 marks)**

Market conditions involve any external factors that lead to the nature of the market changing. This could include commodity prices. If the price of wool increased substantially this would have an impact on the costs of the production of a suit. Consequently, it is likely that Sartorial would have to increase the price of their suits and this would mean that they were less competitive. This may mean that inventory would be difficult to get hold of and this could cause delays in the production of a suit – causing the six-week lead time to increase.

The student has chosen one factor to focus their answer on. They could have discussed market conditions other than commodity prices. It is always worth taking your time to plan your answers and consider the best issues to discuss.

Exam-style practice

The following exam-style questions apply to the concepts covered in Units 2.3.2 and 2.3.3 and refer to the case study on page 101.

1 Explain how ratio analysis could be used by Sartorial Ltd to evaluate business performance.   **(4 marks)**

> To answer this question it might be useful to use examples of specific financial ratios.

2 Assess how Sartorial Ltd could improve its profitability in the future.   **(10 marks)**

> To improve profitability a business can focus on increasing revenue or lowering its costs. How could you apply these approaches to Sartorial Ltd? Remember that you are required to justify the best approach in your conclusion.

3 Assess how internal factors could lead to the failure of Sartorial Ltd.   **(12 marks)**

> This is a very open question about business failure. You can choose from a range of factors to discuss in your answer. Try to choose the internal factors that are most likely to lead to the failure of Sartorial. You are required to identify the main factor or most likely cause in your conclusion.

4 Assess the value of Sartorial measuring its performance based on the quality of its suits.   **(12 marks)**

> Consider how quality might add value to performance beyond simply using financial measures. You may also consider the difficulties in measuring quality.

Between 2016 and 2017 Sartorial's gross profit margin fell from 55% to 49%.

5 Assess the importance of financial performance for Sartorial.   **(12 marks)**

> Remember to apply your answer to Sartorial. Bring additional performance measures into your answer.

> In your answer you will need to show an understanding of the objectives hierarchy and how functional objectives support the aims of the organisation.

Case study

Sartorial Ltd provides a bespoke tailoring service for men. The company runs a network of trained tailors operating from temporary offices around the country. Customers visit their 'Sartorial Expert' at a local office where they can be measured, consulted and advised in order to design a completely bespoke suit considering every detail.

The board of directors have set the corporate objective to be the UK's market leader in bespoke tailoring within the next 5 years. Their mission statement is:

To give every customer a special experience and a suit they are proud to wear.

A Sartorial suit is designed in the UK but made in the Czech Republic. The lead time on a suit being ready for first fitting is 6 weeks. However, the operations director believes that the company would be able to reduce this lead time to 2 weeks if production was moved to the UK. Reducing the distance a suit travels and the use of sustainable materials is very important for the business and something customers value in a bespoke suit. In order to achieve the corporate objectives several functional targets have been set, including:

- 100% customer satisfaction rating of good or better
- zero defects or complaints
- 90% of all materials supplied from sustainable sources within 2 years.

Figure 1: Extracts from income statement 2016–2017

Statement of comprehensive income	2017 £(000)	2016 £(000)
Revenue	1390	1240
Cost of sales	(698)	(558)
Gross profit	692	682
Other operating expenses	(497)	(270)
Operating profit	195	412

Figure 2: Extract from statement of financial position (balance sheet) as at 31 May 2017

Balance sheet	£(000)
Non-current assets	3001
Current assets	252
Less current liabilities	(219)
Less non-current liabilities	(1734)
Net assets	1300
Financed by	
Share capital	450
Retained profit	850
Total equity	1300

Methods of production

Production occurs when raw materials or components are changed into products. Production occurs when the factors of production (land, labour, capital and enterprise) are brought together. There are different approaches to production.

Job production

Production of single unique units. This could be bespoke for the customer and will require a highly skilled workforce, e.g. a bespoke house extension.

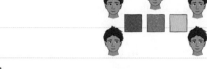

👍 Highly flexible and bespoke

👍 High profit margins

👎 High unit costs (premium price)

👎 Labour intensive – high labour costs

Batch production

As production increases a business may use a batch approach. Here, standardised components can be made in relatively large quantities, but the system can be modified to adjust the specification e.g. changing the size, colour and features. A bakery will use batch production.

The benefits of batch production lie in its flexibility while still being able to deliver some economies of scale through automation and standardisation.

Flow production

Flow production involves a dedicated and highly automated production process. Production is standardised and continuous to achieve economies of scale, e.g. a car manufacturing plant.

👍 Very low unit costs

👍 High levels of productivity

👍 Modern production plants offer some flexibility

👎 Huge set-up costs

👎 Low motivation of workers

👎 Breaks in production can be expensive

Cell production

Traditional flow production involves a production line whereby a single product will go through a number of stages. An alternative approach is to use cellular production whereby teams of workers work together to produce an entire product or part of a product.

Cell production eliminates some of the drawbacks of flow production because:

👍 workers are more motivated operating as a team

👍 production is more flexible

👍 movement of resources (waste) is minimised.

Choosing the optimal mix of resources

A business's production process can either be labour intensive or capital intensive. The balance of the two might depend on the nature of the product and the target market.

Labour intensive: high level of human input in the production process

Capital intensive: high level of capital investment (e.g. use of machinery)

Labour intensive: highly specialist, personal, service industry, high level of skill required

⟷

Capital intensive: mass production, standardisation, efficient production

Now try this

1 What are the benefits of job production?
2 Why might a company choose to adopt cell production over traditional flow manufacturing techniques?

Productivity

Productivity is the amount of output that can be produced with a given input of resources in a specified time period. Maximising productivity means getting the most out of the resources available to the business.

Labour productivity

One way of measuring productivity is through calculating labour productivity. This measures the output per employee in a certain time period, e.g. an hour or a week, and is a measure of how productive the workforce is. Productivity is a measure of output in relation to the input in a time period – in this case, the workers. However, a business may use other inputs (resources) to calculate productivity.

It is calculated using:

For example...

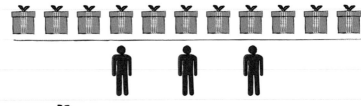

= 3.7 🎁 per employee

$$\text{Labour productivity} = \frac{\text{Total output (in a time period)}}{\text{Number of employees}}$$

Improving productivity

By effectively managing the following factors a business can improve its productivity. Productivity is closely linked to people management – human resources.

Education and training – to improve the skills of the workforce.

Specialisation – an employee becomes a specialist in a specific role.

Motivating workers – happy workers work harder and faster.

Factors affecting productivity

Capital intensity – introducing automation to increase output.

Working practices – this may include the layout of production, team working, quality management.

Difficulties in increasing labour productivity

There is sometimes a trade-off when increasing labour productivity.

Increasing productivity can improve the competitiveness of a business as cost per unit is reduced. This allows a business to increase its profit margin or offer customers a more competitive price.

Increasing the output of a worker may increase productivity and unit costs in the short term. But high levels of output can cause stress and burnout. It is also true that a focus on output can compromise quality, customer service and creativity. Costly mistakes and faults are also more likely to occur, leading to product returns and complaints.

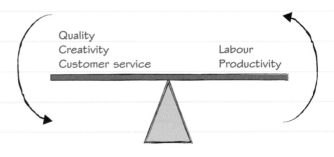

Quality
Creativity
Customer service

Labour
Productivity

Now try this

1 Identify **three** ways in which a business could increase labour productivity.
2 What is a potential drawback of increasing labour productivity?

Efficiency

Efficiency is about making the best use of all the resources of a business. When a business is running efficiently there is minimal waste (waste can be considered anything that does not add value to a product). Average costs (unit costs) will also be at their lowest when a business is operating efficiently.

Unit costs

The unit cost (average costs) takes into account the total costs of a business (fixed + variable) and divides this by the level of output.

It is calculated using:

$$\text{Unit cost} = \frac{\text{Total costs}}{\text{Total output}}$$

For example:

= £X per 🎁

Productivity and efficiency are directly connected. Greater productivity means the workforce is more efficient and efficiency across the business allows more resources to be devoted to production. Where efficiency falls, wastage and unit costs tend to rise.

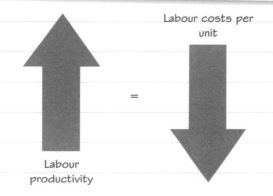

Labour productivity = Labour costs per unit

The benefits of improved efficiency

👍 Labour productivity increases

👍 Unit costs fall

👍 Resources such as labour, expertise and time can be reallocated

👍 Profit margins increase

👍 Improved flexibility across the business

👍 Opportunity to explore new ventures – e.g. a new product line

👍 Ability to charge lower prices and therefore improve competitiveness

Efficiency can be influenced by the level of employee skills, management decision-making and effective systems for production and communication.

Waste

In business, waste can be considered anything that does not add value to the product. Waste is a key factor that influences the efficiency of a business. There are seven types of waste a business can reduce:

Transport – unnecessary movement of the product or materials

Motion – unnecessary movement of people

Inventory – too much stock

Overproduction – making products that cannot be sold easily

Reducing waste and adding value

Defects – faulty products

Overprocessing – adding features that do not add value

Waiting – for processes to finish before others can begin

Now try this

1 Why is efficiency important?

2 What are the **seven** types of waste a business might experience?

Capacity utilisation

Capacity utilisation is about the use that a business makes of its resources. When a business is unable to increase output then it is said to be at 100 per cent capacity utilisation. Capacity utilisation is linked to productivity and efficiency.

Capacity utilisation

The capacity of production is the maximum a business can produce over a period of time given the resources it has available. Capacity utilisation measures existing output as a percentage of the maximum possible output.

It is calculated using:

$$\frac{\text{Existing output}}{\text{Maximum possible output}} \times 100$$

For example:

Under-/over-capacity utilisation

Operating at either under-capacity utilisation or over-capacity utilisation can cause a number of efficiency problems for a business, as well as opportunities:

Under-capacity utilisation e.g. 60 per cent

👎 Idle resources costing money but not being used

👎 Unit costs rise

👍 Opportunity to increase capacity utilisation by taking on new orders – easier to grow

Over-capacity utilisation e.g. 115 per cent

👎 Employees over-worked and unhappy

👎 Mistakes are more likely

👎 Unit costs rise due to the above

👍 Opportunity for growth

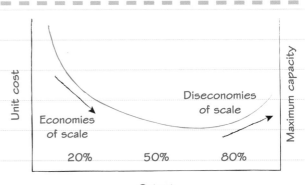

As capacity utilisation increases, unit costs will fall as the business experiences economies of scale. Unit costs may rise as a business approaches maximum capacity due to stress, mistakes and diseconomies.

Changing capacity utilisation

As we have seen, low capacity utilisation is inefficient and can increase unit costs. Similarly, reaching maximum capacity can also cause problems. A business can use a range of techniques to control its capacity in the short term.

Increase capacity

- Sub-contract out production to another business.
- Offer overtime pay to the workforce.
- Employ workers on temporary contracts.

Decrease capacity (or utilise idle resources)

- Rationalisation (redundancies or sale of assets).
- Sub-contract in work from another business.

Now try this

1 How is capacity utilisation measured?
2 How can a business increase its capacity utilisation?

Exam skills

The following exam-style questions explore the topics covered in Units 2.4.1 and 2.4.2 and relate to the Tasty Tapas case study on page 112.

Worked example

Calculate capacity utilisation for the Cleethorpes branch on Friday 12 June. **(4 marks)**

$$\frac{\text{current capacity}}{\text{maximum capacity}} \times 100$$

$$\frac{40}{65} \times 100 = 61.53\% \text{ capacity utilisation}$$

Always start your answer to a calculation by writing down the formula and then what the answer represents – capacity utilisation.

Worked example

Explain **one** way that Tasty Tapas could improve labour productivity in its restaurants. **(4 marks)**

Labour productivity is the output per worker per hour that they work. Improving labour productivity lowers the costs per unit and means that more customers will be served. The best way for Tasty Tapas to do this would be to ensure all of its staff have sufficient training to use the IT system, which has recently been having 'teething problems'. If employees are better trained to use the system it will not take them as long to process customer orders and will allow them to turn over a greater number of tables each hour.

Where possible, try to define any key terms at the start of your answer. This will ensure you secure the marks for knowledge. In this case, the student opens by defining labour productivity.

Worked example

Despite some of the teething problems with the new integrated IT system, Katie has decided to persist and ensure all employees have comprehensive training in using the hand-held devices.

Assess the importance of technology, such as the touch screen device ordering system, to achieving operational efficiency. **(12 marks)**

... In conclusion, technology is very important in a restaurant business because the key to an effective restaurant is being able to provide a fast and efficient service. Technology such as the touch screen devices can do this by streamlining communication and speeding up the process. However, many other factors are important in maintaining operational efficiency, such as the stock management system. If the right stock is not delivered to the restaurant the touch screen ordering devices will have little impact on improving service.

In this type of answer you might consider factors other than technology in delivering operational efficiency.

Ultimately, the extent to which these devices improve operational efficiency depends on whether Katie's employees make use of the system as it will fail in the long term if staff keep resorting back to the paper-based system. For IT to be a success Katie must make sure that all staff are trained sufficiently and any problems with the system are resolved very soon.

The student's assessment shows an awareness of important technological factors related to operational efficiency.

Stock control and lean production

Inventory refers to the supplies and stock held by a business. Inventory includes raw materials, work-in-progress and finished goods. Coordinating inventory and managing stock effectively can influence the competitiveness of a business.

Inventory control charts

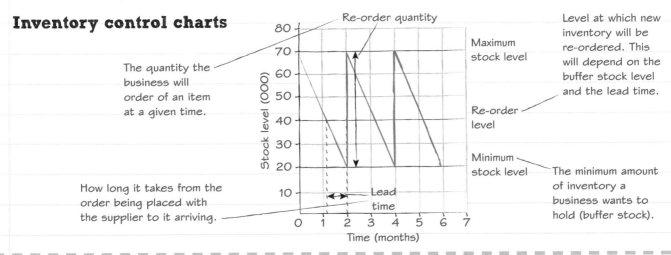

Re-order quantity

The quantity the business will order of an item at a given time.

Maximum stock level

Level at which new inventory will be re-ordered. This will depend on the buffer stock level and the lead time.

Re-order level

Minimum stock level

The minimum amount of inventory a business wants to hold (buffer stock).

How long it takes from the order being placed with the supplier to it arriving.

Lead time

Stock level (000) / Time (months)

The cost of poor stock management

👎 Opportunity cost – over-stocking means tying up cash that can't be used elsewhere.

👎 Shrinkage – stock being stolen, damaged or lost.

👎 Financial costs – storing stock and managing it can be time-consuming and costly.

👎 Too little stock – having too little stock means that orders cannot be met, which leads to unhappy customers and loss of sales.

Waste minimisation

- Store inventory appropriately, e.g. perishable goods in refrigeration.
- Rotate stock – so old stock gets used/ sold first.
- Pricing strategies – adjust prices to clear stock through sales promotions.
- Computerised stock management systems – to track all inventory.

Lean production

Lean production involves practices that reduce waste in the operational process. The main forms of lean production are focused on reducing defects, time wasted and inventory levels.

Lean management should remove anything that is not necessary. For example, the following aspects of an organisation could be re-designed to be more efficient.

Meetings   Processes   Organisational structure

Effective lean production can lead to competitive advantage. Not only do lean techniques help minimise waste and reduce average costs, they can also help improve flexibility and reduce lead times, leading to greater customer satisfaction. In times of difficulty, lean organisations are more able to survive and continue to make a profit.

Just in time (JIT)

Supply of products and raw materials triggered by demand from customers.

Supply of products and raw materials triggered by demand from customers

Supply of materials and services

Demand for products and services

JIT is where stock levels are kept to a minimum and resources and capital are freed up. This relies on effective communication and systems for order processing and delivery. JIT can help improve working capital by freeing up illiquid stocks so trade debtors are decreased, as excessive stock is one form of waste.

Now try this

1 Identify **three** pieces of information shown on an inventory control chart.
2 How can a business increase flexibility when managing inventory?

Quality 1

Quality is the extent to which a product or operation meets its customers' requirements. This means that it is 'fit for purpose'. Achieving the desired quality has a number of benefits for a business, but quality is a subjective concept. What one customer considers high quality, another may consider low quality.

The importance of quality

Quality is the key to meeting customer needs. A high quality product is one that meets customer expectations. A pizza for £2 can have a higher quality than a more expensive pizza priced at £15 if it is more 'fit for purpose' (i.e. it is tasty with good quality ingredients).

Products must have high quality to be able to compete at the right price point. Some businesses will differentiate themselves on having a premium quality. For example, Steveston Pizza Company in Vancouver, Canada sells a pizza for $850 featuring ingredients such as smoked salmon, caviar and other exotic seafood.

Achieving quality improvement

Have a clear understanding of customer needs

Train employees in quality procedures

Invest in technology

Achieve a quality award/mark (recognition from external organisation)

Methods of achieving quality

Adopt processes that assure quality

Involve all employees in managing quality

Work with high quality suppliers

Achieving high levels of quality can improve customer satisfaction, help the business differentiate its product from competitors and above all, add value to the product allowing a premium price to be charged.

Quality control and quality assurance

Below are two perspectives on implementing quality management systems.

Ⓠ = focus on quality

Start ——————————→ Ⓠ End

Start ├—Ⓠ—Ⓠ—Ⓠ—Ⓠ—▸ End

- Quality control is about the **product**.
- Quality is checked at the end of the production process.
- Focus on identifying faults.
- Quality control is a specific role – maybe one person.

- Quality assurance is about the **process**.
- All employees are involved in quality assurance.
- Quality is considered at every step of the production process.
- Focus on continual improvement of quality.

Difficulties in improving quality

Quality can be difficult to improve because:

- customers' perception of quality is constantly changing
- a successful business could let quality slip if there is no incentive to outperform rival businesses
- improving quality can add more work so might be naturally opposed by the workforce
- measuring quality can be difficult and expensive.

Consequences of poor quality

Poor quality can cause a number of problems for a business:

👎 If products need recalling this can be extremely expensive.

👎 Poor quality can damage brand reputation.

👎 There may be legal costs if customers sue the company.

👎 Correcting poor quality can be very expensive.

Now try this

1 Why is quality important?
2 How can a business improve quality?
3 Why can improving quality be difficult for a business?

Quality 2

A company can implement a variety of strategies to improve or maintain quality.

Total Quality Management (TQM)

TQM is a system of management based on quality being the priority throughout the organisation. Quality is everyone's responsibility no matter what their role. TQM is underpinned by a number of principles:

- **Quality chains** – the concept of the internal customer. Each person in the production chain is a customer of the preceding link (process). As such, their needs need to be fully met.

- **Quality policies** – clear policies are established on the expectations of all employees and how they should achieve the highest quality.

- **Controls** – a range of controls are put in place to guarantee quality is achieved.

- **Team work** – people work in teams to solve problems and identify opportunities.

- **Customer views** – feedback from customers is taken into account to improve the process and product.

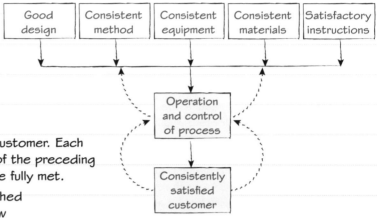

Feedback channel

Control is a feature of TQM – the diagram shows how a business needs to be in control of the factors that affect a product's quality to ensure customer satisfaction.

Quality circles

A quality circle is a small team (about 6 to 12 people) who voluntarily form to work on a specific issue or problem where quality is a concern or an opportunity for improvement has been identified. Quality circles should have representation from across the organisation and all parties have an equal voice in the development process. Quality circles ensure all aspects of the supply chain are considered and give people the opportunity to work closely as a team.

Quality and competitive advantage

Quality is a significant route for a business to add value to its products. Achieving high levels of quality will allow a business to charge a premium price and ensure customers are highly satisfied.

However, quality is a highly subjective concept that is unique to any one customer. Businesses must continually aim to improve quality and adapt to the needs of customers if they are to maintain any competitive advantage.

Kaizen

Kaizen (Japanese for continuous improvement) is a key concept in lean production and quality management. Kaizen may actually involve a wide range of management techniques, but the main principles are that the business, through techniques such as TQM and quality circles, will look to identify areas of improvement across the organisation instead of settling for 'good enough'. The diagram opposite compares Kaizen with a traditional approach to improvement that may involve big shifts in practice.

Kaizen may include processes to continually identify opportunities for improvement or radical change, for example PDCA (Plan, Do, Check, Action).

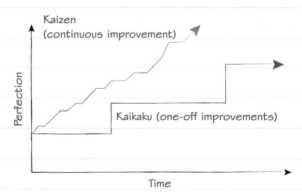

Small teams work together to identify small changes that can build to large-scale improvements over time.

Now try this

1 What is Kaizen?
2 What are three characteristics of TQM?

Exam skills

These exam-style questions relate to the Tasty Tapas case study on page 112.

Worked example

Assess how Katie Collings could improve the customer reviews of Tasty Tapas. **(12 marks)**

Katie Collings could reduce the number of negative reviews at her restaurant by adopting quality assurance. Quality assurance would ensure that every step of the production process is of the highest quality. For example, this would help ensure the ingredients are of the highest quality right through to the service given by her waiters. As each restaurant is operating at near full capacity it will allow her to analyse whether the high level of capacity utilisation is affecting the quality of service. It might also allow her to focus on how effectively the touch screen ordering system is working. One limitation of this system is that she might not have the time or money to train employees properly in how to monitor quality in their particular area.

> An 'assess' question requires you to make a judgement from the available evidence.

> There are a number of ways that a student could answer this question and a number of functional issues they could consider. This is an example of how you might start your answer. The student has begun by discussing how quality assurance could help reduce the number of negative reviews at Tasty Tapas.
>
> The second paragraph could go on to explain how introducing a system of employee rewards could also help Tasty Tapas reduce the number of negative reviews.

Worked example

Explain **one** factor Tasty Tapas might consider when managing its inventory. **(4 marks)**

Tasty Tapas might consider the speed at which it is able to convert its inventory into a finished meal ready for serving. Tasty Tapas are operating at high capacity utilisation and this has led to poor reviews for slow service. By focusing on processes to increase the turnaround of an order it will be able to avoid poor reviews. As a result, this will also allow Tasty Tapas to increase its capacity and turn over more tables each day, with the possibility of increasing revenue.

> The student has chosen a relevant factor in 'speed' because this directly links to one of the issues identified in the case study. The student goes on to explain why speed is important and gives at least one consequence of serving meals faster.

Worked example

Below is an inventory control chart for a Tasty Tapas restaurant. Using the chart, identify the following pieces of information. **(4 marks)**

(a) The maximum inventory level
(b) The size of each delivery
(c) The buffer stock level
(d) The lead time on an order

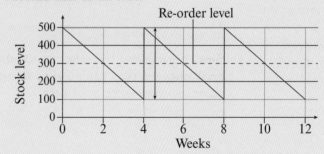

(a) 500 units   (b) 400 units   (c) 100 units   (d) 2 weeks

> This question involves interpreting information on an inventory control chart. (a) is a relatively straightforward question and most students would guess this even if they were not sure what it meant. Some students might think the answer to (b) is 300 units. This is the re-order level and not the re-order quantity that can be interpreted by how much the chart increases by when the inventory is delivered – the size of each delivery. (d) is the trickiest question. From the line at 300 units to the re-order level it takes from this point before the inventory arrives. The lead time is the difference from the point inventory is ordered (shown as 300 units on the chart) to the point that it arrives. Each time inventory is ordered it takes two weeks to arrive according to the chart.

Exam-style practice

The following exam-style questions apply to the concepts covered in Units 2.4.1, 2.4.2, 2.4.3 and 2.4.4 and refer to the Tasty Tapas case study on page 112.

1 What is meant by batch production? **(2 marks)**

What distinguishes batch production from flow or job production?

The table below represents information taken from the Cleethorpes restaurant for one week of trading in June.

Cost of sales	£12 000
Running costs	£7000
Other operating expenses	£5750
Average customers served per week	1300

2 Calculate the unit costs for one week of trading at the Cleethorpes restaurant. **(4 marks)**

Start by writing down the formula for calculating unit costs and then substitute the relevant information from the table.

3 Explain how introducing new ovens into the kitchens of each restaurant could improve productivity at Tasty Tapas. **(4 marks)**

Use the information from the case study to link the benefits of new ovens to the impact they could have on the output of the workforce. You could start by explaining what labour productivity means.

4 Explain how Tasty Tapas might benefit from operating at high capacity utilisation. **(4 marks)**

If you can use calculations from the case study this will show good application to the context.

5 Assess whether outsourcing some of the basic food preparation will 'ease pressure on the kitchens'. **(12 marks)**

Remember to consider this question from both perspectives. What could be the drawbacks of outsourcing? Remember to ensure your answer is rooted in relevant operational concepts.

6 Assess how improving efficiency at Tasty Tapas is likely to lead to a competitive advantage. **(12 marks)**

Case study

Tasty Tapas (TT) operates a small chain of tapas restaurants serving 'an authentic variety of Spanish food and drink'. The chain is owned by Katie Collings who set up the first restaurant in 2007. In every TT venue the aim is to deliver a traditional Spanish-style customer experience, ranging from the food and drink on the menu to the classic iron railings and hand-painted tiles inside every restaurant, as well as each member of staff speaking Spanish as their first or second language. The chain currently consists of four restaurants situated in seaside towns on the east coast of the UK.

One initiative Katie recently introduced is a sophisticated and integrated IT system. Every manager and waiter uses a small touch screen device to place orders. Each of these is wirelessly connected to the restaurant's intranet and can be used to record data. This allows staff to manage customer bookings, take food and drinks orders and to issue or redeem special offer vouchers. There have been some 'teething problems' with the technology, occasionally leading to some staff having to revert to using the old-fashioned paper-based systems.

All four restaurants are successful, and are fully booked on most nights of the week. In particular, customers at the Cleethorpes restaurant have to book several weeks in advance to reserve a table at the weekend. During the weekend the manager of the Cleethorpes restaurant believes the restaurant can serve a maximum of 65 tables in an evening shift.

The table below shows the number of tables the Cleethorpes restaurant served during the weekends of June 2015.

Date	Fri 5/6	Sat 6/6	Fri 12/6	Sat 13/6	Fri 19/6	Sat 20/6	Fri 26/6	Sat 27/6
Tables served (evening)	52	62	40	62	64	68	63	71

Recently Katie has been concerned with some of the reviews her restaurants have received on a well-known review website. Several people have given TT poor reviews, stating that service was poor and complaining about long wait times for their meal. One customer wrote, 'I almost felt like marching into the kitchen to cook the food myself'.

To maintain this success and grow the business, Katie has decided to install new ovens in each of the kitchens. These new ovens will increase the number of dishes that can be cooked at one time and lower energy costs by 20 per cent. To ease pressure on the kitchens Katie is also considering outsourcing some of the basic food preparation tasks, such as chopping vegetables and preparing sauces, to a contractor who will deliver the ingredients each morning.

The business cycle

The economic environment includes a range of economic variables such as GDP, inflation, unemployment and consumer confidence. Governments use a range of policies to influence economic activity and economic change creates a number of opportunities and threats for businesses that will have an impact on strategic and functional decisions.

Gross domestic product

Gross domestic product (GDP) is a measure of a country's total output of goods and services over a period of time. GDP changes over time are represented by the business cycle.

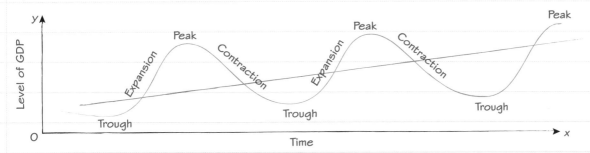

	Boom	Recession	Slump	Recovery
	High rates of economic growth and production.	Output starts to fall, growth declines.	Prolonged period of economic decline.	Economy starts to pick up after a period of decline.
Features	• High profits • Low unemployment • High inflation • Shortages in supply	• Production declines as demand falls • Governments use policies to stimulate growth • Consumer/business confidence starts to fall	• High levels of unemployment • High rates of business failure/ closure • Low interest rates • Low levels of spending and investment	• Increasing consumer confidence • Businesses start to invest/take on new employees • Spare capacity is used up
Impact on strategic and functional decisions	• Firms make strategic decision to expand into new markets through market development. • Functional decision to expand workforce/increase recruitment. • Businesses seek opportunities for efficiencies and cost reductions as a result of economies of scale.	• Expansion plans are 'shelved'. • Market penetration strategies become more attractive as they are low risk. • Businesses stockpile products. • Functions try to increase efficiency and cut costs – such as flexible working implemented.	• Businesses adopt a strategy of rationalisation. • Functional decisions may include redundancies, scale down of production and reduction in capacity. • Businesses reduce prices and focus on their most profitable product lines. • Businesses may decide to cease trading or leave certain markets.	• New business start-ups emerge. • Business investment rises – product development strategy. • Businesses take on new employees and increase contracts to meet growth in demand. • Functional decisions focus on ways to increase productivity – training, growth in production, increased marketing activity.

Now try this

1 Identify **two** features of a boom.
2 Identify **two** features of a slump.
3 Identify **two** features of a recovery.

Exchange rates and inflation

The exchange rate is the price of one currency expressed in terms of another. A UK business will purchase a foreign currency in order to buy products and services from overseas. The exchange rates change owing to fluctuations in demand for a currency, economic growth and interest rates.

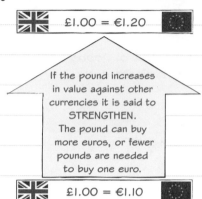

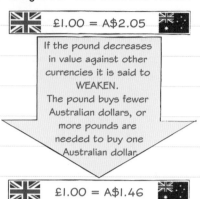

Exchange rates and decision-making

- Businesses will try to avoid uncertainty when exchange rates are volatile. Businesses may set an agreed rate for future transactions.
- A business may choose to target a specific international market (or economy) when the exchange rate is favourable.

Importers:

👍 may switch international suppliers when the exchange rate is less favourable

👍 stockpile raw material and products when currency is strong.

Exporters:

👍 lower prices to limit the impact of a strong currency

👍 increase promotion in foreign markets when currency is weak.

Inflation

Inflation is the general rise in prices over time. Inflation is measured by the consumer price index (CPI). A low rate of inflation can be managed by businesses but a high rate of inflation will increase costs and reduce demand.

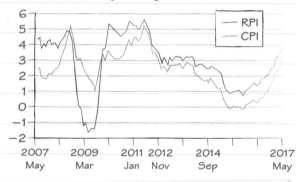

Graph showing UK inflation May 2007–May 2017

High inflation

- Businesses may increase prices to pass costs on to consumers or may decide to absorb the cost rises.
- Businesses will look to reduce internal costs to protect profits.
- Price rises may fuel further inflation.

Low inflation

- Businesses feel confident in a stable economic environment.
- Businesses may look to invest and grow.

Deflation

- Businesses may struggle to pay debts – assets may have to be sold to pay off debts if deflation persists.
- Low demand may lead to redundancies and rationalisation.

Now try this

1 How does the exchange rate affect importers and exporters?
2 Why do businesses want a steady rate of inflation?

Government spending, taxation and interest rates

A government will use policies to influence economic activity in order to maintain growth and limit negative factors such as high levels of inflation, unemployment and the negative externalities of growth.

Interest rates

Manipulating interest rates is a policy to adjust the amount of money in circulation and therefore influence spending and economic activity. The interest rate is the cost of borrowing money and the reward for saving. Increasing or decreasing interest rates can also be a strategy to influence the value of a country's currency.

Money exchange outlets at an airport

The impact of the interest rate on business activity

High %

- Consumer and business spending falls
- Inflation falls
- Stronger £

Interest rate

- Consumer and business spending rises
- Inflation may rise
- Weaker £

Low %

Government spending and taxation

Government spending and taxation is a means of controlling economic activity. The difference between government income (mainly taxes) and expenditure in a fiscal year is known as the budget balance.

Taxation – income tax, national insurance payments, VAT, corporation tax, customs and excise duties

Government expenditure – infrastructure, human capital, physical capital

Expansionary policy	Contractionary policy
Reduces direct and indirect tax to increase disposable income. Increases borrowing (PSNCR).	Increases direct and indirect taxes to slow down growth and reduce the budget deficit.
Increase spending in areas such as health and education. Spending stimulates demand for businesses and creates jobs. Budget deficit may rise.	Reduce spending in areas such as health and education. Pressure on inflation slows. Budget deficit may fall or reach a surplus.

Taxation – income tax, national insurance payments, VAT, corporation tax, customs and excise duties.

Government expenditure – infrastructure, human capital, goods, services.

Now try this

1 What is meant by an interest rate?
2 What is meant by government spending?

Exam skills

The following exam-style question relates to Extract D on page 122 and the topics covered in Unit 2.5.1.

Worked example

Assess the long-term impact of interest rates on UK businesses. **(10 marks)**

The extract suggest that UK interest rates are likely to rise in the second quarter of 2016. Although this is only a small rise, it will increase the costs for some businesses that have borrowed money. This is likely to directly impact profits of a business unless it decides to pass the increased costs on to customers. However, if a business does this it may maintain profit margins, but sales may fall if businesses choose to switch to a cheaper alternative....

The student has used the information in Extract D to suggest how rising interest rates might affect UK businesses directly. The student could then go on to explain how rising interest rates could have an indirect impact – through the actions of customers. They would then need to provide a conclusion justifying the extent to which interest rates will affect UK businesses.

Worked example

Assess the impact a slowdown in economic growth in China is likely to have on UK businesses. **(12 marks)**

World economies are closely linked and should there be a slowdown in economic growth in China this could result in less demand for UK and other European products that are considered luxurious in China. Furthermore, many Chinese tourists visit Europe and the UK each year. If there is a slowdown in economic growth, incomes may also slow down and this might mean that some tourists choose to holiday within China instead of visiting the UK.

The initial paragraph outlines some of the threats to the UK economy. In the second paragraph, the student has analysed one benefit to UK importers.

On the other hand, UK importers may find that it is easier and cheaper for them to import products from China. This is because there will be less pressure on prices and fewer shortages in supply. Furthermore, as China's growth slows, it is likely that the value of the Yuan will fall. This will increase the buying power of UK importers and in turn reduce their costs.

In conclusion, China is the world's second largest economy and any slowdown will inevitably have a negative effect on the UK economy too. Nevertheless, the Chinese economy is still growing and growth is anticipated to be 2% between 2017 and 2020. Although this is not fast growth it could still lead to more jobs and prosperity within the UK regardless of what happens in China.

The conclusion is balanced and suggests that the impact of a slowdown in China's economy may have a limited impact over the coming years. The answer uses evidence from Extract D.

Legislation

The legal environment covers the laws that govern how our society operates. Businesses must abide by legislation set out by the UK government and the EU.

Consumer protection

Consumers want to have clear information on what they are buying, and they want to buy goods at a fair price and of good quality. Consumer protection laws are in place to ensure businesses do not exploit customers. They ensure that:

- products are safe
- products are of an approved standard/quality
- consumers are treated fairly if they are unhappy
- product information is readily available.

An example of consumer protection legislation is the Sale of Goods Act 1979.

Competition policy

Competition legislation is put in place to protect the interests of consumers and businesses. It aims to restrict anti-competitive practices such as:

- cartel activity – businesses working together to manipulate the market and limit competition
- abuse of market power, e.g. imposing unfair conditions on small suppliers
- anti-competitive practices, e.g. anti-competitive mergers and acquisitions.

Competition policy ensures that markets are fair places where responsible businesses can flourish.

Examples of UK legislation governing competition include the Competition Act 1998, Enterprise Act 2002 and Enterprise Regulatory Reform Act 2013.

Employee legislation

Labour laws aim to prevent exploitation of workers. They legislate for issues such as pay, working conditions and grievances. Legislation also governs the powers of trades unions.

Individual labour laws include:
- The Working Time Regulations 1998
- National Minimum Wage Act 1998
- Equality Act 2010.

Collective labour laws include:
- Trade Union Act 2016
- Employment Relations Act 2004.

Environment protection

Environmental legislation aims to internalise any negative externalities associated with business activity, therefore making business pay for the full cost of cleaning up or repairing any damage to the environment caused by their production process. Much of the UK's environmental legislation comes from EU directives. It governs factors such as:

- pollution
- destruction of wildlife
- traffic congestion
- resource depletion.

Specific environmental legislation includes:
- The Environmental Protection Act 1990
- The Environment Act 1995.

Health and safety legislation

Health and safety legislation ensures that businesses have to provide a safe and healthy workplace and facilities that are similarly safe for customers. This may include:

- maintaining temperature and noise levels
- providing adequate breaks and rests
- providing facilities for disabilities
- guaranteeing hygiene levels
- preventing social and emotional stress.

The Health and Safety Executive (HSE) is an organisation that investigates health and safety incidents within industry.

The impact of legislation on business

It is not necessary to understand the different acts or political policies. Instead, it is important to understand how a changing legal environment might impact a business at a functional level, and the threats and opportunities it could create.

Legal change can impose costs. Not implementing the necessary changes could limit competitiveness, damage the business's reputation or worse. However, legal change can also create new opportunities for some businesses and encourage innovation.

Now try this

1 What is the drawback of legislation for a business?
2 How can new legislation create opportunities for a business?
3 How can legislation make a business pay for the full cost of production?

The competitive environment

The threat of competitors is one of the most significant factors that can influence a business's chances of success. All industries have different competitive environments that influence the way businesses act and respond to one another.

Factors affecting competitiveness in a market

There are different factors that might determine how attractive or changeable a market is. These factors may determine how responsive and flexible a business needs to be in order to succeed within its market.

The typical profit margin that businesses can generate

The number and size of competitors in the market

The pace of innovation and new product development

The growth rate of the market

Determinants of competitiveness

The bargaining power of suppliers and customers

The level of regulation within the industry (is there a regulating body?)

The volatility of costs incurred by businesses, e.g. commodity prices

The seasonality of the product

The level of differentiation between competitors

> For more on Porter's Five Forces – a business model for analysing the issues within a competitive market – see pages 132 and 133.

The impact of competition on businesses

Businesses may not desire competition, but the presence of competition can have a positive impact not only on consumers, but on businesses too.

Competition can lead to:

👎 a fall in prices (leading to lower profit margins)

👎 increased costs of promotion

👍 improved efficiency (to reduce average costs)

👍 increased innovation

👍 wider product ranges.

High levels of competition can sometimes lead to some businesses acting unethically.

Size of the market

The level of competition is likely to be less in smaller markets, but this is not always the case. Small markets may have a limited population; therefore any two businesses can have significant rivalry. Small businesses can also access global markets owing to online sales.

Global   National   Regional   Local
markets   markets   markets   markets

Large ◄──────────────────────────► Small

Big or small?

There are different benefits and limitations that a business will experience depending on the size of the market.

Large markets

👍 Wider customer base

👍 Less volatility than small markets

👎 More regulation and scrutiny

👎 Potential for international competition

Small markets

👍 Less competition

👍 Opportunities for expansion – regionally, nationally or globally

👍 Easier to build loyal customer relationships

👎 Threat of new entrants

👎 Few economies of scale

🌐 Real world Smartphones

The pace of technology and new product development is a key market factor in the mobile phone industry. Most smartphone manufacturers launch a new product every six to eight months. Furthermore, sales growth for smartphones in Western Europe and the USA is declining, while Africa and Asia Pacific offer considerable growth opportunities for manufacturers and network providers.

Now try this

1 Identify **one** factor that might determine the bargaining power of a customer?

2 What might be the impact of a business operating in a market with a large number of competitors?

Exam skills

The following exam-style questions explore the topics covered in Units 2.5.2 and 2.5.3 and relate to Extracts A and C in the case studies on pages 121–122.

Worked example

The following questions relate to Extract A.

Explain **one** potential legal implication of Uber's alliance with Facebook. **(4 marks)**

Uber's alliance with Facebook could be deemed as anti-competitive. This means that it might not be in the best interests of consumers and the market. Many countries have legislation in place to prevent anti-competitive actions of businesses, for example the Competition Act 1998. As a result, the alliance between these two companies could be stopped and a case taken to court.

The student has shown an understanding of legislation around competition and clearly explained how this could affect Uber. A relevant example of legislation has been given in the answer. However, as there is no context in the answer linked to Extract A, this answer would only score 2 marks.

Worked example

Explain **one** factor that may influence the level of competition within the taxi service industry. **(4 marks)**

One factor that may determine the level of competition within the taxi industry is the extent to which businesses can differentiate. As essentially the service being provided is the same (travel between two locations) it may be difficult for businesses to differentiate and therefore they have to compete directly on price. Uber is able to differentiate by being the first taxi-hailing service to use mobile phone apps. Having first mover advantage may make it more difficult for other taxi firms to enter the market and build a strong brand.

The student could have discussed other factors such as barriers to entry, the level of bargaining power of customers, the pace of innovation or the volatility of costs.

Worked example

The following question relates to Extract C.

Assess the impact on businesses of the UK and EU imposing new legislation to cover the technological advancement of car technology. **(12 marks)**

Extract C suggests that there will be a number of technological advancements and innovations in car technology over the next five years. A number of these technologies will create opportunities for businesses. For example, in-car advertising. As there are a number of safety issues with such technology it is important that legislation is in place to protect consumers who might use the new technology. Without legislation such as the Trade Descriptions Act, consumers could get injured owing to the distractions of in-car advertising. As a consequence, this will create negative externalities such as pressure on A&E and roadside recovery services....

The student has selected relevant information from Extract C to help contextualise their answer. The need for legislation is well developed and appropriate examples have been used. The student could now go on to explain the limitations of legislation, such as its potential to restrict innovation and increase business costs.

Exam-style practice

Use Extracts A, B, C and D in the case studies on pages 121–122 to answer the exam-style questions below, covering the topics in Units 2.5.1, 2.5.2 and 2.5.3.

1 Explain **one** factor that may determine the level of competitiveness in the UK automobile market.   **(4 marks)**

> You should use information from Extract A, B or C to provide context to your answer.

2 Using Extract B, explain the impact of changes in transport costs for UK consumers.   **(4 marks)**

> Make sure that you actually use the data from Extract B to explain the impact of an increase in transportation costs.

3 Using Extract B, assess how public sector spending could impact the competitive environment within the transport industry.
                                                                (10 marks)

> What could public sector spending involve? Could it be spending on infrastructure? Or perhaps subsidies for public transport? For this question consider how government spending could link to the prosperity of transport-related businesses.

4 Use Extract C to answer the following question.

Assess the impact on car manufacturers of new legislation to cover the technological advancement of car technology.   **(12 marks)**

> Remember that the impact of new legislation can have benefits and drawbacks for businesses.

5 Using the information in Extract D, assess the impact of economic growth in the UK if it were to 'remain above 2% between 2017 and 2020'.   **(12 marks)**

> In your answer consider the impact of economic growth and discuss relevant economic factors such as employment, consumer/business confidence and standard of living. In your answer you might also consider the extent to which 2% is good. How might this compare to other nations? Are there any drawbacks of economic growth? What will be the key issue that you use to assess your answer?

Case study

Extract A: Uber's expansion

Uber, the Californian taxi network company that operates the Uber app linking customers to Uber taxi drivers, has agreed an alliance with Facebook Messenger that will allow users to order a ride from within Facebook's Messenger chat app. The agreement gives Uber access to millions of potential new users and marks the first time that Messenger – for which Facebook has ambitions ranging from retail to concierge services – has ventured into transport.

Uber is the biggest ride-hailing company in the world in terms of funding, with about $12bn raised so far – even as lawsuits relating to its treatment of drivers and compliance with local laws work their way through courts in many countries.

Its Facebook Messenger service, initially released in 10 cities on Wednesday, will be rolled out across the USA before Christmas, with the goal of expanding internationally in 2016. Uber would not disclose whether there was a revenue-sharing agreement with Facebook as part of the deal.

Extract B: UK Transport costs

UK transport report
- The total cost of motoring has risen around the same as the cost of living (RPI)
- Rail and bus fares have increased faster than the cost of living (RPI)

Retail Prices Index, transport components: 1987–2013

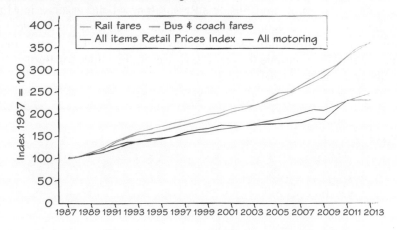

UK public sector expenditure on transport

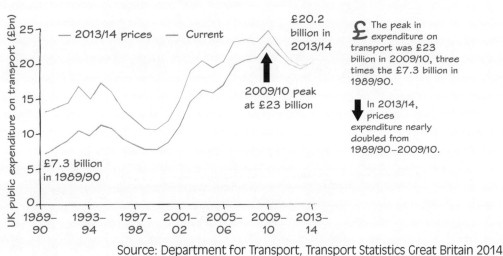

Source: Department for Transport, Transport Statistics Great Britain 2014

121

Case study

Extract C: Cars of the future

A recent Forbes article outlined the following emerging technologies as being some that will change the automobile industry in the next five years.

1 **Comprehensive vehicle tracking** – Insurance companies, and some state governments, are already talking about fees based on how many miles a person drives. By 2020 insurance companies will offer a reduced rate for drivers that agree to full tracking of their behaviour.

2 **Active health monitoring** – For example, seatbelt or steering wheel sensors that track vital statistics. Combine this with basic autonomous technology and you've got a car that can pull over and call paramedics when the driver has a heart attack.

3 **Smart/personalised in-car marketing** – By 2020 the average car will be fully connected to the internet, meaning your vehicle will provide marketers with a powerful set of metrics to customise their message. Hopefully these will manifest as an opt-in feature, but get ready for personalised, location-based ads in your car's display.

Extract D – UK economic forecast

The Bank of England is likely to keep interest rates on hold until the middle of next year rather than raising them sooner, following a gloomier outlook for the global economy, according to the economic forecaster CEBR.

The Centre for Economics and Business Research now believes a rise in May or August 2016 to around 1% is likely. Signs of a global economic slowdown have been growing in recent weeks, especially in the world's second-largest economy, China, and emerging markets. The UK's performance may not be sustainable if economies elsewhere continue to struggle. However, the Office for Budget Responsibility expects growth to remain above 2% between 2017 and 2020.

Corporate objectives

The mission and corporate objectives of a business outline what the business aims to achieve. For this reason the mission and corporate objectives guide the actions and strategy of a business and act as the measures by which we can assess the overall success of the business.

Mission statements

A mission statement sets out the purpose of a business: why it exists. The mission relates to all stakeholders and typically focuses on:

- the values of the business
- the scope of the business (the areas in which it operates)
- the importance of different stakeholder groups
- the impact the business intends to have on society
- the long-term aims of the business.

Influences on mission

The mission of a business will be influenced by a range of factors, including:

- the values of the founder(s)
- the industry the business is in
- the views of society
- the size of the business and type of ownership
- the culture of the business.

Corporate objectives

The corporate objectives of a business quantify the mission of a business and set measurable targets for the whole organisation. Corporate objectives should cascade down from the mission statement and the corporate aims to provide specific and measurable steps that a business should take. A mission statement can also act as a check to guide the objectives of a business.

The mission statement and corporate objectives must be reviewed regularly so that they fit with the direction of the business and its stakeholders. When reviewing its mission and objectives a business might consider:

- What is the purpose of the mission statement?
- Who is the intended audience?
- Does the strategy fit with the mission statement?
- Are the aims and objectives realistic and achievable?

Factors affecting corporate objectives

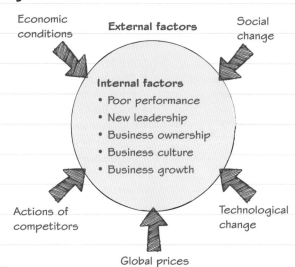

Short-termism is the pressure of achieving short-term gains over long-term success. Sometimes short-termism and the pressure for instant success can influence corporate objectives and decision-making as much as any other internal or external factor.

Now try this

1 Why do businesses have mission statements?
2 What is the relationship between the mission statement and corporate objectives?
3 Identify **three** typical areas that corporate objectives focus on.

Corporate strategy: Ansoff 1

Strategic direction involves a business choosing which markets it will operate in and which products it will provide. Strategic direction is important because the external environment is constantly changing and businesses must develop and compete in areas that make best use of their strengths and core competencies.

The Ansoff matrix

The Ansoff matrix is a strategic tool that businesses can use to help choose the market they wish to operate in and the products they will sell within that market. The model offers four distinct strategies based on the products' degree of newness and the firm's understanding/ experience of the market.

The Ansoff matrix provides a useful framework, but there are always degrees of newness, and a decision might not fit nicely into one strategic option.

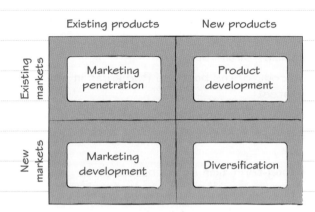

Market penetration

A strategy to boost sales of current products in the current market

→

Possible approaches
- Increase promotional activities
- Change pricing model if product is price sensitive
- Build brand image
- Focus on increasing repeat purchase by developing customer loyalty
- Incentivise customer affiliations

→

Benefits
👍 Low risk
👍 Product and market are familiar to the business
👍 Limited investment required

Limitations
👎 Possibly limited growth potential
👎 Business becomes vulnerable if it does not innovate

Product development

Develop new products for existing customers

→

Possible approaches
- Conduct market research with existing customers to identify areas for improvement/innovation
- Use product portfolio tools to manage product range, e.g. Boston Consulting Group Matrix (this is covered in Unit 1.3.5)
- Divert funds into R&D and product development

→

Benefits
👍 Familiar with customers
👍 Builds on/innovates current products
👍 Responds to customers needs

Limitations
👎 Product development takes time and can be expensive
👎 Product cannibalisation

Now try this

1 What are the four strategic options presented by the Ansoff Matrix?
2 What are the benefits of market penetration?

Corporate strategy: Ansoff 2

Market development

Market development allows a business to enter new customer markets with an existing product or slightly modified product, increasing sales potential.

Take existing products into new market segments (demographic or geographic)

Possible approaches
- Use of penetration pricing to enter new market
- Heavy promotion targeting new customers
- Strategic alliance or takeover of a business already operating in the market
- Develop new channels of distribution to reach new customers, such as an international agent

Benefits
- 👍 Potential for considerable growth
- 👍 No need for expensive product development

Limitations
- 👎 Limited understanding of new customers' needs
- 👎 Competing against established businesses

Diversification

Offer new products to new customers in a new market

Possible approaches
- Often applies to conglomerates with considerable financial power and economies of scale; this power might allow them to adopt such a strategy
- Business may have a particular asset (such as a patent) that allows them to be competitive without having particular expertise
- Could be achieved through external growth – merger or takeover

Benefits
- 👍 Spreads the business risk by engaging in different markets
- 👍 Business can utilise some of its core competencies and apply them to a new context

Limitations
- 👎 Can be extremely high risk
- 👎 No reputation or expertise in the market

Aims of portfolio analysis

The aim of product portfolio analysis is to categorise a company's products with specific characteristics in order to make strategic decisions about them. Portfolio planning models include the product life cycle and the Boston Consulting Group Matrix.

Products will be assessed in terms of:
- current and projected sales
- current and projected costs
- the level of competition
- unique characteristics and strengths
- risks that may affect performance.

Possibly a leading brand in the market. Distribution must be effective to ensure product availability.

Fast growing market but not yet an established product. Normally requires heavy investment to develop and ensure success. Usually lots of competition from rival brands.

relative market share (cash generation)

High   Low

	Stars	Question marks

market growth rate (cash usage) — High / Low

Invest to revitalise or discontinue the product.

Successful products in mature markets. Cash cows generate high revenue for a business that can be invested in other areas. Relatively little promotion is required.

Portfolio analysis models are useful to help apply strategic decision-making to a range of products, but they sometimes oversimplify what can be a very complex reality.

Source: Adapted from The BCG Portfolio Matrix from the Product Portfolio Matrix, ©1970, The Boston Consulting Group

Now try this

1 When might diversification be a suitable strategic option?
2 Identify **three** factors that a business may consider when choosing a strategic direction.

Corporate strategy: Porter

Strategic positioning will involve a business choosing the basis on which it intends to compete within a market. Strategic positioning involves deciding on the right mix of product features/benefits and matching this against price. The aim of a business will be to strategically position itself differently from its competition.

Porter's strategies

Michael Porter suggested that a business should follow one of three positioning strategies in order to compete within its market. These strategies are outlined below. Porter believed that a business must have a distinguishable focus in order to compete with rivals. The strategies are based around the source of the competitive advantage and the scope within the market.

Essentially Porter maintained that companies compete either on price (cost), on perceived value (differentiation), or by focusing on a very specific customer (market segmentation).

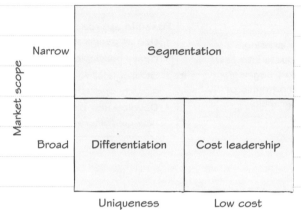

Cost-leadership strategy

Achieve an advantage by being the lowest cost operator in the market

→

Ways to achieve the strategy
- Operate at a scale that keeps average costs low
- Achieve economies of scale through growth
- Have unique access to technology
- Have unique access to skills or raw materials
- Control the supply of a product

→

Benefits
- 👍 Cost-leadership strategy can help to achieve high profit margins as cost per unit is kept low.
- 👍 It can maintain market price and gain higher profit margins (parity).
- 👍 It can lower price and acquire market share (proximity).

Limitations
- 👎 Few businesses can operate as the cost leader within a market as multiple businesses cannot directly compete on cost

Differentiation strategy

Compete by offering a unique product or service to the market or a niche

→

Basis for differentiation might include:
- quality
- customer service
- brand personality
- customer experience
- after-sales service
- speed and efficiency
- meeting the unique needs of a specific market niche.

→

Benefits
- 👍 It can make the business stand out.
- 👍 Differentiation helps develop a unique brand image.
- 👍 Differentiation adds value (special or unique) and therefore higher prices can be charged.

Limitations
- 👎 Other businesses may be able to copy the strategy if it is not sustainable or defensible, e.g. a product is defensible if it is under copyright

Now try this

1 How can a business achieve cost leadership?
2 How might a business differentiate its products?
3 What is a niche market?

Competitive advantage

Segmentation strategy

Segmentation can be achieved through either cost leadership or differentiation. It involves targeting a specific group of customers (niche) and not the whole market.

→

Both cost leadership and differentiation can be achieved through targeting the whole market or a specific segment or niche. The basis of the segment could be its unique needs, geographic or demographic characteristics or a specialist product or service.

→

Benefits
👍 It is easier to target a narrow segment of the market as communications and marketing can be focused.
👍 It is possible to develop a better understanding of customer needs as the segment has narrower interests, needs and characteristics.

Limitations
👎 Customer loyalty is vital if sales are to be maintained – every customer counts.
👎 The market may disappear (or no longer be a viable option) if it shrinks in size.

Competitive advantage

Competitive advantage exists where a business creates unique value for its customers that is greater than that offered by competitors. A sustainable competitive advantage is a distinctive capability that can be achieved through three areas of practice:

Each factor can lead to a **sustainable competitive advantage** because it is unique, not easily copied and may take a long time to achieve.

1 **Innovation** – the ability of a business to create new and unique processes and products. These can sometimes be legally protected through a patent.

2 **Architecture** – This refers to the relationships within a business that create synergy and understanding between suppliers, customers and the employees of a business.

3 **Reputation** – brand values are hard to replicate and may take years to develop.

Choosing a strategy

The expected cost – product development and diversification are likely to be considerably more expensive than the other strategies.

Anticipated returns – a business will conduct investment appraisal in order to consider the potential reward of the strategy.

Risk aversion – the willingness of the owners/managers to take risks.

Stakeholders – apart from financial returns a business will consider the impact of its strategy on its stakeholders.

Factors to consider

Core competencies – a business will look to choose a strategy that makes use of the strengths and advantages possessed by the business.

External environment – could new legislation in a market make a strategy less attractive?

Now try this

1 What might make a competitive advantage sustainable?
2 Identify **three** factors a business may consider when choosing a strategy?

Impact of strategy and tactics

Strategy

- A strategy is a long-term plan or approach that a business will take to achieve its objectives.
- Strategies involve a major commitment to resources.
- Clear strategies guide tactical decisions. A business may have a strategy to become a market leader by having the widest range of innovative products on the market.
- However, a tactical decision to support this strategy might be to divert an extra £5 million into research and development and headhunt some of the most innovative designers in the industry.

Strategy

Current position → Tactics | Tactics | Tactics → Desired position

Strategy and tactics indicate how a company's resources are deployed. For example, a strategy to become market leader might determine capital investment in product development, the creation of new distribution channels and a 50 per cent increase in the size of the employee sales force.

Tactics

- Tactics are the day-to-day decisions taken by middle managers.
- They are frequent and involve fewer resources but are taken to achieve the strategic direction of the business.

The objectives hierarchy

The overall goal or purpose of the organisation — Aims

A statement that communicates the aim and purpose to stakeholders of the business — Mission statement

The directors of the company set measurable targets for the whole organisation in order to meet the aims, e.g. become market leader by 2018. — Corporate objectives
Establish brand in a new international market or to maximise shareholder value

Functional objectives

Finance   Marketing   Operations   People

The functional managers/directors of the business set objectives that support and contribute towards achieving the corporate objectives. For example, the marketing team aim to launch two new product lines in the next year.

Now try this

1 How are strategic decisions different from tactical decisions?
2 Give **one** example of a functional objective.

Exam skills

The first exam-style question relates to the topics covered in Unit 3.1.1 and refers to the Sartorial case study on page 101. The second and third exam-style questions relate to Unit 3.1.2 and the Right Plumbing case study on page 135.

Worked example

Assess how Sartorial's mission statement may contribute towards the success of the company. **(10 marks)**

Sartorial's mission statement will contribute towards the success of the company because it will act as a reminder to its employees of how they should treat every customer and ensure each transaction is a 'special experience'. The mission statement will therefore guide employees in their day-to-day decisions so everything they do contributes towards this aim. By doing this, employees will be giving excellent customer service and customers will be highly satisfied with the suit they receive....

There are several ways that the student could have approached this question. The student could go on to analyse how a mission statement would inform corporate objectives or communicate the aims of the business to other stakeholders such as investors and customers.

Worked example

Explain **one** benefit of Right Plumbing Ltd using a market penetration strategy to expand the business. **(4 marks)**

A market penetration strategy involves targeting the same customers with the same products and services with the intention of increasing the number and value of sales. Right Plumbing may be able to do this through offering a loyalty programme to its customers. This might involve an upfront fee to cover future callouts and maintenance. The benefit of this approach is that it is a low risk strategy involving minimal investment. A market penetration strategy would help Right Plumbing Ltd become market leaders in the North Yorkshire region.

The student starts by defining what a market penetration strategy involves. They then go on to give an example of how this might apply to the Right Plumbing context and then explain one advantage of this strategy for the company.

Worked example

Explain **one** benefit of Right Plumbing Ltd using a differentiation strategy to compete in the market. **(4 marks)**

A differentiation strategy involves a business identifying a unique feature of the business or product to develop and promote. For Right Plumbing Ltd, this might be its fast response times. Promoting itself as the business with the fastest response times should mean that customers will value this and as a result Right Plumbing could charge a higher price for this benefit. As Right Plumbing Ltd move into the renewable energy market, a differentiation strategy will help them avoid competing directly on price with other solar panel installers.

The student has started by explaining what a differentiation strategy is. They have not explained that the theory was developed by Michael Porter, but this does not matter as they have shown good understanding and explained one benefit in the context of Right Plumbing.

SWOT analysis

SWOT analysis is a strategic tool that a business can use to analyse its current position and the external factors that might affect it. SWOT stands for Strengths, Weaknesses (of a business), Opportunities and Threats (that the business might face in the market).

For example, having a strong brand image or a highly skilled workforce. A business will develop a strategy around its strengths.

For example, poor cash flow. A business will try to eliminate these or avoid strategies that require the use of these.

	Helpful to achieving the objective	Harmful to achieving the objective
Internal origin (attributes of the organisation)	Strengths	Weaknesses
External origin (attributes of the environment)	Opportunities	Threats

For example, a fast growing geographical market. A business will attempt to exploit these with its strategy.

For example, a new competitor entering the market. A business will attempt to protect itself against these.

An organisation might split the task of a SWOT analysis into an internal audit and an external audit. An internal audit could include collecting opinions of employees, assessing skills shortages or reviewing different departments. An external audit might involve a thorough investigation into the economy, market conditions and the actions of competitors through market research.

The value of SWOT analysis

Benefits	Limitations
Assists strategic thinking in a structural way	Subjective – depends on opinions of managers
Low-cost, simple approach	Does not offer clear solutions
Can be combined with other decision-making models, such as PESTLE	Classification may depend on perspective

Case study   Case studies and SWOT analysis

A simple SWOT analysis is an effective way to analyse case study information and identify key issues in an exam. It is always worth identifying a firm's objectives in any case study as this is often an effective way to justify decisions. For example, if an action can lead a business to achieving a certain objective then you can justify it.

Now try this

1 What does SWOT stand for?
2 Why might a business use SWOT analysis?
3 What are the limitations of SWOT analysis?

Impact of external influences

One way to analyse the external influences that impact businesses in a positive and negative way is a PESTLE analysis – Political (P) Economic (E) Social (S) Technological (T) Legal (L) and Environmental (E).

Using PESTLE to analyse external influences

Political – covers actions taken by national and international authorities. Their actions are designed to maximise economic activity, while protecting businesses, individuals and the environment. Political decisions have a direct impact on market regulation, enterprise initiatives, national infrastructure and international trade.

Economic – the general state of the economy. For a full description see Unit 2.5.1.

Environmental – government tries to ensure businesses pay for the total cost of production, including the external costs such as pollution, paid for by society as a negative externality. Society is increasingly concerned about the environment and the effect on it from industry and business. There are benefits and drawbacks for a business being environmentally friendly. It may benefit a business that can be shown to be environmentally sensitive but it might add extra costs.

PESTLE

Social – social change is the changing demands of society for different goods and services and the way society spends money and accesses products and services. Social change can include changes in demographics (such as the ageing of the population or migration), and lifestyle changes – how people spend their time and money.

Technological – developments in technology not only create opportunities for new products and services, but advancements in the way in which businesses produce items and deliver them to the consumer. Technology can completely reshape a market (e.g. Uber) and businesses can be left behind if they don't keep up with technological advances (e.g. Kodak).

Legal – the framework within which businesses operate. For a full description see Unit 2.5.2.

The changing competitive environment

As the market environment changes businesses need to respond and adapt their strategies. A market may change in a number of ways:

- **New entrants** – as new entrants arrive the market will become more competitive.

- **New products** – businesses will need to innovate in order to keep up with rivals.

- **Consolidation** – at times businesses may fail and leave a market. Others may then take control of the available market share. Businesses may also merge or be subject to a takeover. When this happens the dynamic in a market can shift significantly.

Market structures

 1 **Highly competitive markets** exist where there is perfect competition. This is where there are many firms who are able to compete on a number of levels through differentiating what they do.

2 **Uncompetitive markets** may exist where one business dominates – a monopoly. Here, businesses may exploit consumers if there is not close regulation.

3 Alternatively, a few large businesses may dominate the market (**oligopoly**). There is a high level of interdependence in these types of markets where the actions of one business will have a significant impact on its rivals.

Now try this

1 Why does the government impose environmental legislation?
2 What is an oligopoly?

Porter's Five Forces 1

Competitive rivalry refers to the factors within a market that determine how businesses operate and compete in that market. A business must respond and make functional and strategic decisions based on these factors. Michael Porter's Five Forces model presents a framework for analysing the competitive environment.

The Five Forces model

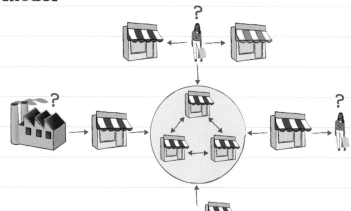

The five competitive forces are:
- competitive rivalry
- bargaining power of suppliers
- bargaining power of buyers
- threat of substitutes
- threat of new entrants.

Porter's Five Forces model can be used alongside other popular models such as SWOT and PESTLE in order to analyse the key issues facing a business and how that business might respond to these competitive forces.

Rivalry within the market

This is the level of competition and aggressive rivalry between businesses within the market. As markets grow and become more attractive, new businesses may enter the market, increasing the competitive rivalry.

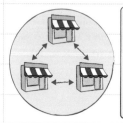

Competition is fierce if:
- easy entry to market
- easy for customers to switch
- little differentiation of products
- little growth or decline in the market

Key problem:
- profit margins are squeezed

Options for businesses to consider:
- lower costs of production and prices to compete
- develop a basis for differentiation
- takeover, merger or strategic alliance

Bargaining power of suppliers

This is the power suppliers have to negotiate terms and prices. The bargaining power of a supplier may change if the supply of a commodity, such as wheat or copper, fluctuates.

Supplier power is high if:
- few suppliers
- supplier's product is essential for production
- the supplier is able to integrate vertically forward and sell direct to the business's customers
- low availability of viable substitutes.

Key problem:
- high production costs and unfavourable terms of supply

Options for businesses to consider:
- build strong relationships with suppliers
- agree long-term contract of supply with favourable conditions
- backward vertical integration

Now try this

1 What are Porter's five competitive forces?
2 What might determine the rivalry within a market?
3 What decisions might a business take where suppliers are powerful?

Porter's Five Forces 2

The bargaining power of buyers

This is the power buyers have to negotiate terms and prices. This might change as consumers gain greater access to information and greater choice between rival businesses.

Buyer power is high if:
- there is little difference between products offered by competitors
- products are price sensitive
- customers buy in large quantities on a regular basis
- it is easy for buyers to switch between competitors.

Key problem:
- Prices forced low and credit terms demanded so there is pressure on cash flow.

Options for businesses to consider:
- Develop a USP.
- Build switching costs into agreements.
- Lower prices to attract customers.
- Forward vertical integration (if buyer is another business).

Threat of substitutes

A substitute is an alternative product that may deliver the same benefits to the customer. The threat of substitutes may change with social trends, for example, the health trend for consumers to use coconut oil as a healthier alternative to sunflower oil or olive oil when cooking.

Threat of substitutes is high if:
- alternative products exist
- alternative prices fall
- customers can easily switch to a substitute.

Key problems:
- Buyers have high bargaining power.
- Competition exists outside of the market.

Options for businesses to consider:
- Develop a USP.
- Build switching costs into agreements.
- Lower prices to attract/keep customers.
- Promote benefits in comparison to substitute products.

Barriers to entry

A barrier to entry is a physical, technological and intellectual factor that makes it difficult for a rival business to enter the market. The existence of large companies can create barriers to entry as they dominate resources and networks. However, disruptive technology and innovation can give small businesses leverage to enter a market.

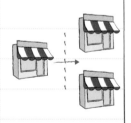

Barriers exist when:
- capital investment to enter the market is very high
- customers are brand loyal to existing businesses
- levels of specialist knowledge and expertise in the industry are very high.

Key problem:
- If few barriers exist it is easy for new competitors to enter the market and increase competitive rivalry.

Options for businesses to consider:
- Innovation – continuous development of new products can keep the business ahead of any new competition.
- Build strong relationships with buyers, making it difficult for new entrants.
- Growth – economies of scale can keep prices low and make it difficult for small businesses to enter the market.

Now try this

1 What factors may give buyers power in a market?
2 What is a substitute product?
3 How might a business compete with new entrants in a market?

Exam skills

The following exam-style questions explore the topics covered in Units 3.1.3 and 3.1.4. The first question refers to the Right Plumbing case study on page 135 and the second to Extract A in the case study on page 121.

Worked example

Explain how **one** external factor may influence the strategy of Right Plumbing. **(4 marks)**

The environment is one external factor that will impact on Right Plumbing. This involves pressures from stakeholders to ensure the company is not having a negative impact on the environment. Right Plumbing is moving into a market for 'green' products and this opportunity has been influenced by consumers' desire for sustainability and energy-saving products as utility bills rise. Right Plumbing is looking to capitalise on the investment from the government which is also looking to encourage environmentally friendly energy sources.

The student has identified one of the PESTLE factors and effectively applied their answer to the context. The student might have discussed other factors, but they effectively chose one that is closely linked to the case study, making the application marks easier to obtain.

Worked example

Assess whether Uber's partnership with Facebook will affect the competitive environment within the taxi market.

(12 marks)

One way in which Uber's partnership with Facebook will affect the market is that it is likely to reduce the competitive rivalry within the market. Uber's partnership gives it another way to reach its customers and makes it easy for them to book a taxi. Uber already has a unique app that allows customers to book taxis and normal taxi firms are finding it difficult to compete. This additional feature will make it even harder for local firms to compete in terms of convenience, especially in large cities. As a result, some taxi firms may close down and this will reduce competitive rivalry and the incentive for Uber to keep prices low.

As other firms may find it difficult to enter the taxi market it will also reduce the threat of substitutes. Some customers who may have driven or taken a bus are more likely to use Uber if its service is more accessible and widely publicised on a social media site such as Facebook....

The student has used the theory of Porter's Five Forces to help them answer this question. The candidate could now go on to discuss other features of the taxi industry that could be affected by Uber's partnership with Facebook.

The student has also discussed a second of Porter's forces and made a link to the market in the context. The final part of this answer would be to go on and explain the extent to which the competitive environment might be affected. The student should try to add some form of counterbalance, perhaps explaining how the partnership might have a limited impact and why.

Exam-style practice

The following exam-style questions relate to the topics covered in Units 3.1.2, 3.1.3 and 3.1.4 and refer to the Right Plumbing Ltd case study below.

1 Explain **one** factor that may influence the strategy of Right Plumbing Ltd. **(4 marks)**

 Think about PESTLE.

2 Explain how Right Plumbing might use SWOT analysis. **(4 marks)**

 Remember that SWOT is a strategic decision-making tool.

3 Assess the impact of political influences on Right Plumbing Ltd. **(10 marks)**

 Apart from political influences, what other external influences might also have an impact on Right Plumbing in the next five years?

4 Assess whether diversification is an appropriate strategic direction for Right Plumbing. **(10 marks)**

 Remember that diversification is a high risk strategy.

5 Assess the factors that may contribute to Right Plumbing Ltd gaining a sustainable competitive advantage. **(12 marks)**

 For this question you could consider the principles of sustainable competitive advantage. 1. Architecture 2. Innovation 3. Reputation.

 Case study

Right Plumbing Ltd is a successful domestic plumbing business that has been established for five years. The company has grown in the North Yorkshire region and now employs over 25 full time independent contractors.

In 2015 Right Plumbing Ltd won a local business award for excellence in customer service. The company has also built up a reputation for having the best response rates for emergency callouts and this has been documented in a number of local press articles.

Jeremy Stokes, the Managing Director, is looking to expand the business and has considered a number of options. The first is to expand across the Pennines into parts of Lancashire. Jeremy anticipates that this will require recruitment of at least another 10 employees who he would personally recruit. The initial workforce of 20 plumbers had been contacts he had made during his 15 years in the industry and the new venture would require him to look further afield.

The second option for Jeremy could be to move into installing renewable energy systems, such as solar panels and wind turbines, into homes around North Yorkshire. Jeremy has little experience with this technology but believes it would be a key market five years down the line with considerable growth potential. The UK government is considering investing £1 billion in the renewable energy market over the next 10 years. Jeremy anticipates that this second option will require an investment of £110 000.

Reasons for growth

Growth is an important objective for many businesses. Business growth can create greater wealth for the owners. It can also leverage a number of benefits and opportunities for the firm that may not be available to smaller organisations.

Ways a business can grow

A business has a number of options when it is looking to grow.

Organic growth is steady and gradual, whereas **external growth** is very sudden and can bring about significant change in an organisation. For this reason organic growth is a lower risk option, while external growth offers the opportunity for fast expansion but with the risk of clashes in the way the two businesses that have been joined together operate.

Synergies – when 2 + 2 = 5. External growth can bring businesses together that complement one another's strengths. For example, one business could be extremely innovative while another might have the financial power to support investment in R&D. Synergies may not occur where there is a clash of cultures.

Economies of scope – operating with a wide variety of products in a number of markets creates benefits through reduced costs which are shared across the different product lines, spreading the risk of any one product failing. Nevertheless, widening a business's scope may lead to a loss of focus on any particular product or market and potentially poor performance.

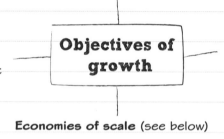

Objectives of growth

Economies of scale (see below)

The experience curve – big businesses typically have more experience than smaller businesses. They have made mistakes and have gained knowledge and experience that smaller businesses simply don't have. However, big businesses can sometimes become complacent – this happened to M&S in the mid-1990s and more recently Blackberry.

Economies of scale

Economies of scale occur when unit costs fall as a business expands – these are the advantages of size. There are several specific benefits a business or industry gains as it grows in size:

Internal economies – benefits a business gains from as it grows:

👍 **Purchasing economies** – bulk buying.

👍 **Technological economies** – larger businesses can invest in the best technology.

👍 **Financial** – large businesses have more collateral and can raise more capital (especially if Plc) and receive a better rate of interest and terms of payment.

👍 **Managerial** – larger businesses can employ specialists to manage a particular aspect of the business. This improves efficiency in different business functions.

External economies – benefits a whole industry gains from as the industry grows:

👍 **Labour** – a concentration of firms in one area may encourage a build-up of a skilled labour force.

👍 **Cooperation** – where firms are concentrated together they are more likely to work together and collaborate.

Now try this

1 What is the difference between organic and inorganic growth?

2 What are economies of scope?

3 What are financial economies of scale?

Limitations of growth

The benefits and drawbacks of growth

Economies of scale result in unit costs falling as the business grows in size. However, at a certain point the business will start to experience diseconomies of scale. Here unit costs will start to rise as the business starts to lose some of the efficiencies it gained from growth.

For many businesses there is an optimal size where they are able to operate efficiently. Furthermore, large businesses can lose some of the advantages they had when they were smaller.

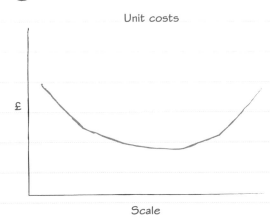

Diseconomies of scale

Diseconomies of scale occur when unit costs rise as a business expands – these are the disadvantages of size. There are a number of specific problems a business might face as it grows:

👎 **Communication problems** – it becomes harder to communicate a clear message across the organisation.

👎 **Control** – in order to control the organisation layers of management are added. This slows down decision-making and quality becomes harder to monitor.

👎 **Flexibility** – owing to the issues of communication and control the business may be less flexible in its ability to adapt to the changing business environment.

👎 **Motivation** – workers in large organisations find it difficult to see the impact they have and feel less significant.

Overtrading

Overtrading occurs when businesses grow too fast and overstretch their financial resources, such as cash. A business may also face logistical problems if it cannot manage operations. Overtrading can lead to business failure.

A business may accept a profitable order but fail to manage the timing of cash flows associated with the order.

A toy manufacturer might anticipate a large order for Christmas but fail to manage the cash flow associated with the production and distribution of the toys from August to November.

When businesses get too big

There may be times when a business needs to reduce its scale. This may be to counteract the problems of diseconomies of scale or to improve efficiency and reduce costs as demand falls, perhaps as a result of a downturn in the economic climate.

Strategies to deal with growing too large may involve:

- redundancies
- closure of branches
- discontinuing product lines
- pulling out of international markets
- de-layering
- reallocating business resources
- cancelling expansion plans
- outsourcing aspects of business operations.

Now try this

1 Identify **two** diseconomies of scale.
2 What are the problems associated with overtrading?

Mergers and takeovers

Takeover ◀— External growth —▶ Merger

Also known as acquisition, this may be hostile or voluntary. One business will acquire another along with its assets. If hostile, the takeover is riskier for the acquiring business. Just 51 per cent of shareholding will mean the predator business acquires full control. However, this can be as little as 15 per cent.

Two businesses come together in a joint venture for mutual benefit. This may be to share strengths or with the purpose of business survival. The business will seek synergies through the merger. A new name may be created out of the two joining companies.

Types of growth

👍 Allows business to acquire materials and resources more cheaply to reduce overall costs.

Backwards vertical taking over a supplier such as a tree farm

Conglomerate taking over an unused business in a different market such as a jewellery retailer

Horizontal merging with a business at the same level of the supply chain such as another Christmas tree wholesaler

👍 Spreads risk and creates new business opportunities – normally adopted by very large businesses.

👍 Economies of scale are achieved and sharing of expertise between businesses – synergies.

Christmas tree wholesaler

Forwards vertical taking over a customer such as a retailer that sells Christmas trees

👍 Manufacturer can determine how products are promoted and build relationships with end users. Allows the business to increase its prices.

Rewards of inorganic growth

There are several benefits of inorganic growth:

👍 Speedy growth – far quicker than organic growth

👍 Higher remuneration for senior staff

👍 Rewards for previous owners – large pay-outs for those selling a company

👍 Greater profitability if merger/takeover is successful

Risks of inorganic growth

There are some risks of inorganic growth.

👎 Regulatory intervention – industry regulators may intervene in some cases of a merger or takeover if they believe it to be anti-competitive.

👎 Resistance – morale and productivity can be very low when a business has been taken over.

👎 Financial strain – both mergers and takeovers can stretch a firm's finances. This is especially the case if a bidding war begins.

Now try this

1 Why might a business choose a merger over an acquisition?
2 Why might a business choose to take over a supplier?

Exam skills

The following exam-style questions relate to the topics covered in Units 3.2.1 and 3.2.2 and refer to the Cloudburst Plc case study on page 143.

Worked example

Explain **one** economy of scale that Cloudburst may experience through the merger with Interact Gaming. **(4 marks)**

One economy of scale that Cloudburst may experience as a result of the merger with Interact Gaming is managerial economies of scale. As the company will have a larger workforce across the USA and China, they may be able to appoint employees and specialists to a particular technical role that they were unable to previously. This might include a business function, such as marketing, or a game development role. This could lead to better ideas, product development or simply efficient working practices. As a result, unit cost could fall and economies be achieved.

The student's answer uses the context to explain how the merger could lead to economies of scale. They could have also discussed technological economies or financial economies.

Worked example

Assess whether Cloudburst Plc will experience synergies through the acquisition of Interact Gaming Ltd. **(12 marks)**

As Interact Gaming is in a different market to Cloudburst it is possible that its expertise might complement that of Cloudburst. Cloudburst is also looking to use a product development strategy and Interact may provide it with fresh ideas and the experience to develop apps for mobile devices. The two businesses will experience synergies if their core competencies complement one another and the two companies can easily integrate their processes and systems, for example the way decisions are made within each business.

However, the process of a merger is never totally smooth and Interact's employees may be used to working in a different way. Furthermore, although it is a mutual merger, some employees may be worried about their roles and status within the organisation. This could lead to demotivation, which is unlikely to lead to synergies in the near future.

In conclusion, the two companies should complement one another because their areas of specialism are aligned and there are opportunities for the companies to share their expertise and enter new markets if the merger is managed well. Overall, the extent to which the companies will experience synergies is likely to be dependent on how closely the organisational cultures can align. However, this might be difficult considering Interact is a Chinese company and Cloudburst Plc is from the USA. The key to a successful merger is open and honest communication across the organisation.

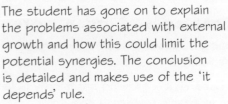

This question requires the student to use the case study to explain the synergies a business might experience through joining with another company. The student has understood the issues in the case study well and applied them to the concept of synergy.

The student has gone on to explain the problems associated with external growth and how this could limit the potential synergies. The conclusion is detailed and makes use of the 'it depends' rule.

Organic growth

Internal, or organic, growth occurs when a business grows naturally by selling more of its products and reinvesting the profit to expand into new areas. The opposite of organic growth is inorganic growth, which involves businesses joining together (external growth).

Methods of organic growth

A business will reinvest its profits to support growth into new areas. See the Ansoff Matrix on page 124 for a description of how a business might use these approaches.

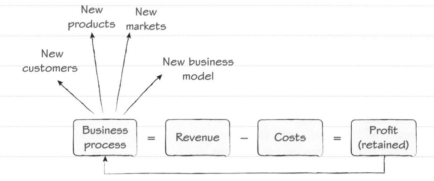

Franchising

One option for a company with a successful business model is to franchise – becoming a franchisor. This will involve the business licensing individuals or companies to trade under its brand using the goods or services it provides. Franchising is a potential route for some businesses to grow without having to necessarily increase the number of outlets, locations or employees. For more on franchising, see Unit 1.5.4.

New business model

Creating a new business model may involve moving from being a retailer to an E-tailer. Alternatively, it might involve moving the opposite way and setting up a 'bricks and mortar' operation. Changing the business operation could also involve changing the way customers access the product or developing the brand image.

Advantages of organic growth

Some of the benefits of a business growing organically are as follows:

👍 **Less risk** – growing organically is less risky than inorganic (external) growth.

👍 **Controlled pace** – a business can steadily increase the scale as and when its internal operations are ready.

👍 **Cheaper than external growth** – less strain on cash and capital investment.

👍 **Diseconomies of scale minimised** – as growth is gradual.

Disadvantages of organic growth

Some of the drawbacks of a business growing organically are as follows:

👎 **Slow pace** – may be too slow for some stakeholders who want rapid returns on their investment.

👎 **External expertise** – organic growth does not take advantage of the resources, skills and knowledge that might exist through a potential takeover or merger.

👎 **Competition** – businesses growing organically might be left behind by others that use external growth to dominate the market.

Now try this

1 Identify **three** ways a business might grow organically.

2 Identify **one** limitation of organic growth?

Reasons for staying small

Not all businesses set objectives for growth. Some business owners prefer to maintain a certain level of trade. This might be through personal preference or a strategic decision to maintain competitiveness.

There are a number of strategic benefits that a business might gain by staying small.

Personal service – a small business may find it easier to provide a personal service to customers.

Flexibility – a small business can make decisions more quickly and adapt to the competitive environment.

Costs – small firms may have lower running costs.

Reasons for staying small

Control and efficiency – small firms may find it easier to operate efficiently and keep control of operations.

Convenience as a USP – small businesses are able to serve a local community and may be more convenient than larger competitors.

Owner preferences – some owners may be happy with the level of profit they are earning as increased earnings would lead to more complicated accounts.

Product differentiation and USPs

To compete against larger firms, small firms may look to find a product or offer a service that is unique and is different from what the large firms can supply or offer. Some people will look to buy products that are different from the mainstream and this market is one that small firms can target.

A small firm has the potential to offer the customer specialist advice and accessories, adding further value to its USP.

Customer service

Smaller businesses often find it easier to provide a personal service. This is partly due to the owners and workers being able to build relationships with a smaller number of customers. This might also lead to a personal service or a bespoke product.

Large organisations seeking economies of scale find it increasingly difficult to provide this type of service to all customers.

Competing through e-commerce

Through e-commerce, small businesses no longer need to expand to be able to operate on a regional, national or international level. Small operations can exist and reach customers via their own or third-party e-commerce websites. Products can then be distributed globally from a small distribution centre without the need for investment in expensive retail space. Small businesses, such as consultants and trainers, can operate online to a large target audience.

Flexibility in responding to customer needs

Small businesses are more flexible because decisions can be made very quickly and the operations can be adapted. For example, they can change the product range, pricing or how the product is made. In large companies, these sorts of decisions might take months to implement and communicate across the organisation. This often means that smaller businesses can be the first to adapt to the competitive environment and customer needs.

Now try this

1 Why might a small business be more efficient than a large company?
2 How could a small business provide better customer service than a large company?

Exam skills

The following exam-style questions relate to the topics covered in Units 3.2.3 and 3.2.4 and refer to the Cloudburst Plc case study on page 143.

Worked example

Explain the benefit for Cloudburst Plc of expanding into new markets. **(4 marks)**

As Cloudburst Plc enters new markets it will be increasing its scale by creating more computer games, apps and software. As the business grows it will experience economies of scale, for example technological economies. As the business is a technology company it will be able to invest in the latest gaming technology, which it may not have been able to do if it were a smaller company. This may give it a competitive advantage over other software developers through developing innovative games in the future.

This is a rather open question and the student could consider the answer from a number of perspectives. In this extract the student has discussed economies of scale and applied this to the Cloudburst context. The student could also discuss some of the benefits of inorganic growth relating to the plans Cloudburst has to merge with take over associated businesses.

Worked example

Assess the importance of Cloudburst Plc continuously innovating in the computer games industry. **(12 marks)**

Innovation in the computer gaming industry may involve bringing out new games on a regular basis or developing technology to improve the processes by which Cloudburst makes its games.

The computer game market is very competitive and new games are brought out each year. Furthermore, customers do not stick with one game for long, so products have a relatively short life cycle. For this reason Cloudburst must develop new games in order to keep up with the demands of customers. Computer games are developing all the time and Cloudburst must also innovate in order to improve the experience of customers when playing its games.

However, Cloudburst became successful through a very successful product. This is a cash cow for the business and may continue to make it significant revenue. There is also no guarantee that investment in new games and technology will be successful. Indeed, innovation is very expensive and a high risk strategy for a business that already has a number of very successful products.

In conclusion, the key issue in the case of Cloudburst is that it operates in a technology-based industry where innovation is constantly pushing game design forward. For this reason Cloudburst would be naïve not to invest in innovation, but it must also maximise the potential of current products. The need for innovation might depend on the competitive environment, such as a new console being launched or a competitor launching a desirable new game. Overall, the merger with Interact Gaming might be the best way to remain competitive as this company already has a strong track record for innovation.

The word 'continuously' in this question is significant. It might be important for a business to innovate, but should they continuously innovate? The student might discuss some of the limitations and risks associated with innovation in their answer.

This is a complete student response to this question. The student has used business concepts very well in their answer. The analysis is also well developed and it is rooted in the Cloudburst context.

The evaluation is well balanced, provides a clear decision and uses value judgements.

Exam-style practice

The following exam-style questions relate to the topics covered in Units 3.2.1, 3.2.2, 3.2.3 and 3.2.4 and refer to the Cloudburst Plc case study below.

1 Explain **one** diseconomy of scale that Cloudburst Plc might experience as it grows. **(4 marks)**

After identifying an appropriate diseconomy remember to explain the impact this may have on Cloudburst Plc.

2 Explain why Cloudburst Plc might face pressure to grow. **(4 marks)**

Consider the type of business Cloudburst is and how this might affect strategic decisions.

3 Assess the reasons why Cloudburst Plc might have decided not to grow organically. **(10 marks)**

You might discuss the benefits and drawbacks of organic/inorganic growth in your answer in the context of Cloudburst Plc.

Cloudburst Plc's two options for the long-term success of the company are to merge with Interact Gaming Ltd or to develop a joint venture with a leading game console manufacturer.

4 Evaluate these **two** options and recommend which option might be more suitable for the business.

(20 marks)

The case study offers two options as to how Cloudburst could grow externally. Which of these could provide the company with the greatest opportunity for long-term success? Perhaps consider the risks involved with either approach.

 Case study

CLOUDBURST PLC

Cloudburst Plc is a large computer software company that makes computer games for platforms such as Xbox 1, PlayStation 4, PC and Mac computers. The company's most successful product is a Massively Multiplayer Online Role Playing Game (MMORPG), which is market leader in the MMORPG gaming segment. Subscribers pay a monthly fee to play alongside other players from Europe and North America in a fantasy world completing quests and challenges. In addition to regular updates to its MMORPG, Cloudburst Plc also releases one to two new games each year. Nevertheless, Cloudburst Plc's popular MMORPG still brings in around 70% of the firm's revenue.

Cloudburst Plc is looking to expand into new sectors of the industry. Recently the board have been negotiating terms for a merger with a Chinese gaming company, Interact Gaming Ltd, which specialises in developing apps for smartphones. Interact Gaming Ltd is considered to be a very innovative company which could benefit from the considerable cash reserves held by Cloudburst Plc. Even with its extremely successful MMORPG, Cloudburst Plc knows that computer games have a life cycle of around three years and a merger with Interact Gaming Ltd would not only add the expertise of its game designers, but allow it to acquire a number of successful app brands into its product portfolio.

Cloudburst Plc has also been in negotiations with a popular console manufacturer to integrate its MMORPG with the new version of the manufacturer's gaming console. This would give players free access to content updates and exclusive access to in-game features. Cloudburst Plc believes this joint venture could increase the reach of its popular game.

Quantitative sales forecasting 1

Forecasting future sales figures is vitally important to a business as this information informs key decisions about production, marketing, recruitment and finance. One way to predict future sales trends is by using historical data to predict future sales figures.

Time series analysis

Time series analysis and extrapolation can help a business work out whether there is an upwards trend, downwards trend or a constant trend in sales figures. It can also help businesses take into account seasonal variations and anticipate future sales figures with varying levels of accuracy.

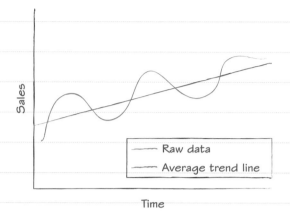

Calculating trends with a moving average

A moving average takes a three-period or four-period time span and finds the average of the three/four periods. The first period's sales then drop out and the next period is included in the average, as shown below for a three-month moving average. These figures plot the trend line.

	Raw data (monthly sales)	Three-month moving average	Method of calculation
Jan	48		
Feb	57	52	(48+57+51)/3
Mar	51	49	(57+51+39)/3
Apr	39	47	(51+39+53)/3
May	53	46	(39+53+47)/3
June	47	45	etc
July	36	44	etc

Centring

If a four-period moving average is necessary, there is no centre point (month or year) to place the average. In this instance, the averages need to be centred as shown below.

Jan   48

Feb   57

Mar   51   48
                      49
Apr   39   50

May   53

Limitations of quantitative sales forecasting

Quantitative sales tools are useful for informing key decisions but there are a number of limitations:

- Relatively short term – data loses value over 1–2 years.
- Dependent on the quality of the market research.
- Less valuable in volatile markets.
- Prior data has little bearing on what will happen in the future.
- Sales forecasts are unlikely to take into account external shocks in the future such as an economic recession.

Now try this

1 How is a moving average calculated?
2 What are the limitations of quantitative sales forecasting?

Quantitative sales forecasting 2

Line of best fit

Having identified the trend line using time series analysis, future sales can be predicted by drawing a line of best fit and extrapolating it to a point in the future. In the case opposite, sales for 2016 have been predicted as £1162 550.

A line of best fit can be drawn by eye, or plotted accurately using a computer or graph paper. The line of best fit should pass through (X, Y), where X is the average of years and Y is the average sales.

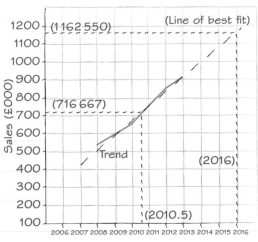

Annual sales of a toy manufacturer

Year	Sales	Four-year moving total	Eight-year moving total	Trend (Four-year centred moving average = Eight-year-moving total / 8)
2006	300			
2007	500			
2008	600	1950	4200	525.00
2009	550	2250	4750	593.75
2010	600	2500	5250	656.25
2011	750	2750	6050	756.25
2012	850	3300	6800	850.00
2013	1100	3500	7350	918.75
2014	800	3850		
2015	1100			

Seasonal variation

Seasonal variation can be used to provide a more accurate prediction than simply plotting the trend line. Here, a variation (+/−) from the trend line is calculated and averaged over a number of years (if several seasons' variations are available). The average seasonal variation is then a more accurate prediction than using the smoothed-out trend line.

For example, seasonal variation for Qtr 4 below should be 320 + 280 / 2 = £300 above the extrapolated trend line for Qtr 4 at any point in the future.

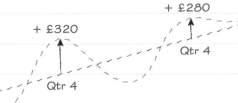

+ £320

+ £280

Qtr 4

Qtr 4

Causal modelling

Causal modelling through correlation looks at the relationship between data. This can be done using a scatter graph comparing two variables to identify whether there is a correlation between the two sets of data. Examples include looking for a link between advertising spend and sales, or between spending on training and the number of customer complaints.

correlation is given as a value between 21 and 11

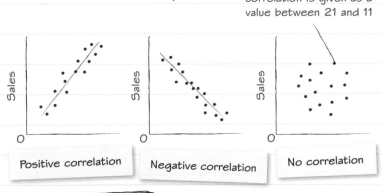

Positive correlation   Negative correlation   No correlation

Now try this

1 Why might a business want to calculate a seasonal variation when predicting future sales figures?
2 What does it mean if there is no correlation between two sets of data?

Investment appraisal 1

Investment appraisal is a series of techniques designed to assist businesses in judging the desirability of investing in particular projects. Investment appraisal may use a range of techniques, including financial and non-financial methods.

What businesses invest in

Investment appraisal may be used to aid businesses in making decisions when investing in:

- non-current assets
- launching new products
- new technology
- expansion
- infrastructure.

Financial methods

Financial methods for investment appraisal include:

- **payback** – calculates the length of time it takes for an investment to recoup its original cost
- **average rate of return** – calculates the annual average return over the life of an investment in order to compare the investment with other alternatives
- **net present value** – can be used alongside other techniques and considers the future value of an investment by discounting the decreased future value of money.

Simple payback

Payback is a quick and simple investment appraisal tool. It simply focuses on the time taken to recoup the initial investment and considers the cash inflows over a number of years. It is useful for firms who need a quick return and may be facing liquidity problems.

Payback can be calculated by using a table.

In this example payback is achieved after two years.

Year	Cash outflow	Cash inflow
0	100 000	40 000
1		30 000
2		30 000
3		30 000

If payback point falls between two years use:

$$\frac{\text{Amount remaining to recover}}{\text{Amount recovered in following year}} \times 12$$

Average (Accounting) Rate of Return

The ARR is useful because it measures the profit achieved on an investment over time, which can then be compared to other investments or the zero risk strategy of leaving money in a bank account. However, profits may fluctuate considerably over the life of a project and this is not taken into account.

ARR is calculated by:

$$\frac{\text{Average annual profit}}{\text{Asset's initial cost}} \times 100$$

13.5% average annual profit as a proportion of the initial investment can now be compared to other projects using the same calculation.

There are three steps to calculating ARR:

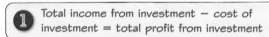 **1** Total income from investment − cost of investment = total profit from investment

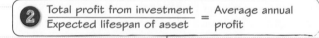 **2** $\frac{\text{Total profit from investment}}{\text{Expected lifespan of asset}}$ = Average annual profit

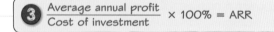 **3** $\frac{\text{Average annual profit}}{\text{Cost of investment}} \times 100\%$ = ARR

The total net profit for a project over 5 years is £1 350 000

Divided by the length of the project = £1 350 000 / 5 = £270 000

Divided by the initial investment cost (£2 000 000) = £270 000 / £2 000 000 = 13.5%

Now try this

1 Why might a business use investment appraisal?

2 Why might a business calculate payback?

3 Why is ARR useful when making investment decisions?

Investment appraisal 2

Discounted Cash Flow (Net Present Value)

Net present value (NPV) takes into account the future value of money by discounting cash flows. NPV considers time in an investment and follows the principle that the value of money depreciates over time. For example, two years from now, £1 will buy less than it does today. NPV is good for considering opportunity cost of an investment, but identifying the appropriate discount factor can be difficult. A project is viable if the sum of the NPV minus initial investment is positive. NPV is calculated by:

Net cash flow × discount factor

Year	Investment A	Investment B
1	40 000	10 000
2	20 000	20 000
3	10 000	40 000

Investment A is preferable as a higher proportion of the return is received towards the start of the investment – year 1.

Year	Discount factor at 10%
1	0.909
2	0.826
3	0.751
4	0.683

Cash flows are discounted using a discount factor for each year, such as 5%, 7% or 10%.

Investment decisions

A business might consider the following factors and use them to form criteria when making investment decisions.

Financial
- The rate of interest – using current rate of interest as a benchmark to judge investments against.
- ROCE – is there an expected minimum % return on the investment?
- Cost – can the firm finance the investment?

Investment criteria

Non-financial
- Corporate objectives – does the investment support business strategy?
- Ethics – does the investment support CSR policy?
- Industrial relations – what will be the impact on employees?

Risk and uncertainty

Risk is the chance of an adverse outcome and the impact it might have. The following might determine the level of risk associated with a particular investment:

 Timescale of the investment

 Knowledge/expertise of the business in the investment

 If the investment is in a new market

 Stability of the external environment (legal, political, social, etc)

Sensitivity analysis

Sensitivity analysis involves using variations in forecasting to allow for a range of outcomes. It allows a business to ask 'what if' questions and put in place plans to deal with these scenarios.

Examples might include:

- comparing NPV using a variety of discount factors
- allowing for a 20 per cent fluctuation in sales and costs
- building in contingency for unforeseen expenses.

Limitations of methods of investment

Method	Limitations
Simple payback	Cash earned after payback is ignored Profitability overlooked
ARR	Effects of time on value of money ignored
NPV	Calculation is more complex If rate of discount is too high, projects will not be profitable

Now try this

1　What **two** non-financial factors might a business use to evaluate a potential investment?

2　Identify **two** factors that may determine the risk associated with an investment.

3　How might a business use sensitivity analysis?

Exam skills

The following questions relate to the topics covered in Units 3.3.1 and 3.3.2 and provide examples of how you might be expected to calculate investment appraisal in an examination.

Worked example

1 Using the data in Extract A, calculate the payback period for Investment Project A. You are advised to show your working. **(4 marks)**

Extract A: Cash flows for Project A

Year	Net cash flow	Cumulative cash flow
0	(500)	(500)
1	100	(400)
2	125	(275)
3	175	(100)
4	200	100

3 Years +

$$\frac{100}{200} \times 12 = 6 \text{ months... Payback} = 3 \text{ years } 6 \text{ months}$$

The student has completed the cumulative cash flow table to show that payback falls between years 3 and 4. The calculation shows this to be 6 months by dividing the amount left to recover the investment after the third year (100) by the cash flow for year 4 (200) = 0.5. This is then multiplied by 12 (months) to get 6.

2 Using the data in Extract B, calculate the average rate of return for Investment Project B. You are advised to show your working. **(4 marks)**

Extract B: Cash flows for Project B

	Project B
Initial cost	£50 000
Return yr 1	£10 000
Yr 2	£10 000
Yr 3	£15 000
Yr 4	£15 000
Yr 5	£20 000
Total net cash flow	£70 000

Profit = £70 000 − £50 000 = £20 000

$$\text{Average annual profit} = \frac{£20\,000}{5} = £4000$$

$$\text{ARR} = \frac{£4000}{£50\,000} \times 100 = 8\%$$

First the student works out the average annual cost by taking the profit from the investment initial cost. This is then divided by the lifespan of the project (5 years). The average annual profit is then divided by the initial investment to give an ARR of 8%.

The following question relates to the Cloudburst case study on page 143.

3 Explain **one** limitation for Cloudburst of trying to forecast its sales in the computer games market. **(4 marks)**

Sales forecasting might involve quantitative sales forecasting using back data and extrapolating a trend using time series analysis. One problem that Cloudburst may face when sales forecasting is that the computer games industry is fast moving and very volatile. Many new games are launched every year. This means that old games could very quickly be replaced by newer versions or superseded by more popular games. Although Cloudburst have a consistently high performing MMORPG which brings in steady sales, as they enter new markets through the merger it will become increasingly difficult to accurately forecast future sales.

The student has made two references to the Cloudburst case study in their answer. They have also opened their answer by demonstrating understanding of sales forecasting techniques.

Decision trees 1

Decision trees are a method of tracing alternative outcomes from a range of business decisions, options or projects. The purpose of decision tree analysis is to place an expected financial or different decision based on the probability of an event occurring.

Decision trees

This is a model that represents the likely outcomes for a business of a number of courses of action showing the financial consequences of each.

Benefits

👍 Clarifies possible courses of action

👍 Adds financial data to decisions

👍 Makes managers account for risk

Drawbacks

👎 Probabilities are often estimated

👎 Does not consider qualitative information

👎 Does not take into account dynamic nature of business

Influences on decision-making

There are other factors that may play a part in shaping management decisions. These include:

- the objectives and mission of the business
- ethics – using a 'moral compass' to guide decisions
- the level of risk involved – some managers and businesses are more risk averse than others
- the external environment including competition – most decision-making models do not take into account these factors which are constantly changing
- resource constraints – a business can only make decisions if it has the resources available (labour, capital, knowledge) and this is where opportunity cost comes in.

Decision tree example

This example shows a business with two investment decisions (or do nothing). The expected value (EV) is highest on the marketing campaign and therefore the option the business should take.

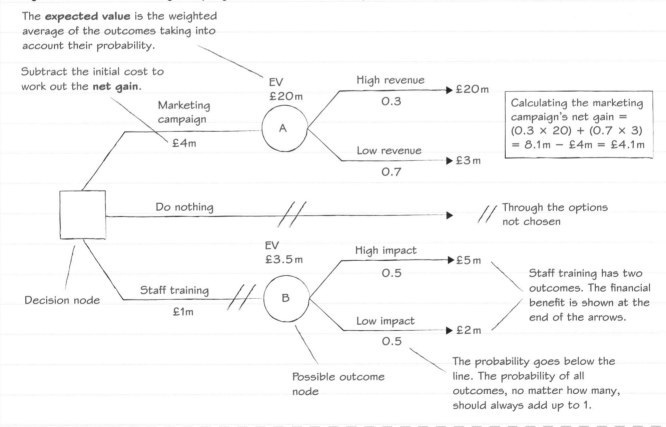

The **expected value** is the weighted average of the outcomes taking into account their probability.

Subtract the initial cost to work out the **net gain**.

Calculating the marketing campaign's net gain =
(0.3 × 20) + (0.7 × 3)
= 8.1m − £4m = £4.1m

Through the options not chosen

Staff training has two outcomes. The financial benefit is shown at the end of the arrows.

The probability goes below the line. The probability of all outcomes, no matter how many, should always add up to 1.

Now try this

1 How might a manager use a decision tree?
2 What is the expected value in a decision tree?

Decision trees 2

Constructing a decision tree

The five stages below will help you to construct a complete decision tree, which can then be used to make investment decisions.

1 Add information to the decision tree, such as:
- decisions
- costs
- outcomes
- financial benefits
- probability.

2 Multiply each financial benefit by its probability for each outcome and add them together to get the **expected value**.

3 If there is an initial cost (£1m to train staff), subtract this to get the **net gains** of the decision.

4 Repeat this process for each decision.

5 Cross through the options not taken.

Decision

Staff training

Cost — £1m

B

Outcome

High impact

0.5 → £5m

Probability

Financial benefits

e.g. staff training = (0.5 × 5m) + (0.5 × 2m)
EV = £.3.5m

Now try this

1 What are the limitations of decision trees?

2 What other decision-making tools might a manager use alongside a decision tree?

3 Using the guide above and using your own copy of the blank decision tree diagram below, come up with your own set of business decisions with probable outcomes. When you have created a scenario that fits the decision tree, work through the five stages to complete the decision tree.

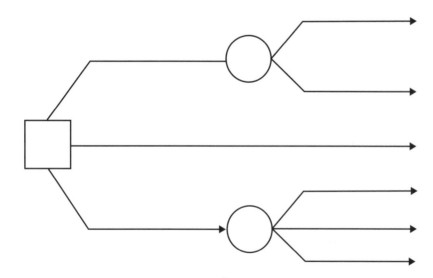

Exam skills

The exam-style question below applies the concepts of management decision-making covered in Unit 3.3.3.

Worked example

Using the information shown in Extract A, calculate the expected value and the net gain of the advertising campaign. You are advised to show your workings. **(4 marks)**

Extract A

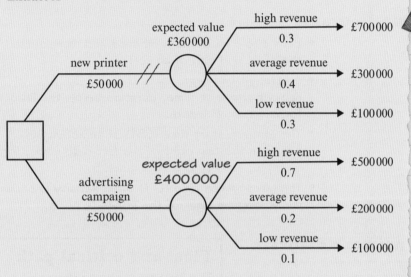

Expected value of new printer calculated by:
(0.3 × 700) + (0.4 × 300) + (0.3 × 100)
= 210 + 120 + 30
= £360 000

$(0.7 \times 500) + (0.2 \times 200) + (0.1 \times 100)$

$= 350 + 40 + 10$

$= £400\,000$ expected value $-$ £50 000 $=$ £350 000 net gain

The candidate has clearly shown their workings. The candidate has also labelled the diagram correctly and crossed through the less profitable option with //.

Critical Path Analysis 1

Critical Path Analysis involves using a network diagram to manage the various tasks required to complete a project. The use of Critical Path Analysis can help a manager to complete a project in the shortest space of time possible and identify critical activities.

Information required to carry out Critical Path Analysis

- Identification of all the tasks necessary to implement the strategy.
- The length of time each task takes to complete it to a satisfactory level.
- The order in which tasks must be completed – the dependent activities.
- Activities that can be completed at the same time – parallel activities.

Interpreting network analysis diagrams

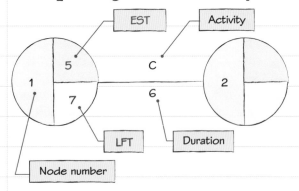

- Each circle (node) is numbered and represents the start and end of an activity.
- A straight line represents the activity. Activity number above the line, duration below the line, for example, 8 weeks.
- The earliest start time (EST) of an activity is shown in the top right of the left-side node; for example, activity C EST is week 5.
- The latest finish time (LFT) of an activity is shown in the bottom right of the left-side node.

The steps in constructing a network diagram

1 If required, construct the network diagram from an activities table showing the activity, what each activity is preceded by and the duration of each activity.

↓

2 All activities start as soon as possible; for example, if three activities can start immediately, three separate lines will be drawn from the first node.

↓

3 Add the earliest start times for each activity. Left to right. EST = EST of previous activity + duration of the activity.

↓

4 Add the latest finish time to each activity working right to left. LFT = previous LFT − activity duration. If there is a choice of numbers, choose the largest to deduct.

↓

5 Calculate the float time for each activity. Float time = LFT − duration − EST.

↓

6 Identify the critical path by hatching the lines of the activities on the critical path (//).

Float and critical path

The float time of an activity is any slack by which an activity can overrun. Float time is important for identifying which activities have flexibility.

The critical path is the route through the network diagram where there is no float time. These activities are critical because, if they overrun, the expected duration of the project will be extended.

Identifying the float time on activities and the critical path is the last stage of completing network analysis.

Carrying out network analysis can help managers to identify key activities, improve efficiency and manage resources effectively.

Now try this

1 What are the EST and LFT on a network diagram?

2 What is the 'float' on an activity?

3 What is meant by the 'critical path'?

Critical Path Analysis 2

Example of a completed Critical Path Analysis diagram

Use the notes below to interpret the information shown in this network diagram.

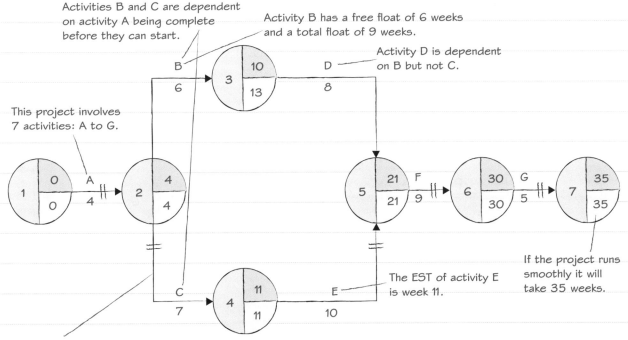

Activities B and C are dependent on activity A being complete before they can start.

Activity B has a free float of 6 weeks and a total float of 9 weeks.

Activity D is dependent on B but not C.

This project involves 7 activities: A to G.

If the project runs smoothly it will take 35 weeks.

The EST of activity E is week 11.

The critical path for the project is ACEFG.

The benefits of Critical Path Analysis

A manager can use Critical Path Analysis to:

👍 identify the exact activities involved in implementing a strategy

👍 effectively plan for the implementation of a strategy

👍 introduce informed deadlines for different activities

👍 allocate resources efficiently to the different activities

👍 identify float time and those activities that are critical to the success/implementation of the strategy.

The limitations of Critical Path Analysis

Critical Path Analysis has a number of limitations, including the following:

👎 Projects and strategies often involve multiple factors, agents and stakeholders – calculating the time taken to complete an activity can be very difficult.

👎 It does not take into account qualitative issues such as employee morale or relationships between workers.

👎 It relies on estimations. If these are correct so are the ESTs and LFTs. Strategies will not be implemented on time if this is incorrect.

👎 It does not take into account unexpected events and significant external factors beyond the business's control, such as key staff on long-term absence.

Now try this

1 What are the benefits of using Critical Path Analysis when implementing a strategy?
2 What are the limitations of Critical Path Analysis?

Exam skills

The following exam-style question relates to the topics covered in Unit 3.3.4 and the Cloudburst–Interact Merger case study on page 166.

Worked example

The Critical Path Analysis diagram represents the activities involved in developing and launching Cloudburst's new smartphone app to support its popular MMORPG.

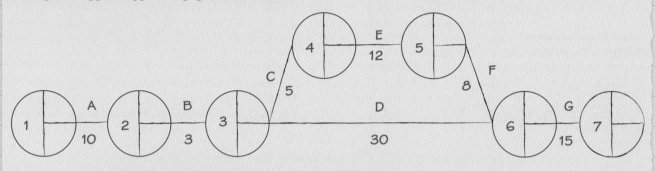

Using the information in the network analysis diagram, calculate:
* the earliest start time of each activity
* the latest finish time of each activity
* the float time for each activity.
Then identify the critical path.

Assume that activity A can start immediately.   **(4 marks)**

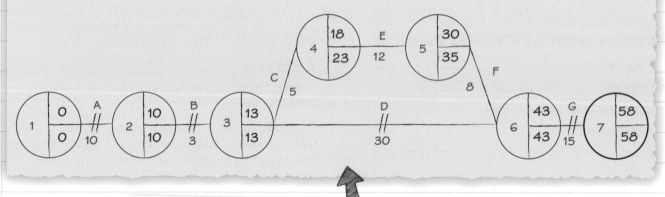

The student has completed the network diagram by identifying the earliest start times and latest finish times. They have also identified A, B, D, G as the critical path. Check the processes outlined on page 153 and see if you come up with the same calculations.

Exam-style practice

The following exam-style questions relate to Units 3.3.1, 3.3.2, 3.3.3 and 3.3.4 and to the Cloudburst-Interact Merger case study on page 166.

1   Using the table below, construct a critical path diagram for the development of a computer game.   **(4 marks)**

Task	Preceded by	Duration (weeks)
A concept development	none	1
B research	A	4
C prototype	A	8
D detailed artwork	B	2
E alpha testing	B	14
F audio production	C	8
G first production	D, E, F	3
H beta testing	G	1
I debugging	H	2
J game launch	G	6

Use the guide on page 152 to help you construct your network diagram. Draft the layout on scrap paper first before you start to add the information to the nodes and lines. You will not be required to produce a network diagram from scratch in your exam, but the process of mapping one out is good practice and will help you understand the logic behind the diagram.

2   Using your network diagram, calculate the:
   • earliest start times for each activity
   • latest finish times for each activity
   • float on each activity.   **(4 marks)**

Before you work this out, write down the steps required to calculate the EST, LFT and project float. Don't forget to show the critical path on your diagram using //.

3   Explain why Cloudburst Plc might use quantitative sales forecasting.   **(4 marks)**

What decisions does a sales forecast allow the business to make? Remember to apply your answer to the context.

A business is considering two new investment projects:
A   Increasing advertising of current products
B   Launching a new product range

4   Using the decision tree below, calculate the expected values of both options and identify the best option.   **(4 marks)**

Remember to multiply the probability by the financial outcome and find the average of the outcomes for each investment.

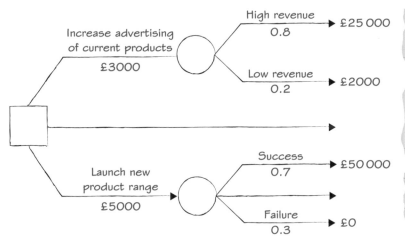

The following question refers to Extract A (Uber) on page 121.

5   Using the information below and Extract A, assess whether Uber should continue its partnership with Facebook.   **(12 marks)**

Consider discussing any risks associated with the venture and any non-financial factors that Uber should take into account.

Uber-Facebook Messenger Investment	
Payback	Approx. 5 years
ARR	4%

Corporate influences

The decisions of senior managers in large corporate businesses have far-reaching and long-term consequences on many stakeholders. As a result, there are far more pressures and influences on large corporations than there are on smaller companies.

Timescales – short-term goals of profitability do not always align with the long-term corporate strategy.

Corporate decision-making

Corporate culture – culture can influence the style of leadership, openness, creativity and trust within an organisation. For more on corporate culture see Unit 3.4.2.

Ethics – corporations with a strong ethical stance are likely to make different decisions from those that do not have strong principles around corporate social responsibility (CSR). For more on business ethics see Unit 3.4.4.

Stakeholder perspective – there are significant pressures for a business to satisfy the demands of shareholders and this may contradict the interests of other stakeholders such as employees and the local community. For more on shareholders vs stakeholders see Unit 3.4.3.

Short-term perspective

Businesses are more likely to:
- maximise short-term profits
- invest less in R&D and training
- return profits to shareholders
- pursue external growth strategies.

Short-term measures of success include: cash position, revenue, productivity, profit.

Long-term perspective

Businesses are more likely to:
- invest in R&D and training
- focus on profit quality
- take an ethical stance on decision-making
- pursue the interests of stakeholders.

Long-term measures of success include: R&D investment, profit quality, employee engagement, sustainability.

Decision-making process

Decisions based on evidence such as financial forecasts or using business tools such as break-even analysis or investment appraisal.

Decisions based on experience and 'gut feeling' without having supporting data.

Evidence-based decision-making (data) ← The extent to which decisions are made at a point along this continuum depends on a number of factors. → Subjective decision-making (intuition)

👍 Data can help reduce the risk in decision-making and help identify the likely outcome. Data can help compare alternative options.

👎 Data can be hard or expensive to collect, especially for small businesses. Sometimes data is unavailable, out of date or unreliable.

👍 Intuition might come from experienced managers, which and this is useful when making qualitative decisions, such as the character of a new employee or the potential success of a new marketing campaign.

👎 Without evidence in the form of data decisions based on intuition will always be risky.

Due to the level of financial risk involved in corporate decision-making, large corporations are more likely to use an evidence-based approach to decision-making to reinforce the opinions of senior managers. They may also have specialist functions and business analysts to produce and analyse evidence, whereas smaller businesses will not.

Now try this

1 What are the causes of short-termism in business?
2 When might a decision based on intuition be better than one that is based on evidence?

Corporate culture

The culture of an organisation includes the traditions, rituals, attitudes and values that make up the way a business is run and the way employees interact with one another. The culture of a business can be described in many different ways; it can be a significant determinant in the success of the firm.

Strong and weak cultures

A strong culture is one that is deeply embedded. It is obvious to the people working in that business and it will influence the way employees work, the relationships between employees, the strategy and the decisions made. The benefits of a strong culture include:

- a sense of identity (belonging)
- a sense of togetherness
- improved commitment from employees
- motivation
- reinforcing the values and beliefs of the business
- people understanding their purpose within the organisation.

Organisational culture

Many things contribute towards the culture of a business. These factors determine the way the business operates and may respond to the external environment and changes within the business.

Physical environment   Rituals – significant events or ways of doing things

Stories – things that have happened, good or bad, in the past

Forming a business culture

Key personalities – leaders and employees who influence others

Rewards – what the business recognises as success and the way it rewards this

Charles Handy's model of culture

Charles Handy's model of culture outlines four distinct organisational culture types.

A few people, or one person, drive the organisation and decisions. The culture is determined by a few individuals. Common in small businesses.

Power culture
(the web)

People associate with a team or function. Very clear structure and cultures may differ across these functions. May develop out of a power culture as a business grows.

Role culture
(greek temple)

Employees associate with a task or project. New groups are formed regularly and cultural norms will frequently change as new groups are formed.

Task culture
(lattice)

Employees have a great deal of independence and may not be strongly affiliated with a specific group.

Person culture
(cluster)

Now try this

1 What factors may contribute to the culture of a business?
2 What is a power culture?

Managing corporate culture

Organisational culture can change over time and many different factors can influence these changes. The nature of culture in a business may be influenced more or less by a number of factors.

Influences on organisational culture

The factors below are likely to influence the culture of a business. These factors overlap and merge with one another, but they will vary in significance across different businesses. For example, in Business A the leader of the organisation is the most significant factor in forming the culture within the organisation. However, in Business B the values and norms (traditions and ways of doing things) are more important.

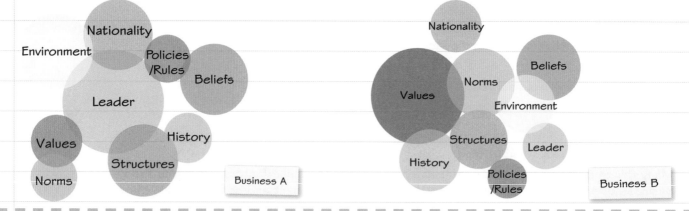

Reasons for changing organisational culture

There are a number of reasons why changing organisational culture might be desirable.

👍 A new leader – who may want to impose their own way of doing things.

👍 Poor performance – a negative culture may have contributed to this.

👍 Corporate objectives – a change in direction and strategy may require a different approach.

👍 Customer needs – expectations of customers or society in general may call for change.

Problems changing organisational culture

Although a change in culture may be desirable, it is not always easy to impose cultural change. Reasons are outlined below.

👎 Changing culture is a long process. It may require significant education and training of the workforce.

👎 Large organisations may have more than one culture across different functions or regions.

👎 Culture is deep set – it extends from people's attitudes and beliefs. These are not easy to change.

Kruger's Change Iceberg

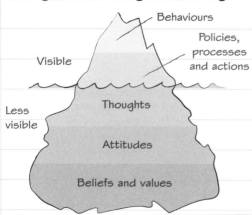

Attitudes and beliefs are part of an organisation's culture. But like the iceberg below the surface, they are hard to see, let alone change.

 Key points

A strong culture – one that exhibits desirable characteristics – can lead to a competitive advantage for a business. For example, it can lead to a creative, innovative, cohesive or highly motivated organisation. However, changing an organisational culture is very difficult and can take a long time as certain aspects of human behaviour are driven by attitudes and beliefs. This is a key point of evaluation that you might use when answering questions on this topic. A strong culture might be desirable, but it will be difficult to change if it is not working.

Now try this

1 Why might a business choose to change its culture?
2 Why is changing organisational culture difficult?

Exam skills

The following exam-style questions relate to the topics covered in Units 3.4.1 and 3.4.2 and refer to the Cloudburst–Interact Gaming merger case study on page 166.

Worked example

Explain **one** factor that may influence corporate decision-making at Cloudburst Plc. **(4 marks)**

One factor that may influence corporate decision-making at Cloudburst Plc is the pressure from shareholders. The shareholders may want to see measures of short-term performance to satisfy them that their investment is safe. This might include seeing quarterly growth in revenue or the regular launch of new computer games on the market. These pressures may lead to new games being developed and released in a tight schedule instead of longer periods of development involving research and development and testing.

The student has shown an understanding of short-term versus long-term decision-making and the pressures from shareholders. The answer is in context by referring to the shareholders of the company (Plc) and the link with the computer gaming industry.

Worked example

Explain why Cloudburst Plc may find it difficult to change the way that the former employees of Interact Gaming work. **(4 marks)**

Cloudburst will find it difficult to change the way that the designers from Interact work because their previous practices such as making many of their own decisions are part of their culture. Organisation culture is formed, among other things, by norms, rituals and beliefs, such as the process adopted to produce a new computer game. People do not change their beliefs easily and the former Interact Gaming designers may believe that they should have the authority to make key decisions without the supervision of line managers.

The student has used the information in the case study to answer the question. They have also shown an understanding of organisational culture and the role it can play in the way employees may act or react to different situations. However, it is not a complete answer.

Worked example

The directors of Cloudburst are concerned that there could be a number of barriers to the successful merger of the two companies: one being cultural barriers and another being the pace of growth.

Evaluate these **two** barriers and decide which is the most significant for the successful merger of the two companies. **(20 marks)**

In order to manage the cultural barriers that exist the directors could set clear objectives so all employees have the same targets to achieve. This will mean they will be striving to achieve the same things and this will encourage them to cooperate. Clear leadership is another way that the culture within a business can be changed. If the directors of Cloudburst are demonstrating the characteristics that they want their employees to have then in time this is likely to influence the behaviour of the workforce. Nevertheless, Cloudburst is now a multinational organisation and it needs to appreciate that different societies have different cultural norms. For example, the former Interact employees may be used to greater power and freedom between themselves and their line managers.

This extract from the student's answer recommends how the culture of the two companies could be aligned. Appropriate examples have been used to put the response in context. The student has also gone on to explain that there are likely to be inevitable differences now that Cloudburst is a multinational.

Stakeholders 1

Stakeholders are groups or individuals who have an interest in a business. It is important for all businesses to manage the needs of their stakeholders if they are to be successful. Stakeholders can have a considerable impact on the actions and fortunes of a business, but not all stakeholders have the same needs and wants. Therefore, the key is being able to manage these often-conflicting interests.

> Shareholders are only internal stakeholders in a private limited company. In a public limited company you would classify them as external because they are often the general public, not owners running the company. The board of directors however, would be internal.

Stakeholders in a business and their interests

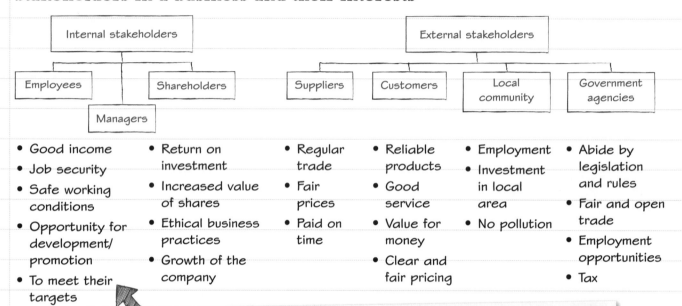

Employees and managers can be seen as separate groups, but have the same interests.

Shareholder vs stakeholder concept

The concept of managing stakeholder expectations is closely linked to that of social responsibility. Meeting the needs of stakeholders, especially the external stakeholders, encourages ethical practices by reducing the negative impact of a business's decisions on a third party. Meeting stakeholders' needs can be expensive and time-consuming. Indeed, it can often compromise profitability in the short term. For example, investing in employee medical cover may benefit the business in the long run, but will increase short-term costs. The major conflict that many large businesses face is focusing on the needs of shareholders or the wider stakeholder groups.

Overlapping and conflicting interests

Sometimes stakeholder interests are aligned, but often satisfying one set of needs can lead to conflict elsewhere. In any situation you should try to consider where conflicts might exist and what the business could do to resolve these conflicts. Look at the diagram and think how a business opening a new high tech factory could have an impact on the stakeholders shown.

Now try this

1 State **three** stakeholder groups.
2 Outline the interests of the local community.

Stakeholders 2

Shareholders vs stakeholders

On the previous page the concept of shareholders vs stakeholders was explained. A corporation will operate somewhere on a spectrum between these two approaches, but may take one perspective over another when making certain decisions. Below is a summary of the conflicts of interest between shareholders and other stakeholders.

```
                          ┌──────────────┐
                          │ Shareholders │
                          └──────────────┘
     ┌─────────────┬──────────┴──────┬──────────────┐
┌──────────┐ ┌────────────────┐ ┌────────────┐ ┌─────────────┐
│ Customers│ │Directors/managers│ │ Government │ │ Environment │
└──────────┘ └────────────────┘ └────────────┘ └─────────────┘
```

Customers	Directors/managers	Government	Environment
Shareholders want to see increased revenue and one way to achieve this is through increasing prices.	Conflicts may arise when the directors of a business look to increase the rewards and remuneration of the board or invest in long-term growth rather than short-term profitability.	Government want to maximise tax revenue from corporation tax. Shareholders and managers often look for legal (and sometimes illegal) means to pay the minimum tax.	Business operations can often deplete natural resources and damage the environment. Governments put in place policies to manage these negative externalities but they do not always work. Profit maximisation will look for the most efficient way to make money. This is not always the most environmental.

Influences on stakeholder relationships

Internal factors			External factors		
Management and leadership	**Objectives**	**Size/ ownership**	**Market conditions**	**Stakeholder power**	**Government policy**
Differing leadership styles will determine how managers view employees.	Profit objectives will be more aligned with shareholder interests. Growth objectives may be more aligned with employees' interests.	A sole trader will not have the pressures of meeting shareholder expectations and may not have as big an impact on the local community.	Demand and the competitiveness of a market will change the priorities of a business.	Majority shareholders and key customers will be given greater focus than a stakeholder with limited power to influence the business.	A business will have to meet its legal requirements, no matter how this impacts its stakeholders. For example, complying with new employment legislation.

Where shareholder and stakeholder interests meet

Shareholder concept – this is the belief that the prime function of a business is to satisfy its shareholders. This means maximising profitability and shareholder returns. Profits will support the long-term success of the business and economic prosperity. Business objectives from a shareholder perspective are profit-based and can be detrimental to the interests of the wider stakeholder group.

Aligned objectives – many businesses now adopt an approach that focuses on shareholder value with a long-term perspective, not just for short-term profitability gains. As businesses adopt a long-term perspective, consideration of other stakeholders becomes more agreeable – such as the investment in training to improve the skills of the workforce.

Stakeholder concept – this is where businesses cater for the needs of all stakeholders, not just shareholders. In doing so, businesses create long-term prosperity and avoid unsustainable business practices. However, focusing on the wider stakeholder groups can hinder short-term profit objectives as the most profitable short-term decisions will not be made.

Now try this

1 What might determine the interests of any one stakeholder group?
2 What is the most important stakeholder group for a business?

Ethics

Ethics are the moral principles that guide the behaviours of individuals and businesses. When making decisions, businesses must consider the impact they have on all stakeholders. Sometimes the drive for profits can conflict with ethical principles. Ethics becomes a more significant factor for large corporations because their decisions and practices have a wide-reaching effect.

Ethics can have a significant impact on the way a business operates and does business. We have already seen how a business's decisions can impact various stakeholder groups.

Environment – Ethical corporations will ensure they are sustainable and not damage the environment. Large corporations may operate in countries with less stringent environmental regulations.

Workers – Ethical businesses will ensure employees have good working conditions, fair pay and care for their overall well-being and health. Many corporations manufacture products in countries where the living wage is low and there are fewer regulations around workers' rights.

Ethical decision-making

Corruption – Ethical corporations will do business in a fair, honest and open way. However, corruption exists in all industries including practices such as tax avoidance, bribery, fraud or profiteering from illegal practices like trading weapons in politically unstable regions of the world.

Technology – There are ethical debates around the development of some new technologies, for example GM crops, fracking, nuclear power and electronic cigarettes.

Ethical business practices

Examples of ethical business practices might include:

- treating workers and suppliers fairly
- being honest with customers
- ethical sourcing of materials
- caring for the community
- meeting government requirements (legislation)
- caring for the environment (sustainability)
- paying suppliers a fair price for their goods
- only trading with other ethical corporations.

Pay and rewards

The practice of pay and rewards is one that large corporations are often crtitcised for. Pay and remuneration is used to attract and motivate a workforce, but the principles behind who gets paid what are not always fair.

In some businesses, senior leaders are paid extremely high bonuses, whereas some workers are paid the minimum wage. There are many industries where the pay gap between men and women is significant.

Pressure groups

Pressure groups are organisations that try to make businesses change their behaviour or operations. Pressure groups focus on issues such as animal rights, workers' rights, the environment and world poverty. A pressure group can cause negative publicity for a business that acts unethically, which can damage the business's reputation.

Profit and ethics

As with the shareholders vs stakeholders conflict. Ethical business practices are not always aligned with profit maximisation unless a business has a long-term perspective on success.

Acting ethically can be expensive and is not the fastest way (but often the most sustainable) to make a profit.

Now try this

1 Give **three** examples of ethical business practices.
2 What is the role of a pressure group?

Corporate social responsibility

Corporate Social Responsibility

Corporate Social Responsibility (CSR) is the belief that a business should act responsibly and protect the interests of all its stakeholders. Going beyond following rules and regulations, CSR dictates that a business should operate in a way that actually benefits society and the environment, not just to behave as a 'good citizen' but for the long-term sustainability and prosperity of the business. CSR shapes the ethics that guide most modern-day businesses.

CSR in practice

Customers	Employees
👍 Fair prices 👍 Transparency 👍 Honesty 👍 Reliable after-sales service 👍 Safe products	👍 Fair pay 👍 Good working conditions 👍 Job security
Suppliers	**Local community**
👍 Fair prices 👍 Frequent and regular orders	👍 Employment opportunities 👍 Investment in infrastructure 👍 Minimal negative externalities

CSR may involve businesses upholding these practices for each of their stakeholder groups.

Corporate Social Responsibility Pyramid

Philanthropic responsibility
Be a good corporate citizen.
Contribute resources to the community; improve quality of life.

Ethical responsibility
Be ethical.
Obligation to do what is right, just and fair.
Avoid harm.

Legal responsibility
Obey the law.
Law is society's codification of right and wrong.
Play by the rules of the game.

Economic responsibility
Be profitable.
The foundation upon which all others rest.

Carroll's CSR Pyramid

This business model sets out four responsibilities that all businesses should meet in order to be socially responsible. The responsibilities are hierarchical, with economic responsibility at the base. Without first meeting this responsibility a business will fail and will therefore be unable to meet its other responsibilities.

The problem with CSR

There is sometimes a short-term contradiction between the first step of the pyramid and the following three. The pressures for a business to be legally, ethically and philanthropically responsible can require significant financial investment, therefore having an impact on short-term profitability.

The pressures for effective CSR

Appropriate CSR practices can have a significant impact on the competitiveness of a business:

☑ Bad publicity can be shared easily through social media, damaging its reputation.

☑ Ethically orientated customers may choose a business based on its CSR record.

☑ Good CSR will help attract the best employees.

☑ Supporting developing countries through effective CSR policies supports long-term sustainability and growth in these markets.

Exam focus — Evaluating in an exam

CSR can provide you with an effective 'depends on' argument when evaluating. For example, when evaluating the decision of a business to enter a new international market, you can consider the impact this might have on its social responsibility; for example, how might this affect its employees in terms of relocation and job security? Is it exploiting cheap labour?

Now try this

1 What is CSR?
2 Why is CSR important for all businesses?

Exam skills

These exam-style questions relate to the topics covered in Units 3.4.3 and 3.4.4. The questions refer to the case studies Extract A and Extract B on page 121.

Worked example

Explain why it is important for companies like Uber to consider the interests of their stakeholders.   **(4 marks)**

Companies like Uber need to consider the interests of their stakeholders because they can have a direct impact on the success of the business. For example, there is some negative publicity around the way drivers are treated and their working conditions. If this is true, then employee motivation could fall and Uber may find it difficult to recruit drivers in the future. Although saving money on worker benefits and rights may increase profits it is not sustainable in the long term.

> The student has clearly explained how a stakeholder, using the example of employees, can influence a business. The student has also applied their answer to the Uber context.

Worked example

UK consumers are becoming increasingly conscious about the impact they have on the environment. In particular, a growing proportion of society actively seeks ways to conserve energy in their homes, recycle and minimise their carbon footprint.

Using Extract B, assess the impact this social trend is likely to have on businesses providing public transport in the UK.   **(10 marks)**

With UK consumers becoming more environmentally conscious it is likely that more people will look for transport methods that are green and limit the impact on the environment. This may include purchasing electric cars, but also switching to public transport and cycling.

As the costs of public transport rise it is important for businesses to absorb these costs and improve internal efficiencies if they are to attract customers. As costs rise, people may be more tempted to walk or cycle to work and this could reduce trade and revenues for public transport providers such as bus and coach companies. In order to remain competitive they will have to find ways to reduce costs and ensure that the price of public transport is competitive against other alternatives....

> The student has used the extract well and identified that public transport costs are rising. They have then used this information along with the question stem to identify the threats these changes could have on public transport providers and how they may have to react. The student could go on to discuss the pressure for public transport providers to offer environmentally friendly transport, such as low carbon emissions.

Assess whether Uber is failing to meet its corporate social responsibility.   **(12 marks)**

... In conclusion, Uber has not broken any laws and its customers are likely to appreciate the services it provides in order to make calling a taxi more convenient. For this reason Uber is certainly meeting its economical and philanthropic responsibilities as outlined by Carroll's CSR Pyramid. However, a key aspect of CSR is ensuring no stakeholders are affected in a negative way. As Uber currently has a number of lawsuits going through the courts it is yet to be seen whether they are meeting their legal and ethical responsibilities. Uber is meeting the needs of its shareholders and some businesses will set this as a key objective. Therefore, the extent to which Uber is meeting its corporate social responsibility may depend on its corporate objectives and long-term goals.

> Notice how the student has clearly focused on answering the question in their last paragraph. The student has used some good techniques in their assessment, including the 'depends on' rule and using appropriate management theory.

Exam-style practice

The following exam-style questions relate to the topics covered in Units 3.4.3 and 3.4.4 and refer to the Cloudburst Plc–Interest Gaming Ltd merger case study on page 166.

1 Explain **one** factor that might influence the corporate culture at Cloudburst Plc.   **(4 marks)**

To answer this question, you might consider the day-to-day features of a business that help form its culture, or broader factors such as leadership styles or the size of the organisation.

2 Assess the factors that could lead to Cloudburst Plc being considered an ethical business by its stakeholders.   **(10 marks)**

Use specific examples of ethical business practices that might relate to Cloudburst and the IT/computer games industry in your answer.

3 Assess the reasons why the directors of Cloudburst Plc might find it difficult to integrate the two companies.   **(10 marks)**

When answering this question think about organisational culture and managing stakeholder interests.

4 Assess the impact of shareholder influence on decision-making at Cloudburst Plc.   **(12 marks)**

In the case study, look for examples of decisions that might be influenced by shareholders or stakeholders. Discuss the pressures that might be placed on Cloudburst from various stakeholder groups.

Case study

The Cloudburst Plc–Interact Gaming Ltd merger

CLOUDBURST PLC ←－－－→ **Interact**

In 2015 the board of directors agreed terms with Interact Gaming Ltd and in November a merger between the two businesses was completed, leading to a jump in Cloudburst Plc's share value by 30p per share. Cloudburst Plc became the trading name for the company, but the Interact Gaming Ltd brand was kept for existing products launched in the Asian markets.

The first step taken by the board was to move the company from a functional structure to a product structure. This was followed by the voluntary relocation of a number of former Interact Gaming Ltd game designers to Cloudburst Plc's headquarters in San Francisco.

The first new product to be launched by the company was a smartphone app to support Cloudburst Plc's popular MMORPG. The app would allow players to monitor statistics of their characters and complete transactions such as buying items for their characters to use in the game without having to log-in on a computer game console.

Initial meetings ran smoothly, but problems arose when the schedules were put in place. The former Interact Gaming Ltd game designers felt that a March 2016 launch would be feasible for the new app, but key managers at Cloudburst Plc felt that this would be too rushed and the final app might not match the quality they demanded of a Cloudburst Plc product. It also took some time for the former Interact Gaming Ltd designers to feel comfortable with the lack of autonomy they were given. While working at Interact Gaming Ltd, game designers were given considerable freedom to make their own decisions. Whereas, at Cloudburst Plc project managers had to officially sign-off any big decision.

Following complications with the app, the directors of Cloudburst Plc sat down to discuss the issues. Cloudburst Plc had merged with Interact Gaming Ltd to expand into new markets, but also to benefit from the creative skills its employees possessed. It seemed that change might be needed if Cloudburst Plc was to get the most out of the company.

Interpreting financial statements 1

A business will produce a range of financial information to support its stakeholders in decision-making. Two key documents that all companies are required to produce are the **statement of comprehensive income** and the **balance sheet**.

Key information in the statement of comprehensive income

The profit after direct costs have been deducted. Gives a broad indication of the success of a business's trading activity.

Overheads are then deducted from gross profit.

The profit left after other indirect operating costs (overheads) have been deducted.

The direct costs associated with the production and sale of the product or service.

These are general indirect overheads such as office salaries, expenses claims, rent and administrative costs.

	£m
Revenue	300
Cost of sales	(45)
Gross profit	**255**
Other operating expenses	(65)
Operating profit	**190**
Exceptional expenses	(40)
Exceptional income	10
Tax	(35)
Profit for the year (net profit)	**125**

The bottom line – what a business has left to reinvest or return to shareholders/owners after tax has been deducted.

These could be expenses or incomes not associated with the direct activity of the business. They may be one-off items. They are kept separate in order to give a true reflection of the quality of profit.

What we can find out from a statement of comprehensive income:

- ☑ Changes in sales revenue
- ☑ Changes in the direct costs of sales
- ☑ How well a business is managing its operating costs
- ☑ The profitability of a business
- ☑ Unusual incomes/expenses during the year

Shareholders – will be interested in the profit for the year as this may indicate potential returns for shareholders.

Managers – use revenue, gross profit and operating profit to measure performance and set targets.

Stakeholder interests in the statement of comprehensive income

Government – to identify the level of taxation the business needs to pay to HMRC.

Employees – the profitability of the business may indicate the potential for remuneration and rewards.

Now try this

1 Why might employees be interested in their company's statement of comprehensive income?
2 What is meant by the quality of profit?

Interpreting financial statements 2

The statement of financial position

Also known as fixed assets, these are assets used to operate the business and include land and machinery (tangible), brands and patents (intangible).

These are physical assets such as plant, property and equipment. They are used in the production process.

Receivables are debts from trade that a business anticipates will be paid within 12 months.

Total assets − total liabilities = the value of a business

Provisions is money put aside in anticipation of bad debt − customers not paying.

Total equity will always balance with net assets − it represents how a business has been financed.

These are not physical assets. They include goodwill (the value the business is worth above its net assets) and other intangibles such as brand names and copyrights.

Assets that the business expects to use or sell within the year. These can be converted into cash to pay off liabilities.

Inventories is the stock a business is holding.

Payments due within one year.

Borrowings include short-term debts such as an overdraft or short-term loans.

Debts that a business does not expect to pay within a year.

Share capital is the amount of money paid in to the business by shareholders.

		£m
Non-current assets		**70**
Intangible non-current assets	10	
Tangible non-current assets	60	
Current assets		**55**
Inventories	30	
Receivables	25	
Current liabilities		**(35)**
Borrowings	(30)	
Payables	(5)	
Net current assets		**20**
Non-current liabilities		**(50)**
Long-term loan	40	
Provisions	10	
Net assets		**40**
Retained profit	30	
Share capital	10	
Total equity		**40**

What we can find out from a statement of financial position:

☑ The value of a business (equity)   ☑ The liquidity of a business

☑ The current assets a business holds   ☑ The long-term debts of a business

☑ Short-term liabilities the business will need to pay within the year   ☑ How a business has been financed

Shareholders − may analyse the asset structure of the business to see how their investment has been spent.

Stakeholder interests in the statement of financial position

Managers − use the current financial position to analyse liquidity and the level of risk associated with debt.

Suppliers and creditors − will be interested to see whether the business will be able to pay its debts and support any decisions around credit agreements.

Now try this

1 What are receivables?

2 What is meant by the term 'intangible asset' in the context of a statement of financial position?

Ratio analysis

Units 2.3.1 and 2.3.2 explore profitability and liquidity ratios. The ratios in this unit are used to assess financial performance and the financial structure of a business.

Return on capital employed (ROCE) ratio

The ROCE ratio compares operating profit earned with the amount of capital employed by the business. Capital employed is its total equity plus any non-current liabilities.

It is calculated by:

$$\frac{\text{Operating profit}}{\text{Capital employed}} \times 100\%$$

Also known as the 'primary efficiency ratio', ROCE shows how effectively the business was able to generate a profit from the investment placed within the business. It can be compared to previous years and the general rate of interest.

A business can improve its ROCE by increasing operating profit or by reducing capital employed.

Gearing ratio

Gearing analyses how a business has raised its long-term finance. The ratio represents the proportion of a firm's equity that is borrowed.

It is calculated by:

$$\frac{\text{Non-current liabilities}}{\text{Total equity + non-current liabilities}} \times 100\%$$

Interpreting the gearing ratio

A highly geared business has more than 50 per cent of its capital in the form of loans. A highly geared business is vulnerable to increases in interest rates.

A low-geared business may have the opportunity to borrow funds in order to expand. Businesses with secure cash flow or considerable assets may be able to borrow more for this purpose.

The value of ratio analysis

Allows a business to calculate and compare trends over time.	Does not take into account qualitative issues such as brand image or customer service performance.
Shows greater insight than financial accounts on their own.	Does not take into account the impact of long-term decisions, such as investments today that may lower profitability in the short term but boost it in the long term.
Information can be used against benchmark data – such as an industry average.	
Can be used to assess the performance of other functional areas of the business – operations and human resources.	Economic climate – ratios do not take into account economic conditions or the performance of other businesses.

Now try this

1 What issues might a business face if it is highly geared?
2 Identify **one** limitation of financial ratios.

Exam skills

The following exam-style questions explore the topics covered in Units 3.5.1 and 3.5.2 and relate to Extract C in the Winstanley and Walker Confectionery Ltd case study on page 180.

Worked example

Using Extract C, calculate the return on capital employed ratio for Winstanley and Walker Confectionery Ltd.   **(4 marks)**

$$\frac{\text{operating profit}}{\text{capital employed}} \times 100\%$$

capital employed = net assets

$$\frac{2.5}{2.8} \times 100\%$$

ROCE = 89.29%

You should know how to calculate capital employed as it will not necessarily be a direct figure in the financial accounts.

Worked example

Explain how a stakeholder might use the financial accounts of Winstanley and Walker Confectionery Ltd.   **(4 marks)**

One stakeholder group that might be interested in the financial accounts of Winstanley and Walker is their employees. The employees might look at the statement of comprehensive income to analyse how profitable the company has been in 2016–17. As the company has made a £1.1 million profit for the year this would suggest that investment and growth are likely and this would give an indication of job security and future potential for promotion. Employees might also look at this information in the anticipation of a financial bonus.

The student has chosen one stakeholder group and answered the question from their perspective. It is a better approach to develop one reason or factor in an 'explain' question than mentioning several points with limited development of each.

Worked example

Using Extract C, assess the financial position of Winstanley and Walker Confectionery Ltd.   **(12 marks)**

From the statement of financial position, you can see that Winstanley and Walker Ltd have net current assets of minus £700 000. This is a worrying position for an expanding company as it is likely that there will be considerable drains of cash to support the growth of the company, especially if the contract with the large retailer is increased. With growth there is often an outlay of cash before revenues start to increase. Winstanley and Walker's current ratio is 0.5 and this could lead to liquidity problems....

In this first paragraph the student has identified a limitation of the company's finances from the statement of financial position. The student has also used a relevant ratio to support their analysis. A second part to this answer may go on to discuss the positives of the financial accounts, such as the profitability of the company in 2016–17.

Human resources

Managers can use a number of calculations to interpret and analyse the performance of human resources within their business. Understanding human resource performance can help managers make decisions on job design, employee numbers, rewards and remuneration, and human resource policies.

Labour productivity

Labour productivity is a key measure of employee performance. It interprets the output per worker over a given time period. It directly affects profit margins and decisions around pricing.

It is calculated using the formula:

$$\frac{\text{Total output per time period}}{\text{Number of employees at work}}$$

Interpreting labour productivity

Generally speaking the higher the labour productivity the better the business is performing.

However:

👎 it does not take into account **wage rates** – a key factor in employees' performance

👎 it does not take into account **technology** used in the production process

👎 it may be affected by many **other factors** – such as internal disruptions to production, or the nature of the task or product being produced, which will also influence this calculation.

Labour turnover and labour retention

This is an important measure as the number of employees leaving a company can give an insight into a number of issues relating to happiness, motivation and the impact of this on overall labour costs.

Labour turnover is calculated by:

$$\frac{\text{Number of staff leaving in a year}}{\text{Average number of staff}}$$

Labour retention substitutes the average number leaving with the average number employed for one year (the year being measured).

Interpreting labour turnover and retention

- With labour turnover comes increased costs of recruitment and training.
- A higher turnover or low retention figure could indicate that employees are not happy with their jobs.
- This might be used as a key performance indicator as businesses try to retain the most talented workers within their company – having the best employees can be a competitive advantage.
- Some industries will expect high rates of labour turnover – for example holiday companies, due to contracts being seasonal.
- High rates of labour turnover may be encouraged as a business goes through a period of change.

Absenteeism

This compares the number of people absent for a time period by the total number of employees.

It is calculated using the formula:

$$\frac{\text{Number of staff absent for time period}}{\text{Total employees}}$$

Interpreting absenteeism

- A high level of absenteeism increases business costs as productivity falls and costs to cover employees rise.
- High levels of absenteeism may also be an indicator of demotivation or tensions in the workforce.
- A business may also compare its health and safety records with absenteeism data.

Now try this

1 Why is labour productivity important?
2 What are the dangers of high labour turnover?

Human resources strategies

Methods of motivating employees in order to increase business performance are explored in Unit 1.4.4. Below is a range of other strategies that a business may use to increase labour productivity, improve employee retention and reduce absenteeism.

Using financial rewards

Businesses can be creative in the way they use financial rewards to have a direct impact on productivity, retention and absenteeism.

Rewards linked to output – some organisations will link remuneration to the level of output through performance-related pay, bonus systems and commission systems. Increasing any of these can boost output and labour productivity.

Financial rewards

Loyalty bonuses – in many companies financial rewards will also be linked to the length of time employees have been with the company. Other bonuses, such as holidays, may also be tied to an employee's length of service.

Attendance bonuses – some employers may link bonuses to attendance, for example a £500 bonus linked to 100% attendance over a six-month period.

Employee share ownership

Employee share schemes are another way to remunerate employees. Employees can buy into a sharesave scheme that allows them to purchase company shares at a fixed price. Employees make capital gains on these shares as the price increases over time. However, should share prices fall, employees get their investment back in cash. These schemes encourage long-term service and are a low risk investment opportunity for employees.

Consultation strategies

Employees will feel more involved and connected to their company if they feel as though they have an influence on the way the business is run. A company may use a range of consultative strategies and working groups to delegate responsibility and ownership to the workforce. This can often resolve any negative working practices or issues that could eventually lead to labour turnover or absenteeism.

Empowerment

Other strategies to motivate employees may include:

Extra training

Ensure employees are well resourced

Feedback – employees want to know how they are doing and receive praise when it is deserved

Empowerment strategies

Delegate authority – allow employees to make decisions on how they work

Offer flexible working practices

Communication – if employees understand the direction of the company and rationale for decisions they are more likely to feel secure in their roles.

Now try this

1 How might a company reduce absenteeism?
2 Why is employee consultation important?

Exam skills

The following exam-style questions relate to the topics covered in Unit 3.5.3 and refer to the Winstanley and Walker Confectionery Ltd case study on pages 179–180.

Worked example

Calculate labour productivity at Winstanley and Walker Confectionery Ltd for the week commencing 17 July. **(4 marks)**

labour productivity = total output for time period / total number of employees at work

31800 boxes / 65 employees

= 489.23 boxes per employee

> Labour productivity does not need to be expressed as a percentage.

Worked example

In order to improve labour retention, Winstanley and Walker are considering introducing one of two strategies: profit sharing or an additional three days holiday entitlement per year.

Evaluate these **two** options and recommend which strategy would be the best for improving labour retention. **(20 marks)**

Profit-sharing would involve an arrangement where a percentage of net profits is shared among the workforce. This might help retain employees as they would be anticipating a bonus at the end of the financial year. Furthermore, Winstanley and Walker is a growing company and many employees would expect the financial rewards to be significant.

> The case study allows for the labour retention figure at Winstanley and Walker to be calculated. Always calculate and use financial information in your longer answers if available.

However, not all employees are motivated by financial rewards alone and there could also be a spike in the number of employees leaving the company once the profits had been distributed....

> The second paragraph of this answer should explore the benefits and limitations of providing employees with three days of additional holiday.

In conclusion, the best option would be to introduce profit-sharing. This is because employees would feel as though they had a greater stake in the long-term success and performance of the company. In order for this scheme to work, employees should know what reward they can expect and the financial performance of the company throughout the financial year. It might also be useful to distribute the profits to employees on a quarterly basis, to prevent employees from simply leaving once they have been paid the bonus. The success of the profit-sharing scheme will depend on how other factors, such as self-esteem and social needs, are being met within Winstanley and Walker.

> The student has chosen option A and provided a recommendation to Winstanley and Walker. They have also used 'it depends' to explain how a limiting factor might influence the success of this strategy.

The causes of business change

Change happens in all businesses, whether they are growing or adapting to the external environment. Change can bring a number of threats but also a considerable number of opportunities to improve competitiveness and success.

Size – a business will go through a process of change as it grows, but this will also occur as a business consolidates and goes through a process of retrenchment.

PESTLE – external forces may lead to change as a business attempts to adapt and keep up with the demands of legislation, technology, customer needs and political pressures. For more on PESTLE see page 131.

The causes of change

Poor performance – this might mean a dip in sales or a loss in profits. Business failure can lead to drastic changes in personnel, product design and development and how the business operates. Change as a result of poor performance can often be fast-paced.

New ownership – a change in ownership. The move from Ltd to Plc is also a significant step as the company becomes influenced by public share ownership and stock market forces.

Transformational leadership – leaders make change happen. They set a vision and direction for the company and ensure people are on-board. New leadership may come about through succession planning or poor performance. Either way, new leaders will assert their own ideas and strategy.

The effects of change

External forces   Poor performance   Change in size   Ownership   New leadership

Change process

Productivity

Change may come about through the adoption of new technology or ways of working, such as staff training or organisation structure. A driver of change will always be the aim of increasing productivity and improved efficiency.

Competitiveness

Whether the business is growing or fighting to survive. Change is driven by the need to improve or maintain competitiveness. Change through the process of growth can lead to economies of scale and scope, whereas change linked to improved efficiencies can lead to a more flexible organisation with lower costs. Either way, the aim should be to improve competitiveness.

Financial performance

Most businesses have a focus on the bottom line – profits, improving productivity and competitiveness should lead to increased revenue and ultimately profits. Profitability is often the driver for internally imposed change.

Change and stakeholders

With change comes uncertainty and often fear. The role of a leader within an organisation is to manage and support stakeholders through the change process so that all stakeholder groups see it as a positive change.

Stakeholders may respond to change in a number of ways. For example:

- **shareholders** may withdraw their support/investment if they fear that the change will not be successful and might not lead to return on their investment
- **employees** may fear for their job security and status within the organisation
- **customers** may react negatively to new products or processes.

Customer complaining about a new product

Now try this

1 How might a business change as it grows?
2 Why does poor performance often lead to business change?

Key factors in change

Change is often opposed. Any departure from the status quo can lead to fear and insecurity. As a result, business leaders have to understand the change process and ensure it is managed effectively.

Size and culture

Organisations with a strong culture are more difficult to change. Although leaders can quickly change the processes and structure of a business, it is a far longer process to change attitudes and beliefs.

It is also much harder to impose change on large organisations. This is partly due to the efforts needed to clearly communicate and implement the plan and retrain employees. Large organisations may also have different cultures and approaches across the company, especially if the company is a multinational.

Speed and timing

The pace of change may be determined by the external forces imposed on the business, for example the actions of competitors or the introduction of new legislation.

Change can sometimes be easier when the company is in a strong position and is looking to 'stay ahead of the competition'. However, change driven by poor performance can be difficult as leaders have to manage the expectations of customers, re-establish the brand and deal with demotivation and uncertainty from within the workforce.

Reasons for resistance to change

Self-interest	Prefer present state	Different assessment	Misunderstanding
Individuals may lose out in terms of pay, status or anticipating harder work.	Some employees may be very comfortable with the current situation. Change will take them outside their comfort zone.	Some employees may simply disagree and believe that change is not necessary or that a different approach would be more successful.	Employees may not see the need for change or may not understand what the change process will involve – fear of uncertainty.

Change

This may include:
- new technology
- new ways of working
- new products
- new structures
- new processes and regulations
- new members of staff (leadership).

Approaches used to overcome resistance to change

Education and communication	Facilitate and support	Participation and involvement	Manipulation and co-option	Negotiation and bargaining	Explicit/implicit coercion
Clearly share the reasons and logic behind the change and provide necessary training in new approaches.	Give employees what they need to accomplish the change along with encouragement and support.	Involve employees in the decision-making so that they have ownership of the change.	Involve and influence key people. Get individuals with influence on-board and use them to drive the change.	Compromise may involve employees receiving higher wages or better working conditions.	Force change through using authority. Threats may be involved – openly or implied. Long-term success may be more important than short-term agreement.

The factors that may determine which are the most appropriate tactics to deal with the change process include:
- the reason for resistance and the level of that resistance
- the time available and the leadership style of the managers involved.

Now try this

1 What might change within a business that will need planning and managing?
2 Identify **two** reasons why employees might resist change.

Scenario planning

Scenario planning involves the process of a business analysing the current and future environment and anticipating potential risks. Once risks have been identified the business can formulate contingency plans to ensure business continuity and minimise the impact of risk.

Scenario planning

The following steps might be taken as a business conducts scenario planning:

- Identify possible trends and future issues.
- Build possible scenarios.
- Plan response.
- Identify probability and most likely scenarios.
- Put in place plan associated with the scenario.

Risk

Businesses will attempt to calculate the level of any risk associated with a decision or negative outcome.

Risk is the likelihood of a negative event occurring multiplied by the impact of that negative event. Businesses will then adjust their plans in order to minimise this risk or put in place a plan to deal with the negative outcome. The risk of a negative outcome might be low even if the outcome is catastrophic, if there is only a 0.2 per cent chance of it occurring.

Examples of scenarios a business might plan for

Scenario planning and risk mitigation

 1 Natural disasters such as flooding and earthquakes can devastate communities and destroy businesses. Natural disasters can cause external shocks (an unpredictable economic event that can disrupt the economy).

 2 IT systems can fail and many large businesses are also targeted by cyberattacks where hackers will attempt to steal or wipe business data such as customer information.

 3 Key employees can be lost suddenly through resignation, illness and even death. Businesses have to have plans to function without key personnel and replace them if necessary.

Risk mitigation

A business might put in place measures to mitigate against risk. This includes business continuity planning, which can involve the following:

- Ensure sufficient insurance is in place.
- Back up IT infrastructures and install effective security software.
- Carry out an impact analysis.
- Develop recovery strategies.
- Monitor political and economic trends.
- Train staff in disaster recovery.
- Identify multiple suppliers of raw materials and components.
- Fully test new systems on a small scale.
- Ensure emergency plans are in place for all eventualities.
- Ensure all regulations and legislation are met.

Succession planning

To ensure any loss of personnel is covered, and vital knowledge and skills are not lost from the workforce, a business may have continuity plans as part of its human resources strategy.

- Identify future talent and leadership from within the organisation.
- Ensure key knowledge is recorded in Management Information Systems.
- Put in place a recruitment plan.
- Put in place a training plan to develop the skills of potential replacements.

Business continuity

In the event of an incident, a business should take the following steps:

 1 Carry out a business impact analysis.

 2 Put together a recovery strategy.

Now try this

1 What is meant by risk?
2 What might a business do to mitigate against risk?

To make sure that the recovery strategy takes place effectively there should be testing as well as training and monitoring using a development plan.

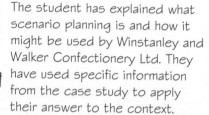

Exam skills

These exam-style questions explore the topics covered in Units 3.6.1, 3.6.2 and 3.6.3. The questions refer to the Winstanley and Walker Confectionery Ltd case study on pages 179–180.

Worked example

Explain how Winstanley and Walker Confectionery Ltd could identify potential risks associated with their growth plans.

(4 marks)

Winstanley and Walker could identify potential risks through scenario planning of, for example, increasing automation. This involves using research, such as market trends, to identify a range of potential negative outcomes. The company would then make contingency plans in order to minimise the risk of any negative event occurring. For Winstanley and Walker this might include having plans in place for any contamination of their chocolate or increases in the price of cocoa. Having these plans in place would allow them to act swiftly and minimise any impact on sales or the reputation of the company.

The student has explained what scenario planning is and how it might be used by Winstanley and Walker Confectionery Ltd. They have used specific information from the case study to apply their answer to the context.

Worked example

Assess the barriers that Winstanley and Walker Confectionery Ltd might face as they manage the change process. **(12 marks)**

One barrier that Winstanley and Walker may face when managing the change process is resistance from employees who do not like the new ways of working. Many employees may prefer the old way of working when there was less automation in the production process. As a result, some employees may not embrace the new way of working and deliberately disrupt the new processes. This could lead to mistakes being made and a fall in productivity....

This is a partial answer to this question. The student has identified a relevant barrier to change within the company. The student should now go on to identify a second barrier before evaluating the significance of these barriers. For example, is employee resistance a bigger problem than the reaction from customers who preferred the brand when it was only sold through small independent retailers?

Worked example

Assess how Winstanley and Walker Confectionery Ltd could resolve the issues of key personnel leaving the company.

(12 marks)

... A second strategy that Winstanley and Walker could use to deal with key personnel leaving the company is to put in place succession plans. This would involve identifying employees within the business who have the ability and desire to be promoted and take on more responsibility. A succession plan would also involve having a recruitment strategy in place to bring in new talent as people leave. A succession plan could ensure employees who leave are replaced quickly with minimal disruption to the workforce and productivity....

This is a partial answer. In this paragraph the student has discussed how Winstanley and Walker could use succession planning. Another option is to discuss working practices that would improve retention and avoid high labour turnover, such as financial rewards. The student could then evaluate by discussing how preventing employees from leaving might be better than replacing them. The student could also use data from Extract B to support their answer.

Exam-style practice

The following exam-style questions relate to the topics covered in Units 3.5 and 3.6 and refer to the Winstanley and Walker Confectionery Ltd case study on pages 179–180.

1 Calculate absenteeism at Winstanley and Walker Confectionery Ltd for the week commencing 14 August. **(4 marks)**

Remember that this ratio is expressed as a percentage of the total workforce. You need to express your answer to two decimal places.

2 Calculate the gearing ratio for Winstanley and Walker Confectionery Ltd. **(4 marks)**

The gearing ratio is calculated using data from the statement of financial position.

3 Explain how Winstanley and Walker Confectionery Ltd could use ratio analysis to assess the performance of the company. **(4 marks)**

Mention specific ratios in your answer, what they demonstrate and the decisions managers might make based on these ratios.

4 Assess the importance of scenario planning for a company like Winstanley and Walker Confectionery Ltd. **(10 marks)**

Scenario planning can minimise risk, but what are its limitations? Consider how reliable any plans based on the scenarios might be.

5 Assess the impact of the factors of change as Winstanley and Walker Confectionery Ltd introduces new working practices to meet the demands of the contract with a large UK retailer. **(12 marks)**

Read the question carefully. Firstly, identify the factors that are likely to influence the change within the company, for example organisational culture or the speed of the change. Then consider the specific issues that might be a barrier to this change using information from the case study. You should evaluate the main issues and provide the management of the company with recommendations on how they could manage this process.

In order to analyse the performance of the workforce, Winstanley and Walker Confectionery Ltd has decided to conduct an investigation into one of two human resource performance measures so that it can develop a strategy to improve productivity. The two options include an investigation into labour productivity and an investigation into absenteeism.

6 Evaluate these **two** options and recommend which option would help Winstanley and Walker improve productivity of the workforce. **(20 marks)**

Extract B will allow you to calculate labour productivity and absenteeism. It also gives an indication of employee numbers during this period. Consider what the trends might tell us about employee attitude within the company. What might Winstanley and Walker do to address any issues?

Case study

Extract A: Winstanley and Walker Confectionery Ltd

Winstanley and Walker Confectionery Ltd specialises in high-end luxury confectionery. The company was established in 1964 and supplies independent retailers across the UK, but primarily the North West. Over its 50-year history the company has grown and currently employs a workforce of 80 people, 60 of them directly linked to the production of 15 different lines of boxed chocolates and sweets. In 2017 the directors secured a contract for the Winstanley and Walker brand to be stocked in a large UK supermarket chain. The terms of the contract dictate sole rights to the brand, meaning that the directors agree not to supply any other large supermarket chain. The deal will initially involve a trial of the company's three most popular products. To meet the deal, Winstanley and Walker will need to increase production by 300%.

Winstanley and Walker are traditional confectionery manufacturers, with most of their products being hand-made by skilled chocolatiers. In order to meet the demands of the new contract with a large UK retailer the company has invested £1 million in a semi-automated production facility. The company has budgeted a further £200 000 for the retraining and restructuring of the workforce. The first trial of stock was distributed and appeared in the retailer's stores in March 2017.

Extract B: HR performance data July–Aug 2017

Week beginning	3/7	10/7	17/7	24/7	31/7	7/8	14/8
No. of employees	60	65	65	64	64	62	62
Output (boxes)	21 800	31 100	31 800	36 850	43 000	44 000	49 600
Average staff absent (per day)	2	5	6	8	9.4	8.5	8

Eight employees left the company between July and August.

Case study

Extract C: Financial accounts

Statement of Comprehensive Income
Dec 2016–Dec 2017

	£m
Revenue	18
Cost of sales	(8)
Gross profit	10
Administrative expenses	(4.5)
Selling expenses	(3)
Operating profit	2.5
Exceptional expenses	(1.2)
Interest	(0.2)
Profit for the year (net profit)	1.1

Statement of Financial Position
15th December 2017

		£m
Non-current assets		6.5
Intangible non-current assets	0.5	
Tangible non-current assets	6	
Current assets		0.7
Inventories	0.5	
Receivables	0.2	
Current liabilities		(1.4)
Borrowings	(0.9)	
Payables	(0.5)	
Net current assets		(0.7)
Non-current liabilities		(3)
Long-term loan	2	
Provisions	1	
Net assets		2.8
Retained profit	0.4	
Share capital	2.4	
Total equity		2.8

Extract D: Confectionery market trends 2017–2022

Key findings from international market research in the UK confectionery market:
- Between 2011 and 2015 there was a 42% growth in luxury boxed chocolate.
- Growth of the market over this period was mainly due to product development and marketing from industry leaders.
- Consumers are experimenting with even more exotic tastes.
- Consumers are becoming more conscious of cocoa levels when buying chocolate.
- Cocoa prices will continue to increase by up to 5% over the next five years.
- Economic uncertainty related to Brexit is expected to impact sales of chocolate confectionery over the next five years.

Growing economies

The growth rate of economies around the world is very different. Over recent years, growth rates in BRICS (Brazil, Russia, India, China and South Africa) and MINT (Mexico, Indonesia, Nigeria and Turkey) have been faster than in the developed economies of the USA, Japan and Western Europe. This rapid growth creates opportunities and threats for international businesses.

Growth rate of UK economy and emerging economies

The UK was once a major producer of manufactured foods exporting all over the world. Nowadays it is the service industry that dominates, with manufactured goods being predominantly produced in emerging markets.

In the emerging markets, growth rates have been rapid over recent years. This growth results in higher average incomes and the development of new industries and markets within these countries.

An increase in incomes leads to greater demand, both domestically and from international markets. As markets grow, so does the infrastructure in these countries, the quality of education and the skills of the workforce.

Out of the emerging markets come competitive multinational corporations (MNCs) that pose significant competition to established global market leaders.

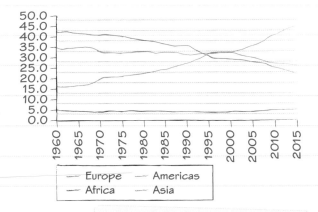

Percentage share of world real GDP

Economic growth of countries

Opportunities for rapid growth are created in countries with higher than average growth rates. However, these markets can often be uncertain and also present greater risk than countries with an established economy and infrastructure.

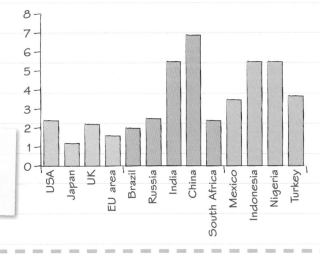

The graph shows percentage change in GDP from the previous year. The figures are forecast figures for 2017. Growth in China, India and MINT nations has far outpaced growth in the UK over recent years, creating opportunities for export markets, but also international competition.

Trade opportunities

The growth of emerging economies creates a number of trade opportunities for international business. These include:

- increased Foreign Direct Investment (FDI), see Unit 4.1.2
- opportunities for exporting to developing economies
- better infrastructure leading to developing economies becoming a production location.

Employment patterns

As economies develop, unemployment rates tend to fall significantly. This can also create opportunities for international trade as increased incomes generate demand in an economy. As economies grow, so do the levels of skilled workers and the quality of education. This offers international businesses the opportunity to recruit to skilled posts when producing abroad.

Now try this

1 What do BRICS and MINT stand for?
2 What opportunities are created through emerging economies?

181

Indicators of growth

A variety of measures might be used to evaluate the potential opportunities in developed and emerging markets.

Gross Domestic Product (GDP)

GDP is a measure of all the goods and services produced in a country divided by the number of people in the country.

Issues with GDP include:

- real GDP – using figures adjusted for inflation
- reported figures for each individual (per capita GDP)
- comparing currencies – GDP can be hard to compare across nations with different currencies. One way to deal with currency differences is to compare the buying power across countries for a standardised basket of goods.

Health

The health of a nation is a good indicator of the standard of living (how much people can buy with their incomes) and the potential demand and prosperity in a country. Measures of health include:

- life expectancy
- infant mortality rates
- access to clean water
- doctors per 100 000 people.

Literacy

As with health, literacy rates give an indication of standard of living in terms of the quality of education and the skills of the workforce in a country. Higher literacy rates lead to a better quality workforce. As literacy rates improve so will the nature of the products and services bought and sold in that country. For example, countries with high literacy rates purchase more luxury goods.

Adult literacy rates

80% 89% | 99% 99% | 75% 86% | 51% 67%

World average | Developed countries | Developing countries | Least developed countries

Human Development Index

The Human Development Index (HDI) combines a range of economic statistics for a country. The purpose of the HDI is to focus on a country's people rather than simply the economic context. A business looking to expand into international markets might use the data to analyse the potential demand, income and skills within a country.

Life expectancy   Mean years of schooling

HDI measures

Gross National Income – GNI per capita (measure of income based on US dollar value of a country's income divided by its population)

Now try this

1 Why is health an important indicator of a country's economic development?
2 Why is literacy an important indicator of a country's economic development?

Exam skills

The exam-style question below relates to Unit 4.1.1 and refers to the CompTech Sports Plc case study (Part A) on page 200.

Worked example

Assess the potential of BRICS and MINT nations becoming areas of future growth for CompTech Sports Plc.   **(12 marks)**

The fast growing nations of BRICS and MINT will certainly offer growth opportunities for CompTech Sports, firstly as a potential market to sell its products to. As economies grow, the middle classes become wealthier and spend more money on leisure pursuits such as sport and fitness. Furthermore, as these countries develop so will the industries within these nations, such as plastics manufacturing, and mining for raw materials, such as sulphur. This creates trading opportunities as CompTech Sports could find suitable suppliers in these countries who can supply raw materials or components for its sports products.

However, CompTech Sports sells products for sports such as mountain biking, sailing and contact sports. The success of these products in developing markets will very much depend on the cultures of these nations and whether consumers engage in these types of sport. Furthermore, developing nations could also offer increased competition from companies with cheaper labour costs and business rates looking to expand into international markets.

In conclusion, developing countries do create opportunities especially for manufacturers such as CompTech. As people become wealthier they will certainly spend more money on leisure pursuits, but CompTech will have to target potential markets very carefully and ensure they are able to adapt to local cultures and traditions, and meet international trading legislation.

The student has discussed the opportunities and threats of international trade. They have considered both perspectives in terms of the opportunities for B2C (selling their sports equipment to customers in these countries) and B2B trade (trading with suppliers in these countries).

The student has used the context by applying the nature of the product and explaining how relevant this might be in developing countries with different cultures and traditions.

International trade

International trade creates growth opportunities for nations and businesses. There are a number of benefits that a business gains from trading beyond its borders and taking advantage of specialisation and comparative advantages.

Importing and exporting

Buying products for resale or importing raw materials and components for the production of goods that are imported from a foreign country.

Selling products and services direct to foreign customers.

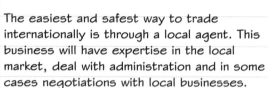

The easiest and safest way to trade internationally is through a local agent. This business will have expertise in the local market, deal with administration and in some cases negotiations with local businesses.

Importing and exporting is the easiest way for a business to trade internationally, but there are risks associated with fluctuations in the exchange rate that will influence costs and demand from foreign buyers.

Comparative advantage

Comparative advantage comes from a country's ability to specialise in the production of certain goods and trade them with other nations, rather than nations producing multiple products themselves.

The concept of comparative advantage is the basis for many businesses to move into international markets to buy and sell products.

You will not be tested on this concept in your exam, but you may find it useful to know that certain countries and the businesses within them are more efficient at producing certain goods.

Competitive advantage

Competitive advantage can be gained from adding value where other businesses cannot, for example using local resources, such as slate in Wales, to produce items that cannot be produced elsewhere for the same price or quality. Other advantages that may be country specific include the knowledge and skills of production techniques which give companies a competitive advantage in international markets. For more on competitive advantage, see Porter's competitive strategies on pages 126–127.

Foreign Direct Investment (FDI)

Unlike importing and exporting, FDI involves direct investment into a country, leading to a business becoming a multinational corporation (MNC). This might include setting up a production facility, a joint-venture with a local firm or buying assets in a foreign country. It is far riskier than exporting or importing, but allows a firm to access the comparative and competitive advantages held by foreign businesses.

Investment in expanding industry and fast growing, profitable businesses

Access to local resources e.g. copper or wine

Reasons for FDI

Access to foreign brands

Access to infrastructure and complementary industries

Access to local knowledge and skills

Now try this

1 What is FDI?

2 Why is exporting less risky than setting up production in a foreign country?

Globalisation

Globalisation is the increasing integration and cooperation between countries and the growth of international trade. Globalisation creates many opportunities for international and domestic businesses. Global restrictions still exist, such as protectionism (see Unit 4.1.4) and caps on migration in some countries.

Key features of globalisation

There are several features of globalisation that lead to business integration and interdependence.

- Multicultural society – the sharing and merging of cultures
- The flow of capital between countries
- Economic interdependency between countries
- Goods and services traded throughout the world
- Collaboration between countries such as interchange of technology and intellectual property

Transport and communication networks have improved significantly, making the sharing of data much faster and the transportation of goods much cheaper. People can reach parts of the globe much faster and more cheaply than ever before.

Migration is the temporary or permanent movement of people around the globe. Approximately 3% of people in the world live outside their country of birth. Migration leads to cultures being imported and therefore the demand for new products but migrants often send a proportion of the money they earn back to their home country.

Investments across the globe through FDI mean countries and businesses have an interest in economic affairs in all parts of the world.

Political reform and political stability have given rise to democracy across the world and better trade relations between countries, allowing globalisation to take place.

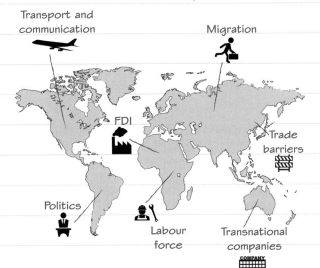

Transport and communication

Migration

FDI

Trade barriers

Politics

Labour force

Transnational companies

COMPANY

There has been a gradual reduction in the level of trade barriers (trade liberalisation) across the globe and the growth of trade blocs such as the EU and ASEAN – for more on trade barriers see Units 4.1.4 and 4.1.5.

The growth of huge multinational corporations that have investments and operations on most continents bring familiar products and services to countries across the globe, e.g. BP, General Electric, Toyota and Vodafone.

The global population increases the size of the labour force. This, in turn, increases global demand for products and the number of entrepreneurs setting up businesses that trade globally.

All or any of these economies will structurally change over time. For example, the growth of the service sector has meant that Western economies rely less and less on income from the primary and secondary sectors. This structural change gives flexibility to expand and set up companies in other parts of the world, made easier by the availability of the internet.

Now try this

1 What are the benefits of migration for international business?
2 How has political reform contributed to globalisation?

Exam skills

The exam-style questions below relate to Units 4.1.2 and 4.1.3 and refer to the CompTech Sports Plc case study (Part A) on page 200.

Worked example

Explain how Foreign Direct Investment could help CompTech Sports Plc.   **(4 marks)**

FDI involves a company investing directly in another country. FDI could help CompTech Sports by allowing it to take over or merge with a plastics manufacturer in a country such as Latvia. This would allow it to access raw materials and cheaper labour costs. As a result, CompTech Sports would be able to lower its unit costs and become a more competitive international brand. Furthermore, it could also increase the possibility of increasing productivity and access the market for sports equipment in Latvia or other developing markets in Europe.

The student has explained what FDI is and outlined two ways that it could benefit CompTech Sports. The answer is in context by referring to 'plastics'.

Worked example

Assess the competitive advantage CompTech Sports may gain when trading in international markets.   **(12 marks)**

CompTech is currently a UK manufacturer and has a respected brand trusted for safety and high quality. Many international markets see products made in Europe as being of better quality and more prestigious than other products. CompTech Sports could use these advantages to add value to its products and charge a premium price. These are sustainable advantages because developing a strong brand image, such as having a reputation for providing quality British products, can take a long time to build.

However, these competitive advantages may have a limited impact if it is unable to keep prices low, and some other nations may have a comparative advantage when producing plastics-based products such as sports equipment. If CompTech Sports pursues FDI then it may be able to invest in a foreign production facility, but this might erode its competitive advantage and brand image if it is unable to maintain the quality that customers have come to expect.

In conclusion, CompTech has a competitive advantage through its brand image and it should think carefully before any investment in production abroad. One option would be to continue production in the UK but import the resources it requires from a cheaper supplier.

The student has identified a potential competitive advantage for CompTech. They have also gone on to compare this advantage to the comparative advantage that other countries might have – the ability to produce sports products more efficiently and at a lower price.

They have then gone on to discuss how FDI might damage this competitive advantage.

Protectionism

What is protectionism?

Protectionism involves protecting domestic business and home industries against foreign competition and limiting the number of imports into the country. The government will impose protectionist policies through legislation, taxation and spending. The key government legislation linked to protectionism is outlined below.

> Free trade can benefit all countries by creating opportunities for growth and economic prosperity. For this reason protectionism is sometimes criticised and may provoke a similar reaction from trading partners.

Benefits of free trade

Free trade provides growth opportunities for home nations as international markets become accessible and profitable. Free trade means that nations can exploit the advantages other countries possess to produce certain goods and services more efficiently than others. Not only does this mean that goods and services become more accessible, they also become cheaper.

For businesses, free trade may allow them to access components, raw materials and finished goods far cheaper than they could do otherwise.

Protectionism in practice

Tariffs – tax on imports that increases the price of imported goods, raises government income and makes domestic businesses more competitive.

Soft loans – generous loan agreements offered to exporting businesses to help them compete in foreign markets.

Subsidies – government grants given to support exporting businesses so that they can lower their prices in order to compete internationally.

Technical barriers – e.g. rules and regulations governing the standard of products entering the country.

State procurement – favouring domestic businesses as suppliers over foreign competition.

Quotas – physical limits set on the number of units that can be imported into a country.

> **Risks** – protectionism may force businesses to use more expensive domestic suppliers, therefore making them less competitive. It may also encourage businesses to move abroad to avoid trading barriers.

Now try this

1 Why might a government impose protectionist strategies?
2 Identify **three** protectionist strategies a government might use.

Trading blocs

Trading blocs are partnerships and agreements between nations to allow free trade and the collaboration and integration of economic, political and cultural practices.

Trading agreements

There are various different arrangements that exist between countries and regions. There is a spectrum of agreements based on the level of free trade and collaboration.

Low   High

Customs unions
Customs unions involve an agreed set of tariffs against non-members but free trade exists between members.

Common markets
As well as free trade between members there is also free movement of labour and capital.

Protectionism
Protecting businesses and markets. For more on protectionism, see page 187.

Economic unions
Economic unions aim for integration of economic, political and cultural factors. This also includes the adoption of a common currency such as the Euro.

Preferential trade areas
Certain products from certain countries receive reduced tariff rates.

Free trade areas
Where there is removal of all trade barriers between countries.

Single markets
As well as free trade, common laws are adopted to harmonise standards and tax.

Global trading blocs

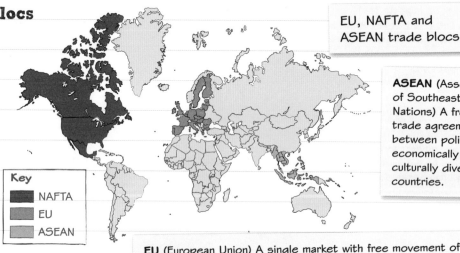

EU, NAFTA and ASEAN trade blocs

NAFTA (North American Free Trade Agreement) A free trade zone including trade, investment, labour, financial dealings and environmental legislation. Member countries negotiate separate deals with outside members.

ASEAN (Association of Southeast Asian Nations) A free trade agreement between politically, economically and culturally diverse countries.

Key
- NAFTA
- EU
- ASEAN

EU (European Union) A single market with free movement of people, goods and services. The EU also adopts common laws around employment and consumer legislation. Most member states are also part of the monetary union – the Euro.

Benefits of trading blocs

👍 Opportunities to expand into new markets.

👍 Allows businesses to benefit from comparative advantage – cheaper and better quality products.

👍 Makes it easier to source labour if free movement is permitted.

👍 Aligns international legislation making markets more efficient.

Drawbacks of trading blocs

👎 Countries and businesses outside the trading bloc may have a better comparative advantage which members are unable to access.

👎 Infant industries are vulnerable to large international competitors.

👎 Tensions with regions outside of the trading bloc.

👎 Inefficient producers may be protected leading to poor quality and high prices.

Now try this

1 What is the difference between a single market and a customs union?
2 What are the benefits for member states of trading blocs?

Exam skills

The exam-style questions below relate to Units 4.1.4 and 4.1.5 and refer to the CompTech Sports Plc case study (Part A) on page 200.

Worked example

Explain how import tariffs could affect a business like CompTech Sports Plc. **(4 marks)**

Import tariffs could be a barrier to trade for a business like CompTech which is looking to expand and sell its products in new international markets. An import tariff is a tax on imports brought into a country. When selling to countries that impose import tariffs its sports equipment will be more expensive to buy. Even though it is considered to be 'reasonably priced' import tariffs may make it less competitive than domestic rivals in that country.

The student has explained what an import tariff is and how the mechanism works. They have explained the impact a tariff may have on the competitiveness of CompTech Sports when trading internationally.

Worked example

Assess the impact of the UK leaving the EU on businesses such as CompTech Sports Plc. **(12 marks)**

As the UK leaves the European Union Single Market it will look to negotiate free trade deals with other countries. If this is successful it could create a number of opportunities for businesses such as CompTech Sports. For example, trade deals with countries such as the USA and India could create significant opportunities for growth as the price of CompTech's sports equipment becomes more affordable for buyers in these countries if free trade deals are in place.

However, if a free trade agreement does not exist between the UK and other EU countries it could create barriers, such as import tariffs and quotas, for CompTech when trading with its closest trade partners. Although the USA and India are significant growth opportunities, these markets are far away and shipping costs will need to be considered when supplying these markets. It is much easier to supply countries such as France and Germany where there are frequent trade routes via road.

In conclusion, Brexit may create a number of opportunities for UK businesses such as CompTech, but the extent of these opportunities will depend on the agreements made between governments. CompTech needs to ensure it is finding opportunities in developing markets to ensure it is able to balance any negative outcomes with new trade opportunities.

The student has shown an understanding of protectionism and free trade. They have considered both the opportunities and the threats of Brexit and the changing nature of the EU Customs Union and Single European Market. Although the student has shown good understanding of the issues surrounding trade in the EU and Single European Market, they have struggled to effectively apply their answer to the context of 'businesses such as CompTech Sports Plc'.

Conditions that prompt trade

A range of factors force and entice businesses to seek trading opportunities with other countries. These opportunities create new ways of competing and chances for growth and profitability.

Push factors

Push factors are adverse situations that force businesses to look for opportunities in international markets. These may include:

- **Market saturation** – as domestic markets become saturated and growth slows businesses will look for international markets with high growth potential.
- **Competition** – domestic competition (or that of other international firms) can make competing at home unprofitable.
- **Shareholder pressure** – pressure for return on investment can cause businesses to seek new opportunities for growth.

Pull factors

Pull factors are opportunities for businesses to take advantage of lower production costs or new growing market places. They include:

- **Acquiring brands and intellectual property** – foreign businesses may own intangible assets that are difficult to develop or replicate so buying them is a more desirable option.
- **Economies of scale** – there are significant cost savings to increasing the scale of operations. Risk spreading economies can also be gained from operating in several different international markets.
- **Cost savings** – in some developing countries certain costs (e.g. labour, tax) are cheaper than in the UK.

Off-shoring and outsourcing

Two approaches to becoming a multinational corporation are off-shoring and outsourcing.

Off-shoring

Outsourcing

UK business

Moving manufacturing or service industries to a part of the world with lower production costs.

Benefits

👍 Lower wage rates

👍 Access to raw materials

👍 Access to a skilled workforce

Drawbacks

👎 Damage to business reputation in home country

👎 As economics develop production costs also rise

👎 Cultural and language barriers

Moving a business function to a specialist external provider in another country.

Benefits

👍 Allows the business to upgrade

👍 Takes advantage of a country's comparative advantage

👍 Access to specialist facilities and knowledge without having to directly invest

Drawbacks

👎 Reliance on third parties – limited control

👎 Cultural and language barriers

👎 Businesses are less flexible if tied into a contract with a specialist provider

Extending the product life cycle

Moving into international markets gives a business the opportunity to extend the life cycle for any products that have reached maturity or have entered the decline phase. This might simply involve exporting the product to international markets or using a process of innovation to ensure the product meets international standards or addresses cultural or social factors. For more on adapting to international markets see Unit 4.3.3.

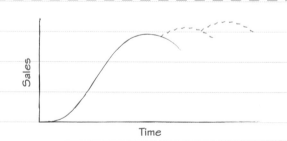

International markets create opportunities to extend the product life cycle by opening up new markets.

Now try this

1 What is a push factor that may lead to a business trading internationally?
2 What are the benefits of outsourcing a business function to an international supplier?

Exam skills

The exam-style question below relates to Unit 4.2.1 and refers to the CompTech Sports Plc case study (Part A) on page 200.

Worked example

CompTech Sports are considering two routes to increasing their presence in the global market for sports equipment. They are considering one of two options: off-shoring or outsourcing.

Evaluate these **two** options and make recommendations to the directors of CompTech Sports Plc as to which option would be best. **(20 marks)**

Outsourcing would involve a third-party manufacturer being licensed to produce some of the products that CompTech Sports sells. The benefits of outsourcing are that it would allow CompTech Sports to focus on other aspects of the business. For example, certain product lines, perhaps new ones, could be made by a third party abroad and then branded by CompTech. This would help it increase its product range without having to invest capital in new production facilities. However, CompTech has a good reputation for safety and quality and this could easily be damaged if the quality is not as high through a third party.

Off-shoring would involve CompTech opening its own factory abroad. One option for this could be Latvia, where it has investigated the opportunity for a new factory. The benefit of this route is that it could maintain control of production and use some of its own highly skilled workforce to set up and manage the factory. This option is less likely to have a negative impact on the brand image. However, off-shoring and setting up a new factory in Latvia could require considerable capital investment and CompTech Sports may be unfamiliar with business interactions, legislation and policy in Latvia.

 Both options have been discussed. The first two paragraphs of the answer offer a balanced analysis of the two options.

In conclusion, both of these options are likely to damage its 'made in the UK' brand as both are likely to involve production in a foreign country. However, the best option would be off-shoring. Off-shoring production to Latvia would be much cheaper because labour costs will be considerably lower than in the UK and operating from Latvia may reduce the costs of exporting to foreign markets. Overall, the main reason to off-shore is that CompTech Sports will have full control of the factory to ensure all products meet its high standards.

 A recommendation has been made by the student. They have justified their choice and identified what they consider to be the main reason based on the context of CompTech Sports Plc.

Assessment of a country as a market

Businesses will consider a range of factors when analysing which international markets to trade with or which countries they want to invest in through FDI. The purpose of this analysis is to reduce risk by identifying the countries with the greatest opportunities and structures to support trade and stability.

Assessing a country

Overall, a business will want to ensure that it is easy to do business in a foreign country. Often, trading abroad can result in additional costs and complications, which most businesses will want to avoid. The checklist opposite considers some of the factors that a business may focus on when making a choice.

The scenarios below present a commentary on the analysis of two different countries.

Country trading market checklist

☐ Growth in disposable incomes (will there be demand from customers?)

☐ Ease of doing business (time and cost of setting up and running a business)

☐ Developed infrastructure (transport links, maturity of complementary industries and communications network)

☐ Political stability (political unrest and relationships with other countries/trading partners)

☐ Stable exchange rate

Country A

- GDP per capita increased by 8 per cent between 2013 and 2017 leading to a growth in disposable incomes
- Four different permits required to set up a new international business
- 15 per cent corporation tax
- Minimal legislation surrounding trade and consumer safety
- Extensive rail and road networks
- IT and communications infrastructure improving. Extensive investment planned for 2020
- Government has poor relationships with international organisations such as WTO – several violent protests against government in the past six months
- Imposed import tariffs on many goods bought from Europe. For more on tariffs, see page 187.

Country B

- GDP per capita fell by 0.2 per cent between 2013 and 2017. The poorest in the society have seen disposable incomes in real terms fall by 3 per cent
- No permits required to set up a business
- 4 per cent corporation tax
- Legislation harmonised with close trading partners
- World's fifth largest port
- Excellent investment in broadband throughout major cities
- No trading barriers
- Stable exchange rate

Now try this

1 After analysing the information shown for each fictional country, which country do you think is the most attractive as a new market for international trade?

2 Why is infrastructure an important factor when considering a country as a market to trade with?

3 Why is political stability an important factor when considering a country as a market to trade with?

Assessment of a country as a production location 1

Businesses will consider a range of factors when analysing and choosing a country to off-shore their production facility or services. The purpose of this analysis is to reduce risk by identifying the countries that have the greatest opportunities, with structures to support Foreign Direct Investment by welcoming multinational corporations (MNCs).

Assessing a country

When reviewing and choosing a production location abroad a business will take into account the costs of setting up that production, the potential risks and the conditions within the country. Parts of Eastern Asia have traditionally been favoured locations for the production facilities of western MNCs because there is plenty of cheap labour and access to natural resources. Setting up production in a foreign country is a significant investment for any business and it will analyse the likely return on this investment across different countries.

Proximity to markets

One factor that MNCs will take into account when choosing a production location is the proximity of that country to its international markets. In some cases, large MNCs will have multiple production facilities around the world that make it easy for them to transport their products (export) into that geographical region. For example, Renault the French car manufacturer has production plants in Morocco, Slovenia, Turkey, Russia, Romania and Argentina.

Production location checklist

☐ Costs of production (including labour costs)

☐ Skills and availability of labour

☐ Location in a trading bloc (making it easier to export goods to local trading nations and international markets)

☐ Government incentives (governments may provide subsidies and reduced rates to encourage MNCs to invest in their country)

☐ Ease of doing business (time and cost of setting up and running a business)

☐ Developed infrastructure (transport links, maturity of complementary industries and communications network)

☐ Political stability (political unrest and relationships with other countries/trading partners)

☐ Natural resources (access to local resources that can be used in the production process)

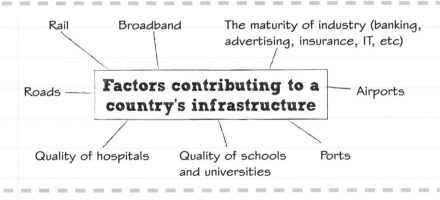

Rail   Broadband   The maturity of industry (banking, advertising, insurance, IT, etc)

Roads — **Factors contributing to a country's infrastructure** — Airports

Quality of hospitals   Quality of schools and universities   Ports

A container port

Now try this

1 What incentives might a government give to an MNC?

2 Why might an MNC have production facilities across multiple countries?

Assessment of a country as a production location 2

Analysis for two fictional countries (A and B).

Country A	Country B

Country A

- Standard of living has increased by 5 per cent over the past 10 years
- 90 per cent of the natural resources to support the production process can be sourced in this country
- 25 per cent corporation tax
- Literacy rates improved by 10 per cent in the last 15 years
- Minimal legislation surrounding trade and consumer safety
- Country not part of a trading bloc
- 22 per cent unemployment rate
- Shares a land border with Europe and has excellent road and rail networks
- Grants provided to MNCs that invest in the poorer south of the country
- Import ban placed on goods from this country by a large European country

Country B

- The standard of living has declined over the past 3 years
- Government offers a reduction in VAT for new MNCs
- Country home to two reputed international universities
- Natural resources need to be imported from a neighbouring country
- 15 per cent corporation tax
- 12 per cent unemployment rate
- Country part of ASEAN
- An island with one major port and a small airport
- Minimal regulations and controls on setting up new businesses

Now try this

1 Study the analysis of the two fictional countries (A and B) and decide which you believe is the most attractive to establish a new production location for an MNC.

2 Why is it often cheaper to off-shore production?

3 How might the level of unemployment affect an MNC's decision to set up a production location in a country?

Exam skills

The following questions relate to Units 4.2.2 and 4.2.3 and refer to the CompTech Sports Plc case study (Part A) on page 200.

Worked example

Explain the importance of disposable incomes for a business such as CompTech Sports Plc when choosing international markets to trade with. **(4 marks)**

A disposable income is the amount of money a person has to spend on non-essential items. Economic organisations measure the disposable income and GDP per capita of a nation as this gives an indication of wealth. The wealthier a country is, the more demand there will be for a company's products. As CompTech Sports sells high quality sports equipment it will need to target markets where customers have the spending power to buy its products to maximise sales potential.

This answer starts with a definition of disposable income. The student then goes on to give several linked strands of development to explain why this is important for an exporter such as CompTech Sports. However, as this answer only has one developed strand of context, it would probably only score 3 marks.

Worked example

Assess the factors CompTech Sports should consider when deciding whether to invest in Latvia as a production location.
(12 marks)

One factor that CompTech Sports should consider is the natural resources that can be found in the country. If Latvia provides many of the raw materials required for the production of plastic products then it might be a suitable location. This means that these resources will not need to be imported and will therefore be cheaper. As a result the production facility will be more flexible as the lead time on deliveries will be lower and the overall unit cost of products will fall.

Another factor that CompTech should consider is the skills of the Latvian workforce. CompTech will need to find experienced and qualified employees to work in their factory. As 98% of the population have at least some secondary education compared to 88% average across the EU this might suggest that education and training in Latvia are good and could contribute to a skilled workforce.

The student has offered two alternative factors that CompTech Sports should consider when choosing an international production location. They have also used evidence from Extract B to apply their answer to the CompTech Sports context.

In conclusion, for CompTech the skilled workforce might be more important than the raw materials. The raw materials for plastic production could be found in neighbouring countries, but it is far harder to find workers with the necessary skills to work in its factory and training employees is expensive and can take a long time.

The evaluation justifies why the second factor is more important than the first.

Reasons for global mergers and joint ventures

A merger is where two companies join together to create one organisation. A joint venture involves two separate businesses collaborating to achieve a shared goal. International mergers and joint ventures are often agreed to achieve certain ends.

Barriers to entry

There are significant barriers for a business when attempting to access an international market. These barriers might include:

- low brand awareness
- cultural/language differences
- knowledge of the market
- additional costs incurred through exporting.

Some of these mergers have not been wholly successful, e.g. Time Warner and AOL.

Global mergers

Some of the biggest global mergers ever:

- ✓ SmithKline Beecham Plc and Glaxo Wellcome Plc merged to form GlaxoSmithKline: $76bn (pharmaceuticals)
- ✓ Time Warner and America Online (AOL): $165bn (media)
- ✓ Vodafone and Mannesmann: $180bn (telecommunications)
- ✓ SABMiller and AB InBev: $90bn (brewing)

Spreading risk – by operating in different global markets businesses are spreading the risk of any one market failing. For example, economic recession in one part of the world might be offset by growth in another.

Global competitiveness – as other global brands merge and collaborate a merger may be one way to stay ahead and remain competitive.

Securing resources and suppliers – in order to ensure that a company has access to the supply of certain raw materials or services, it may choose to acquire the business that provides it with these things. Not only does this ensure the long-term stability of the company, but it also reduces costs by removing the value added by the supplier.

Entering new markets – some international markets are difficult to enter, especially those where established businesses dominate. By merging with or taking over a domestic business a foreign company can instantly gain a presence in the foreign market.

Acquiring national and international brands – a strong brand can give a business a competitive advantage and add value to its products. Buying a brand is much quicker than investing the time and money into marketing and brand development.

Reasons for global mergers and joint ventures

Gaining access to intellectual property – as with patents and brands, taking ownership of a company means taking ownership of its assets. Apart from patents, a business may hold copyrights and trademarks that are highly desirable. Intellectual property may also reside in the creative skills of employees who work for the company that has been acquired.

Acquiring national and international patents – a patent provides a company with the right to use an invention and protects it from being copied or stolen by a rival firm. One option for a rival firm is to buy the company (and therefore the company's assets) that owns the patent. Another option might be to pay a licensing fee to use the invention.

In 2012, Disney bought Lucasfilm, the company behind the Star Wars franchise, in order to acquire the licence and copyrights. Disney Studios is now able to create its own Star Wars films and stories.

Now try this

1 Why might a business want to acquire an international patent?
2 How could a merger help a business enter an international market?

Global competitiveness

A range of factors can determine how competitive a business is operating across the globe. Many aspects of competitiveness depend on the size of the company and the assets it owns (such as international brands). However, competitiveness can be affected by external influences.

Exchange rate fluctuations

Unit 2.5.1 explores the impact of changes in exchange rates on businesses, especially those that trade internationally. Exchange rate fluctuations can be very unpredictable and have a significant impact on the competitiveness of a global company. The significance of these fluctuations might depend on:

- elasticity of demand – the demand for some products is less responsive to a change in price caused by exchange rate fluctuations

- the relative economic growth in international markets – economic growth in an economy may counterbalance a fall in demand for exports as a result of an appreciation in the currency

- the use of fixed contracts (pre-agreed exchange rate) – this mitigates the impact of exchange rate fluctuations.

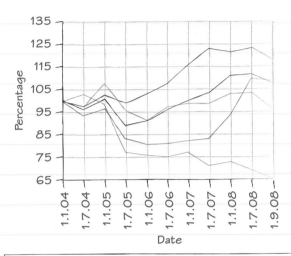

— Chinese renminbi (CNY)　— South Korean won (KRW)
— Taiwan dollar (TWD)　— Brazilian real (BRL)
— Japanese yen (JPY)

Exchange rate of the US dollar against other currencies 2004–2008

Cost competitiveness and differentiation

Operating on a global scale offers a business an alternative route to achieve competitiveness.
For more on using a polycentric approach to marketing, see Unit 4.3.1.

Cost competitiveness

Also referred to as cost leadership, MNCs may find it easier to gain economies of scope and economies of scale because they have multiple operations across the globe. Operating on a global scale helps businesses reduce unit costs. Through vertical integration MNCs can remove the mark-up added by their suppliers. For example, MNCs are likely to have their own fleet of trucks instead of using a delivery firm.

Differentiation

Global firms can use a polycentric approach to marketing (see Unit 4.3.1) and adapt their products to meet the needs of local markets. This might include differentiating a brand to ensure it fits a specific niche in an international market. One route might involve buying companies or brands in a foreign country that allow it to do this, while maintaining its core product.

Skills shortages

The skills and knowledge within a company can lead to competitive advantage. However, at times a business will face skills shortages and this can reduce the effectiveness and productivity of its workforce. Operating at an international level gives businesses the opportunity to access labour internationally. This allows them to access unique skills that may not exist in their home nation, for example, artisan cheese production techniques unique to Italy.

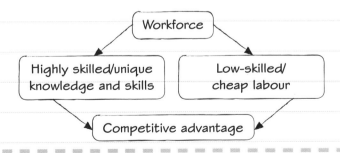

Artisan cheese production in Italy

Now try this

1 How might a company protect itself against the uncertainty of exchange rate fluctuations?

2 How are global businesses better placed to achieve cost leadership?

Exam skills

The following exam-style questions relate to Units 4.2.4 and 4.2.5 and refer to the CompTech Sports Plc case study (Part A) on page 200.

Worked example

Explain **one** reason why CompTech Sports Plc may find it difficult to break into a new international market.   **(4 marks)**

One reason CompTech may find it difficult to break into a new international market is the fact that its brand may not have a reputable brand image. CompTech has developed in Europe and the USA but at present there is little brand awareness in other parts of the world. Customers around the world will be brand loyal to local manufacturers or global brands such as Nike and Adidas. As a result, CompTech may have to position itself differently in a new international market and set a low price point in order to break into the sports footwear market.

> Brand awareness is one reason why a business may struggle to compete internationally. Often firms will look to acquire international brands through mergers or acquisitions in order to enter a new international market.

Worked example

Assess the impact on CompTech Sports of a skills shortage in its workforce.   **(10 marks)**

As CompTech Sports employs a highly skilled workforce, a skills shortage is likely to lower productivity in its factories. This is because it will take time and investment to build the skills of a new workforce to the standards of that at the UK factory. Should the company choose to open a factory in Latvia then this could be a realistic outcome. This is supported by the fact that the number of years in school is lower than the EU average, which might lead to skills shortages....

> This first paragraph of the answer provides an analysis of the reasons why a shortage of skills in the workforce could have a negative impact on CompTech Sports. This first paragraph has used several pieces of information from the case study to provide context. The rest of the answer should go on to provide a counterbalance as to how the impact of a skills shortage could be mitigated.

Worked example

The following question refers to Extract C.

Assess the impact of exchange rate fluctuations on CompTech Sports Plc.   **(12 marks)**

....However, CompTech Sports sells its products to markets in Europe and has a home market in the UK. The appreciation of the pound against the dollar may have a limited impact on overall sales if the Euro is relatively stronger than the dollar or sales in the US are a relatively small proportion of total sales revenue.

> The paragraph provides an example of counterbalance. The student's initial paragraph may have used Extract C to explain that an appreciation of the pound against the dollar (as indicated in the graph) could lower the demand for exports of sports products to the USA. However, the impact on CompTech Sports may depend on a number of factors.

Exam-style practice

The following exam-style questions relate to the topics covered in Units 4.1 and 4.2 and refer to the CompTech Sports Plc case study (Part A) on page 200.

1 Explain how CompTech Sports might use information from the Human Development Index (HDI).   **(4 marks)**

Think about the information that the HDI contains and the context of CompTech Sports Plc.

2 Explain how protectionism may impact on how CompTech Sports Plc trades internationally.   **(4 marks)**

Use specific examples of protectionist policies such as tariffs, quotas and non-tariff barriers in your answer.

3 Assess the factors that CompTech Sports Plc may consider when choosing which countries to trade with.   **(10 marks)**

Mention specific ratios in your answer, what they demonstrate and the decisions managers might make based on these ratios.

4 Assess whether Latvia would be a good place for CompTech Sports Plc to set up a new production facility.   **(12 marks)**

Use the information from the table in Extract B to provide context to your answer. Rather than discuss a wide range of factors, try to focus on two or three in your answer.

In order to compete in the USA, CompTech Sports Plc is considering a merger with a smaller manufacturer of sports equipment in California or developing contracts with a wider range of sports retailers in the USA.

5 Evaluate these **two** options and provide recommendations on which option would be best for improving their competitiveness in the USA.   **(20 marks)**

Use your understanding of the benefits of mergers to answer this question and compare this to the benefits of developing 'Place'. You should try to identify at least one limitation of each option and provide a clear justification for your recommendation.

Case study

CompTech Sports Plc: Part A

CompTech Sports Plc

Extract A: CompTech Sports Plc

CompTech Sports Plc is a UK company that manufactures a wide range of sports equipment requiring high-tech composite plastics. The company has developed a worldwide reputation for safety and durability with products tested to withstand high levels of impact and stress. CompTech's product range includes rackets, sports protection, such as shoulder pads and helmets, kayaks and sailing equipment.

CompTech exports its products to parts of Europe and the USA. Although the brand is less well known than some other market leaders, it has a good reputation with sports specialists for supplying safe, high quality equipment at a reasonable price. CompTech has a highly skilled workforce at its UK factory and believes its 'made in the UK' brand helps boost sales in some foreign markets. Fierce competition from Asia has led to CompTech considering foreign direct investment in Eastern Europe, moving production from the company's factory in Burton-upon-Trent.

Extract B: Economic indicators – Latvia

Development indicator	Score	Change (1990–2015)	EU average
Life expectancy	74.3	5.2 years	79.4
Mean years of schooling	11.7	4.1 years	11.8
GNI per capita	22 589	44.2%	39 605
Population with some secondary education	98%	–	88%

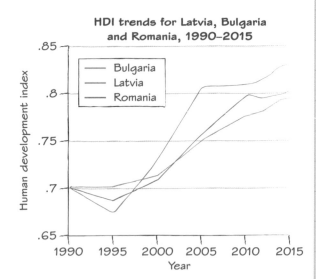

HDI trends for Latvia, Bulgaria and Romania, 1990–2015

Extract C: Pound (£) Exchange Rates

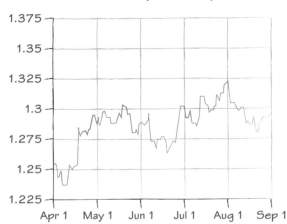

US dollars (USD) per British pound (GBP)

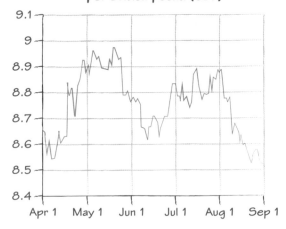

Chinese Yuan renminbi (CNY) per British pound (GBP)

Global marketing

As companies expand into international markets they will often need to adapt their marketing strategies to meet the needs of an international customer. The level of adaptation might depend on the branding and core competencies of the company and the nature of its products or service. There are four generic approaches to marketing in international markets.

Ethnocentric (domestic) approach

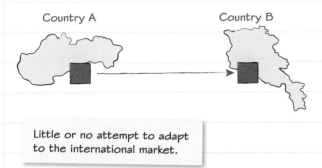

Little or no attempt to adapt to the international market.

This approach maximises the appeal and unique features of such things as regional food that would be exported or made identical for a foreign market. Benefits include standardisation and economies of scale but this approach may not take into account cultural differences across nations.

Polycentric (international) approach

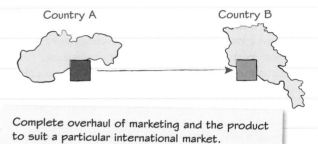

Complete overhaul of marketing and the product to suit a particular international market.

This approach is expensive and it may be difficult to launch new versions in order to compete with established local brands. Products are better targeted to meet the needs of specific countries and cultures.

Geocentric (mixed) approach

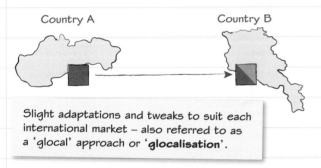

Slight adaptations and tweaks to suit each international market – also referred to as a 'glocal' approach or 'glocalisation'.

Products may be tailored to the local market with lower development costs.

Ansoff Matrix and international markets

Unit 3.1.2 explores the Ansoff Matrix as a strategic marketing tool. This strategic model can be applied in international markets and aligns with the three approaches outlined here. As a business moves into an international market it will either adopt a market development strategy (ethnocentric or geocentric) or a diversification strategy (polycentric), as both of these approaches involve entering a new market.

Marketing mix in international markets

Entering international markets will affect a business's approach to the marketing mix in the following ways:

Product	Price
To what extent does the product need to be adapted to suit the needs of an international market?	What pricing strategy is best suited to the local market, including the demographic, economic and competitive environment?
Promotion	**Place**
What are the most effective promotional methods in different countries? How does language and culture influence the brand and message?	What are the best channels of distribution in international markets? Is it better to export, use a local agent or set up as an MNC?

Now try this

1 What is the difference between an ethnocentric marketing strategy and a geocentric marketing strategy?
2 How might a business adapt its marketing mix for an international market?

Exam skills

The following exam-style questions relate to Unit 4.3.1 and refer to the CompTech Sports case study (Part B) on pages 213–214.

Worked example

Explain **one** reason why CompTech might use a geocentric approach to marketing its products abroad. **(4 marks)**

A geocentric marketing strategy involves a business adapting its products slightly to cater for the needs of a local market – also known as glocalisation. CompTech Sports may use this approach when entering the Chinese market for lacrosse equipment as there are a number of slight changes in sizes and colours that would be needed to cater for the Chinese market. A geocentric approach would help ensure products are suitable, but the company can still achieve economies of scale as there would be little or no change to the function of the equipment.

The student has started their explanation by defining the key term. The benefits of a geocentric approach have also been explained.

Worked example

Assess the impact of CompTech using an ethnocentric strategy to market its products in Latvia and other Eastern European countries. **(12 marks)**

An ethnocentric strategy involves a company making a limited attempt to adapt its products to the nature of a local market. For CompTech, this approach would be attractive as it would allow it to achieve economies of scale through standardising its production processes. This would help the company lower its unit costs and achieve higher profit margins. This strategy could be a suitable option as the use of sports equipment is the same in all countries if the rules are the same. As CompTech Sports makes sports equipment, it is likely that minimal changes would be required.

The first paragraph outlines the reasons why an ethnocentric approach might be beneficial to CompTech Sports in relation to the products it sells. The second paragraph then goes on to discuss reasons why failing to adapt products to a local market might have limitations.

However, as identified in the Chinese market, there are some slight changes that would be required to completely meet the needs of a local market. If CompTech does not take these local differences into account it may struggle to compete with other local brands. Furthermore, sports equipment needs to meet safety standards and these can differ across different countries. If CompTech Sports fails to adapt its products they may not be suitable for other international markets....

The final paragraph should provide a justified evaluation to make a judgement on whether an ethnocentric marketing strategy would have a positive impact or not.

Niche markets

Sometimes businesses identify global niche markets that can be highly profitable if they are able to meet the needs of subcultures and specialised markets.

Features of global niche markets

Businesses that operate in global markets, but target niches instead of mass global markets, have features such as:

- a clear understanding of the needs and wants of customers
- an emphasis on quality
- excellent customer service
- expertise in the product area
- prioritising profit rather than market share
- innovation.

Competing internationally

Sometimes businesses that offer a highly specialist product in one market find it easier to expand internationally. This is because the innovation, expertise and specialist knowledge may not already exist in other countries, unlike the situation for most mass markets.

The challenge for niche marketers is not developing desirable products, but being able to find, attract and supply their products to a small group of particular customers.

Transmission of desirability

Highly desirable and exclusive brands in one country are often just as desirable in another country. In many situations, they may even be more desirable because they are seen as more exclusive and perhaps exotic. Some Italian designer brands are more desirable in some other parts of the world than they are in Italy.

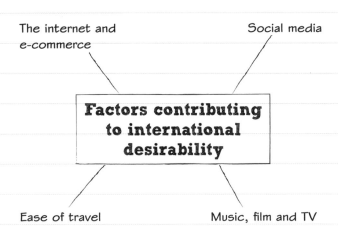

The internet and e-commerce   Social media

Factors contributing to international desirability

Ease of travel   Music, film and TV

International niches

Although common niches with similar characteristics can exist across countries, it is also possible for businesses to find niches that are unique to a country. Even though niche markets are small by definition, they can also differ through the fact that people have different cultures, values and interests in different parts of the world. Mass markets transcend international boundaries, but a niche market may only exist within a country.

Niches and the marketing mix

Product – niche marketers design products with a focus on quality, excellence and a premium service.

Price – the nature of niche markets dictates that pricing must deliver a high profit margin on each unit sold.

Promotion – branding is vital in niche markets; promotional tools will emphasise exclusivity and carefully target customers.

Place – a narrow range of channels using specialist agents and dealers will support an image of quality and exclusivity.

Now try this

1 Why might a niche market exist across international borders?
2 How does a niche market affect a business's approach to the marketing mix?

Cultural/social factors

One significant barrier to successful marketing and business relations in international markets is cultural and social factors. These issues can sometimes be unforeseen and difficult to plan for, but businesses have to be aware of cultural norms and expectations when conducting business.

Cultural and social barriers

Cultural differences – culture includes the beliefs and values of a society and also the norms of a society. This is the way people behave. This will range from the way people greet one another to what sort of behaviour is considered appropriate. Unit 3.4.2 explores the topic of culture.

Unintended meanings/bad branding – there are many examples of marketing that has gone wrong because the meaning has been lost in translation. The box below identifies some famous examples of unintended meanings.

Language differences – these can cause confusion and misunderstanding. Subtleties in body language, idioms and tone can be missed resulting in a message that can seem blunt or insensitive. Some nations are also more direct in their communications and say what they mean (such as parts of Europe and the USA) while others (such as parts of Asia) will take longer to consider information and make a decision.

Different tastes – taste can include actual taste for flavours, such as how sweet, bitter or spicy a culture prefers its foods, but also tastes in styles and fashion.

The reason that businesses sometimes get marketing and communications wrong when operating in international markets is ethnocentrism: the fact that people tend to view their own ethics, culture and norms as absolute and superior to others.

Business cultural norms

- ✓ Parts of Asia prefer to use formal salutations and surnames whereas many western cultures will accept the use of first names when conducting business.
- ✓ In Norway organisational hierarchies are more flat and communication in general is less formal than in most parts of the world.
- ✓ In parts of Italy or Mexico being several minutes late for a meeting is considered acceptable, but it is poor manners in the UK.

Branding mishaps

- ✓ KFC made Chinese consumers a bit apprehensive when 'finger-licking good' was translated as 'eat your fingers off'.
- ✓ Pepsi's slogan 'Come alive with the Pepsi generation' was introduced in China as 'Pepsi brings your ancestors back from the grave'.
- ✓ Coors beer translated its slogan, 'Turn it loose', into Spanish, where it is a colloquial term for having diarrhoea!

Now try this

1 What problems can cultural barriers cause when carrying out international business?
2 Why do businesses need to be careful when translating marketing material into a different language?

Exam skills

The following exam-style questions relate to Units 4.3.2 and 4.3.3 and refer to the CompTech Sports Plc case study (Part B) on pages 213–214.

Worked example

Explain **one** cultural or social barrier CompTech Sports Plc might need to overcome when trading internationally.

(4 marks)

One barrier CompTech Sports may experience when conducting business internationally is a language barrier. CompTech Sports is a UK business and with the opening of the new factory in Latvia, workers from the UK will need to deal with workers and managers from the local community. In a manufacturing business there may be many examples of jargon or idioms used among footwear technicians and these may not transfer well into another language.

The student has used the fact that CompTech Sports might choose to open a factory in Latvia as context along with economic information from Part B Extract B.

Worked example

CompTech Sports Plc is looking for a way to increase awareness of its brand in the USA. Two options it has identified are to target a mass market for sports equipment or to target a niche market for sports equipment.

Evaluate these **two** options and recommend which option the company should take. **(20 marks)**

By targeting a mass market, such as clothing and equipment for American Football, CompTech Sports will have more potential customers to trade with, especially as the US market is so big. This would allow the company to achieve economies of scale allowing it to lower the unit cost of a product. This might help CompTech Sports counteract any additional costs, such as import tariffs, that US customers would incur from importing its equipment. This could help CompTech Sports remain competitive when competing against local American brands. Nevertheless, the US market will already be saturated with many big global brands such as Nike and Adidas....

....In conclusion, it would be better for CompTech Sports to identify and target a niche market in the USA, such as a small, growing sport that requires protection/safety equipment. There will be less competition in this market and it may find it easier to target a narrower range of customers. The success of this strategy will depend on how well CompTech Sports is able to identify the needs of the niche and develop a brand and reputation in that sport.

The student's response includes the first paragraph of an answer and then an evaluation. The missing paragraph would include an analysis of the second option.

The analysis of operating in a mass market has been discussed. There are several points of context and the student has shown some counterbalance in the last sentence.

This final paragraph provides a supported judgement. The student has recommended that a niche market would be the best strategy and they have picked out a factor that CompTech Sports will need to address if this strategy is to be a success.

The impact of MNCs (local context)

The arrival of MNCs in local communities is generally welcomed. This is because a new factory is likely to create jobs and generate contracts in the supply chain for local businesses.

Job creation

The establishment of a new factory or plant can create hundreds of jobs for a local community. It also brings opportunities for the development of skills and a growth in the population as people choose to relocate to work at the factory. The growth in population may generate demand for local businesses too.

A new factory will not only provide jobs for local people but will have other positive knock-on effects.

Wages and working conditions

The increased demand for labour in a local area is likely to create more competition for skilled workers if unemployment is low. If supply does not increase sufficiently to meet this demand wages will rise, as will the quality of working conditions and fringe benefits.

Local businesses

A large MNC will have a supply chain made up of smaller local businesses. In the case of a large production facility, such as a car plant, this might involve hundreds of smaller suppliers of components and services. This will create new opportunities for entrepreneurs in the area.

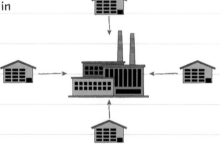

Community and environment

A large MNC is likely to cause negative **externalities** in the local community and environment, for example congestion and pollution. To counteract this, an MNC may invest money to enhance the local area. For example, it might build parks or community facilities, or support local schools and organisations and improve transport links.

Companies might support funding of green areas to improve the local environment.

Infrastructure

Sufficient transport links and other aspects of infrastructure may not already be in place to support the MNC. In such cases the MNC may build access roads and rail links, and invest in local utilities. The whole community, including other local businesses, will then benefit from this investment.

Social enterprise

Large MNCs may set up charities and social enterprises to support the local community. They might choose to do this to fulfil their social responsibility or to develop a positive image in the local area. These charities and social enterprises will support local people. Examples might include setting up food banks or health schemes, or the regeneration of run-down areas in a town.

A social enterprise is a business that is set up with the objective of benefiting society instead of a profit motive.

Now try this

1 What are the positive results of an MNC setting up a factory in a local community?
2 Name **one** drawback of MNCs.

The impact of MNCs (national context)

FDI flows

When an overseas business locates a factory, offices or a facility in a foreign country it invests a huge amount of capital into that country (Foreign Direct Investment). This investment leads to spending in the economy, which creates jobs and lowers the level of unemployment – FDI creates wealth in a country.

FDI may lead to:

- reduction in national debt
- increased employment
- increased incomes
- increased tax revenue.

Balance of payments

The initial FDI flow is one boost to the balance of payments in a foreign country, but products and services created by the MNC may also be exported around the world. This brings a second flow of money into the country.

Technology and skills transfer

An MNC may have created its success through developing new technologies and processes in its home nation. It will also train and develop the knowledge and skills of its workforce. This knowledge and technology will naturally transfer into the foreign country. This may help develop local industries and improve their competitiveness.

Consumers

The introduction of an MNC will increase the level of competition within a national industry. Although this has negative consequences for national businesses, it may create benefits for consumers such as:

- lower prices
- more choice
- improved quality
- better living standards – a wider range of products and services to meet their needs and make life more enjoyable.

Culture

Business culture (the way we do things around here) will naturally transfer to local businesses through the growth of MNCs. This might include working practices, decision-making and entrepreneurialism. For example, the growth of Japanese MNCs has led to quality management techniques being introduced around the world.

Tokyo business district

Transfer pricing

Transfer pricing is where an MNC will ensure it is selling its products through a country with the lowest tax levels, even where the product might have been produced in a country with high tax levels. MNCs sometimes operate across countries to avoid paying high levels of taxation. However, this can have a negative impact on government tax revenues.

Phones are made and sold all around the world by MNCs

Now try this

1 How can an MNC support skills development in a local community?
2 What impact does an MNC have on the balance of payments in a country?

Exam skills

The following exam-style questions relate to Unit 4.4.1 and refer to the CompTech Sports case study (Part B) on pages 213–214.

Worked example

Explain **one** way that CompTech Sports Plc could contribute to economic growth in Latvia.   **(4 marks)**

One way that CompTech Sports could boost economic prosperity in Latvia is by supporting Latvia's balance of payments. In setting up the new factory, considerable investment would be made by employing a workforce and training them in the production of sports equipment. This investment in skills would support the development of skills-related industries such as clothing.

Furthermore, as CompTech Sports exports its products to Europe and the USA this will create a flow of FDI into the Latvian economy, which will also improve the balance of payments.

The student has explained how CompTech Sports opening a factory in Latvia will create an initial flow of FDI and then support the balance of payments due to export sales.

Worked example

Assess the impact on the local community of CompTech Sports Plc's factory in Latvia.   **(10 marks)**

CompTech Sports has brought FDI into Latvia and this investment is likely to boost the local economy. The new factory has created 300 jobs in the area. This will lead to a rise in incomes and the standard of living by increasing wealth and disposable income in the region. Employment opportunities will also be created through the 24 suppliers it uses in the local area. As CompTech Sports has also provided employees with health insurance we can assume that more people will also have access to healthcare and this could increase life expectancy. However, 300 employees may not have a significant impact on this figure.

Although FDI has a positive impact on a local economy, there is the chance that the factory will cause some negative externalities, such as the disposal of waste from the factory that has already been noted by the media. These negative externalities could outweigh some of the benefits that the new factory will bring to the local area.

In conclusion, the new factory will have a positive impact on the local community because the key to economic prosperity is employment. The extent that the factory will contribute to this will depend on how CompTech Sports manages the negative externalities mentioned above and the wage rates that it pays its Latvian workforce.

This answer shows a good understanding of how an MNC can positively impact on a local community. The student has used a range of information from the case study to apply their answer to the CompTech Sports context. The evaluation gives a supported judgement and highlights factors that the positive impact of the factory may depend on.

Global ethics

For MNCs there is greater pressure to act ethically, but there is also more scope to break ethical codes of practice. As businesses operate across nations there are more discrepancies between laws, expectations, values and cultural norms. What might be considered ethically acceptable in one nation may not be in another.

Stakeholder conflict

Unit 3.4.3 looks at stakeholder conflict. These conflicts can be more profound when operating as an MNC.

Other key stakeholder groups for international business include suppliers, managers and employees and local competitors.

Governments and NGOs (non-governmental organisations) – international governments will place pressure on MNCs to ensure they pay the correct tax levels, invest in the local community and look after their workers.

International stakeholder conflicts

Shareholders – shareholders will seek the greatest return on their investment and profit maximisation can lead to other stakeholders' interests being sacrificed.

Communities – although MNCs will bring employment opportunities to a region, they may also bring negative externalities such as pollution. If not managed effectively this can cause bad publicity for a business.

Customers – customers are becoming increasingly conscious of where their products have come from. It is not always clear whether products have come from sustainable and ethical sources, especially when produced abroad.

Pay and working conditions

Standards for health and safety and employment legislation differ considerably across countries. This can sometimes lead to production facilities operated in LEDCs (Less Economically Developed Countries) being below an acceptable standard. Ethical business practices may relate to:

- acceptable pay levels of workers – a 'living wage' is paid
- provision of suitable working conditions, such as ventilation and number of breaks
- human rights – no inhumane treatment or excessive working hours.

Environmental considerations

Some forms of legislation, such as the Climate Change Act 2008, do not exist in LEDCs and there are no pressures from government for businesses to report on greenhouse gas emissions. Legislation on how businesses dispose of and manage waste may also not be enforced rigorously in some countries. Managing these negative externalities incurs costs and this can conflict with the profit motive for some MNCs.

Supply chain considerations

Global sourcing of products has become extremely complicated as components of raw materials may come from a wide variety of countries. This can make it very difficult for governments and consumers to track where, with what and how products from MNCs have been produced. This complication also means it is far more difficult to be certain that workers or a community have not been exploited somewhere down the supply chain, for example the use of child labour or slave labour. This problem makes it easier for MNCs to hide unethical behaviour.

Marketing considerations

Unethical practices in marketing may involve the way a business promotes its products to consumers, but also the way it negotiates and deals with potential customers and suppliers. Unethical marketing practices might include:

- misleading labelling on packaging
- false claims in advertising
- use of company finances to entertain potential customers and suppliers
- the giving of gifts to customers and suppliers
- using business connections with a personal or family tie.

Now try this

1 Why is there scope for unethical practices in MNCs?
2 Why might an MNC indirectly exploit workers?

Controlling MNCs

MNCs can bring many benefits to a country, but their actions need to be controlled by governments and NGOs. There are many ways that the actions of MNCs can be influenced to ensure their business practices are in the best interests of all stakeholders.

Influences on MNCs

Political influences – businesses and industries can be directly controlled through state ownership (privatisation) to ensure business is conducted in the best interests of society. Government policies such as tariffs and quotas are another way to influence trade. Government subsidies are a further option to support home industries. The danger with political intervention is that it can open up opportunities for state corruption.

Social media – allows all stakeholder groups to access and share the actions and behaviour of companies. This creates a transparency and a social authority that can directly challenge unethical behaviour.

Pressure groups – pressure groups, such as the Animal Liberation Front and Climate Camp, act as a control against MNCs. Even where businesses have not broken any laws, unethical practices can be exposed through naming and shaming companies, lobbying (taking issues directly to government) or direct action, which might involve protesting or sabotage.

Political influences

Social media

Pressure groups

MNC

2

Legal controls

Taxation policy

Legal controls – MNCs can be controlled through regulation such as competition laws, employment legislation and consumer legislation. Where MNCs breach these laws, governments can take direct action. This may involve heavy fines or even criminal prosecution against individuals within a company.

Taxation policy – taxation raises revenue for a government to run a country. However, taxation policy can also influence business activity. Low corporation tax levels might be applied in order to attract FDI. Taxation policy might also be used to ensure any negative externalities are 'internalised' e.g. forcing companies with high carbon emissions to pay a higher tax rate. Tax evasion is also a big issue for some nations where large MNCs exploit tax laws to evade paying tax.

Now try this

1 Why are pressure groups important?
2 How can taxation be used to control the actions of MNCs?

Exam skills

The following exam-style questions relate to Units 4.4.2 and 4.4.3 and refer to the CompTech Sports Plc case study (Part B) on pages 213–214.

Worked example

Explain **one** way that the Latvian government could influence CompTech Sports Plc. **(4 marks)**

The Latvian government could influence the actions of CompTech Sports Plc by imposing new safety regulations. An example would be legislation around containment of crude oil in the production process. This regulation might increase the cost of producing sports equipment for CompTech. CompTech Sports may have to make considerable adjustments and capital investment to adhere to the new legislation, which will reduce its profit margins. These unforeseen costs may make it difficult for CompTech to expand into new markets such as China, where sports like lacrosse are booming.

The student has identified political influences as a control of MNCs. They could have chosen other methods such as taxation or legislation.

Worked example

Explain why the Latvian government might be concerned about the actions of CompTech Sports Plc. **(4 marks)**

It is claimed that CompTech Sports has provided unsatisfactory working conditions for its employees. This might involve employees being paid below the living wage and not operating in a safe working environment. This could lead to greater pressure on Latvia's healthcare system if this results in illness and injuries. As a member of the EU, employees in Latvia have certain rights, but paying minimum wages could result in employees having insufficient income to live on. This could lead to poor levels of growth in the economy.

The student has drawn information from the case study to link their answer to CompTech Sports context. However, an 'explain' question requires two linked strands of context to achieve full marks. The student could have applied other information from Extract A or Extract B.

Worked example

In order to improve its reputation with the media and stakeholder groups, CompTech Sports Plc is considering investing money into working conditions at its factory or carrying out a full review into its ethical sourcing of raw materials.

Evaluate these **two** options and provide a recommendation on which option will have the biggest impact on CompTech Sports Plc's reputation. **(20 marks)**

If CompTech Sports Plc invests more money in working conditions it is likely to improve the poor reputation and publicity caused by the magazine article because workers will be happier and they are likely to explain why if interviewed or when sharing information with friends or on social media. Furthermore, this may not only repair the reputation of CompTech Sports, but also boost productivity as employees will be happier and more motivated. However, investing in working conditions may require capital investment to renovate the factory or increase labour costs if employees work shorter shifts....

This is a good opening paragraph for this answer. The student has used information from Extract B and clearly identified several consequences of improving working conditions at the factory. They have also identified a limiting factor for this option. You could have a go at completing this answer by explaining the issues with reviewing ethical sourcing and providing a recommendation on which option would have the biggest impact on the company's reputation.

Exam-style practice

The following questions relate to the topics covered in Units 4.3 and 4.4 and refer to the CompTech Sports Plc case study (Part B) on pages 213–214.

1   Explain **one** way that CompTech Sports could improve government revenue in Latvia. **(4 marks)**

> There are several ways that the actions of CompTech Sports Plc could boost economic activity in Latvia and generate revenue for the government. For example, CompTech Sports Plc could help contribute to several forms of taxation.

2   Explain **one** cultural factor that CompTech Sports Plc will need to consider when trading in China. **(4 marks)**

> You may not be able to identify specific cultural differences, but think about the ways businesses and consumers are different around the globe. This might include tastes, language and values.

3   Assess whether CompTech Sports should target the lacrosse market in China. **(10 marks)**

> The case study suggests that lacrosse is a niche sport in China. Therefore, CompTech Sports will be marketing in a niche. What benefits and drawbacks might this present?

4   Explain **one** limitation of CompTech Sports Plc adopting a polycentric marketing strategy across international markets. **(4 marks)**

> Polycentric involves a complete overhaul of the product to suit the international market. What evidence can you find from the case study to suggest this is a bad idea?

The Latvian government has introduced two new policies to help control the actions of large MNCs. The two policies are new legislation around product standards and safety, and an increase of 5% on import tariffs.

5   Evaluate these **two** policies and provide a recommendation to the directors of CompTech Sports Plc on which it should be most concerned about. **(20 marks)**

> In this evaluation question you are not providing a recommendation on a course of action or strategy. Instead, you need to evaluate which of the two government interventions is likely to have the biggest negative impact on the company. Your evaluation could suggest how CompTech Sports could respond.

Case study

CompTech Sports Plc: Part B

Extract A: A Latvian factory

In 2017 CompTech Sports set up a regional distribution centre in Latvia. The new factory allowed the company to reduce production costs by 35% and access to growing markets in Eastern Europe and Asia. Throughout 2017, demand from the USA had started to slow down due to increased competition from South American manufacturers and the rising value of the pound. Market research suggested that CompTech may find further opportunities in Eastern Europe and Asia where growing incomes were leading to people playing more specialist sports.

CompTech Sports has few links with agents and distributors in these parts of the world, but believes that its reputation in key developed markets such as Europe and North America would help it successfully establish the brand in new developing markets.

Extract B: Problems at the factory

CompTech Sports Plc suffered several incidents of bad publicity in 2017 when a US sports magazine published a list of what it claimed were the most ethical sports brands. The report ranked top brands in terms of their ethical sourcing of materials, carbon footprint and working conditions of its workforce. The article ranked CompTech Sports Plc at number 87 out of 100 companies. The main reasons for the low ranking were the company's shift to cheap labour in Eastern Europe and the disposal of chemicals used in the production of its plastic sporting equipment and clothing.

Shortly after the article was published, CompTech Sports Plc distributed a press release highlighting the positive impact the company had on the local community where its factory was based.

CompTech Sports Plc press release: key facts
• Creation of 300 jobs
• Contracts with 24 local businesses
• Sponsorship of local sports teams and schools
• Free health insurance for all employees

Case study

Extract C: Market growth in China

Market research into Asian markets by the marketing team at CompTech Sports Plc identified lacrosse as a significant opportunity for growth in China. China has recently gained full membership to the Federation of International Lacrosse (FIL) and participants in the sport had more than tripled in a four-year period to 2017.

Although still considered a niche sport, lacrosse posed a significant opportunity for growth with the safety equipment and stick required to play the sport. The marketing team believed adjustments would be required to the current product range in order to break into the Chinese market. Modifications included marginal size adjustments to clothing and bolder colours used in branding.

Answers

1.1.1

1. The market

1 Marketing is the process of understanding customers in order to develop products and services which can then be communicated to customers through promotion.

2 A niche market is a narrow/small segment of the market with specific interests and needs.

2. The dynamic nature of markets

1 Market size can be measured in terms of value or volume.

2 The benefits for customers of a highly competitive market are that prices are generally lower and they are likely to receive better quality products and better customer service because businesses have to try harder to gain their trade.

1.1.2

4. Market research

1 Market research allows a business to understand the needs of its potential customers, to establish the level of demand in the market and assess the nature of competition from other businesses.

2 Secondary research might be an appropriate form of research for a business start-up. This is because it is relatively cheap and start-ups rarely have money to invest in market research. However, it is important for new businesses to clearly understand the market so focus groups and sampling may also be important.

5. The limitations of market research

1 The limitations of market research are that it is very time-consuming and it is extremely difficult for a small business to conduct research that is representative of the whole market.

2 The purpose of sampling is to gather a representative sample of the population in order to effectively carry out market research.

1.1.3

6. Market positioning

1 A large supermarket chain could use market mapping to identify the perceptual position of the business in relation to other supermarkets in the market. This would allow it to make decisions on the types of consumer goods it stocks and the prices it should charge.

2 A business should be cautious when using a market map because it is a simplistic model for decision-making. There are many other factors that should be taken into consideration when making decisions about the strategic position the business takes in the market.

7. Competitive advantage and differentiation

1 A business may develop a unique selling point by developing product features that no other products have. If these features provide customers with unique benefits

and the business is able to promote these features, then the business may be able to develop a reputation for this that will benefit them in the long term as customers come to naturally associate them with these benefits.

2 A business can achieve a sustainable competitive advantage through innovation, architecture or reputation. Innovation refers to the business's ability to create new ideas, products and processes that are better than those of competitors. Architecture refers to the internal relationships between stakeholders that build synergy, understanding, trust and effective working relationships. Reputation refers to the brand image that the business builds over time.

8. Adding value

1 The speed of service and response time will add value as some customers may require products and services at short notice. This means that they will be happy to pay a higher price for this service.

2 Added value is linked to price because the more value a business is able to add to its products and services, the higher the price that customers are willing to pay. This is because they will perceive the products to have more benefits.

1.2.1

12. Demand

1 As price falls, there will be a shift along the demand curve. The quantity demanded will rise.

2 If consumer incomes rise then the demand curve will shift to the right (increase). This is because customers are wealthier and more people are willing and able to buy the goods at any given price.

3 An external shock is a factor in the economy, such as a political decision, that has an impact on the conditions in a market. An external shock is beyond the control of a business.

1.2.2

13. Supply

1 If the price rises, so will supply. This is because more producers are willing and able to supply goods at a higher price.

2 One factor that could shift the supply curve to the right is government subsidies. A subsidy will make it cheaper for producers to supply a good, so more will be willing and able to do so.

3 Supply might not be affected by price if the level of supply is fixed. For example, on a plot of land there may only be the room to build 10 houses. No matter what the price, only 10 houses can be built.

1.2.3

14. Markets

1 Excess supply refers to the condition where there is more supply in the market than there is demand at a given price. In this situation, prices will fall to an equilibrium where the market clears.

2 All markets will eventually find their equilibrium price because producers do not want to be left with unsold products. Furthermore, producers will also take the opportunity to increase prices where there is excess demand as some customers will always be willing to pay a premium for a good that is in short supply.

1.2.4

16. Price elasticity of demand

1 A PED of 0.2 represents a relatively price inelastic product where a change in price causes a smaller change in quantity demanded.

2 Successful branding should have the impact of making the price elasticity of demand for a product more inelastic. This is because successful branding will make a product more desirable and so more customers will be willing to buy the product at a higher price.

1.2.5

17. Income elasticity of demand

1 A YED of +1.5 represents a relatively elastic product. This means that should consumer incomes fall the business would expect demand for its goods to fall by a relatively greater percentage.

2 A business selling products that are income inelastic may decide to do nothing during an economic recession. This is because it would expect demand to stay relatively stable during a downturn in the economy, although it may choose to improve efficiency and offer special deals or product discounts to customers.

1.3.1

22. Product/service design

1 The three elements of the design mix are function, aesthetics and cost.

2 Three social trends that businesses may consider when designing products and services are: the importance of minimising waste, such as packaging; the importance of using recycled materials; and the importance of using ethically sourced resources, such as Fairtrade products.

1.3.2

24. Promotion

1 The purpose of promotion is to create awareness, interest and the desire of customers to purchase a product.

2 Three promotion methods include advertising, public relations (PR) and sponsorship.

3 A promotion method suitable for targeting children aged 5 to 8 years might include TV advertising early in a morning or around 4pm when children are typically watching television. Adverts might follow children's TV programmes.

25. Branding

1 The benefits of a strong brand are that businesses can charge a premium for their products and services and consumers will naturally trust a product with a strong brand over another that they may not be familiar with.

2 A business may want to associate its brand with that of a celebrity in order to link the brand characteristics with that of the celebrity. For example, a celebrity seen as being fashionable will project this image onto any brand they endorse.

1.3.3

27. Price

1 The profit margin is an important factor when setting the price of a product because it directly determines the contribution each unit will make towards paying off fixed costs and ultimately the net profit of a business.

2 A business might choose to set a premium price for a product if it believes the product is of premium quality, unique or will be highly desirable.

3 Penetration pricing is where a business offers a low price when it launches a new product in order to attract customers and break in to a market. As the product becomes more established the price will gradually rise to match that of other competitors in the market as consumers become brand loyal.

4 Price is a subjective concept because all people will place a different value on money and a different value on a product or service. Price is subjective because it depends on a number of factors including competition, incomes and necessity.

28. Pricing strategies

1 Cost-plus pricing is where a business will take into account the cost per unit and then add on a mark-up (percentage) in order to determine the price of a product.

2 Price comparison sites have led to businesses having to be very competitive in their approach to pricing to ensure they are offering good value for money. This is because customers can easily compare rival brands in order to make an informed decision. Customers have far more information on the potential options than ever before.

1.3.4

30. Distribution (place)

1 A retailer adds value to the product by providing the customer with advice, customer service and a shopping experience.

2 The role of a wholesaler is the breakdown of bulk and to help a manufacturer distribute its products to retailers.

31. Online distribution

1 A manufacturer might sell direct to its customers in order to keep its prices low and increase competitiveness. It may also allow the manufacturer to build relationships with its customers and guarantee a certain level of customer service.

2 The internet has led to a growth in on-demand services because people can now access services through their smartphone and place orders immediately. The software allows customers to customise their orders and track them without having to make a phone call.

1.3.5

33. Product portfolio analysis

1 When a product goes through growth it is important that the business can keep up with demand and ensure distribution channels allow the product to reach the customer.

2 The benefit of a cash cow is that it will generate regular inflow of revenue for a business. This revenue can support other projects such as new product development or promoting the 'question marks'.

3 The limitations of product portfolio analysis are that it simplifies what can be a very complex reality. For example, it can be hard to identify the growth potential in a market or the market share of a product. Products do not always go through the same cycle and are subject to numerous external factors that can alter demand for a product.

34. Marketing strategies

1 One way that a niche marketer might operate differently from a mass marketer is through the pricing strategy that it uses. As a niche market is specialist and offers a unique feature or benefit for customers, it will add more value than that of a mass-marketed product. This means a niche marketer can use a premium pricing strategy.

2 Inbound marketing is any technique that directs customers to a business's website or store. This may include search engine optimisation or adding links to social media posts.

1.4.1

38. Approaches to staffing

1 By multi-skilling a workforce, workers are more flexible and can cover for one another; this helps to limit the impact of absenteeism or staff turnover.

2 In many organisations, employment (staff costs or human resources) is the largest cost for the organisation. By lowering these costs businesses can improve profitability. This is why some managers may view employees as a cost to be managed.

39. Employer–employee relations

1 A trades union is an organisation established to protect and improve the economic and working conditions of workers, such as the National Union of Teachers (NUT).

2 A works council is different from a trades union because it is not an external organisation with a specific remit and legal right to protect its members.

3 The drawback to individual bargaining is that agreements might differ between employees.

1.4.2

41. Recruitment and selection

1 The recruitment process includes drawing up a job description and person specification, advertising the job, short-listing applicants, requesting references, inviting candidates to interview and the necessary selection processes and identifying the best candidate and offering a contract of employment.

2 Recruitment is a key aspect of human resource management because it is the process of bringing new talent and skills into the organisation. The effectiveness of the recruitment process will directly determine the quality of a company's workforce.

42. Training

On-the-job training is less expensive than off-the-job training because it is not being provided (generally) by an external trainer and employees can remain on the job and working. This limits the productivity lost while training takes place.

1.4.3

44. Hierarchies

1 An organisation chart shows the relationship between employees, the lines of authority and the teams that employees are part of.

2 A team leader will support and coordinate work within a small team of employees doing the same task. A supervisor has authority over a workforce and will monitor the standards of that work.

45. Organisational design

1 Delegation frees up managers and allows them to focus on strategic decision-making. Delegation also benefits junior employees who benefit from the responsibility and experience of carrying out new tasks.

2 Centralisation might be appropriate for a business when the senior leaders within the organisation want to keep close control of decision-making and standardise processes and products across the organisation.

3 When considering the design of the organisation, a manager should consider the level of autonomy they want to give employees, how decisions will be made and the need for structure and authority.

46. Organisational structures

1 A tall organisation structure works best when the nature of the product or business requires close control and management with clearly distinguished roles and lines of authority.

2 A flat organisation structure works well with a highly skilled workforce who require little supervision and businesses where decisions need to be made quickly.

1.4.4

48. Theories of motivation 1

1 Two principles of scientific management include efficiency through standardisation and the division of labour. Frederick Taylor believed that man is a rational being and is primarily motivated by financial means. Work and reward were, therefore, organised accordingly.

2 Elton Mayo's theory of motivation differs from that of Frederick Taylor in that Elton Mayo believed that human beings are primarily motivated by social interaction, whereas Taylor believed that people are rational beings and primarily motivated by financial reward.

3 Maslow's five human needs include physiological needs, security needs, love and belonging, self-esteem and self-actualisation.

49. Theories of motivation 2

1 Three hygiene factors include clean working conditions, employee healthcare and a good wage.

2 Maslow believed that people are motivated to achieve a hierarchy of needs and that they aim to achieve these needs in a systematic order in all aspects of their life. Although Herzberg also identified similar motivational factors to Maslow, he believed that some factors, known as hygiene factors (similar to the lower order needs identified by Maslow), did not in fact motivate employees but prevented demotivation if they were sufficiently satisfied. Herzberg's 'motivators' correspond to the 'higher order' needs identified in Maslow's hierarchy.

3 A manager could use motivational theory to develop job design and plan remuneration so that employee needs are being met in order to maximise motivation.

50. Financial methods of motivation

1 A business might use commission as a financial motivator to reward sales staff.

2 The benefits of profit-sharing are that employees are only financially rewarded if the business performs well and generates an end of year profit. It also ensures employees are focused on the overall performance of the company and not just their own jobs.

3 The limitations of financial rewards are that they will only motivate employees to a certain extent. Financial rewards will not aid employees in achieving job satisfaction through social interactions, self-esteem and self-actualisation.

51. Non-financial methods of motivation

1 Employee training might motivate a workforce because it shows employees that the company is investing in their skills and knowledge. This helps build job security and the long-term prospects of career progression.

2 The drawbacks of team working are that it can be difficult to identify the performance of individuals and in some circumstances social interactions at work could reduce labour productivity if they become a distraction from the task.

3 It is important to help employees achieve their 'higher order' needs as, according to Herzberg, without sufficient opportunities for career progression and personal satisfaction within a job, employees will not be motivated at work.

52. Choosing motivational methods

1 A manager might decide not to delegate decisions if the decisions are key ones or the manager does not believe their subordinates have the relevant knowledge or experience.

2 Three benefits of a highly motivated workforce are that they are more productive, will freely contribute and engage with the business and are less likely to leave the organisation.

3 The skill level of the workforce is important when considering methods of motivation because the more highly skilled the workforce, the more likely it is that employees will seek opportunities for self-actualisation. The nature of the job may also dictate the most appropriate method of payment and financial reward.

1.4.5

54. Management and leadership

1 The traits of a successful leader include confidence, communication skills and strategic thinking.

2 The characteristics of a laissez-faire leader are trust in their employees, openness to new ideas and a relaxed approach to supervision and monitoring.

1.5.1

57. The role of an entrepreneur

1 Entrepreneurs are important because they create businesses that solve economic and social problems and create jobs.

2 A person might set up their own business if they are unsatisfied with their own job or see a gap in the market that they believe they can fill with a new business venture.

58. Running a business

1 Three functions of a business include finance, operations and marketing.

2 Intrapreneurship refers to the innovation of employees within a business. This is important because these employees solve problems and create new products that can lead to success and growth of the business.

3 Setting up a business involves risk. This risk can be personal and financial. Some people may prefer not to set up their own business, but instead work for someone else where there is more certainty.

1.5.2

59. Characteristics and motives of entrepreneurs

1 One factor that might lead to the success of an entrepreneur is their determination to succeed. Many entrepreneurs give up, but the most successful are those that have the resilience and drive to keep going in the face of adversity.

2 Three reasons why a person might want to set up their own business include: freedom to make their own decisions, the potential to make a large profit and their interest in a certain subject, e.g. a hobby.

1.5.3

61. Business objectives

1 Objectives should be specific, measurable, agreed, realistic and time-related so that they are effective in helping the business achieve its aims.

2 Some objectives might be more important than others if they are linked to the survival or competitiveness of a business. The importance of an objective depends on the priorities of the business.

1.5.4

63. Forms of business 1

1 A sole trader has complete control over their business, it is easy to set up and the owner keeps 100% of the profits.

2 A public limited company is allowed to raise capital through selling shares to the general public through a stock market.

64. Forms of business 2

1 A person or group may decide to open a franchise in order to save the time and energy creating a unique business concept. Furthermore, franchisees receive support and training from the franchisor.

2 When a business becomes a Plc it has external shareholders so its objectives might focus on keeping these shareholders happy and improving its share price. This might lead to the directors making decisions that are not in the long-term interest of the business but made in order to generate profits and shareholder value.

65. Stock market flotation

1 The share price of a company may change due to its performance, the anticipated future performance of the company and the condition of the economic environment.

2 The share price of a business directly affects the value or worth of the company. The value of shares may also affect a company's ability to raise finance.

1.5.5

67. Business choices

1 An example of opportunity cost might be a business investing in a marketing campaign, but losing the opportunity and benefits of giving its workforce a bonus.

2 A business may survey stakeholders before making key decisions because they care about the impact those decisions might have on the stakeholders. Any decision is more likely to be successful if it is based on the perspectives of all stakeholders.

1.5.6

68. Entrepreneur to leader

1 An entrepreneur of a growing business might find it difficult to delegate responsibility because they feel very connected to the business and are used to being the sole decision-maker. They may also lack the skills required to delegate or the trust to allow another employee to make important decisions.
2 A leader of a large organisation might be expected to set a vision and strategic direction for their company. This may exist within a smaller business, but the entrepreneur may not have to motivate and share this vision (take people along with them) in a smaller business with few employees.

2.1.1 and 2.1.2

73. Sources of finance 2

1 Three examples of short-term sources of finance include trade credit, an overdraft and debt factoring.
2 Retained profit is low risk because it does not have to be paid back.
3 Private limited companies (Ltd) and Public limited companies (Plc) can raise finance through share capital.

2.1.3

75. Limited liability

1 The dangers of unlimited liability are that the owners of a business are directly responsible for the debts of the business and subject to any legal action taken against the business.
2 A secured loan is a suitable source of finance for a limited company because the assets of the business can be used as collateral and are not the personal assets of the owners.

2.1.4

77. The business plan

One stakeholder group that might use a business plan is any potential lender, such as a bank. The bank will use the business plan to calculate the level of risk. For example, a well-produced and detailed business plan will indicate that the owner has researched and thought out the details of the business. This is likely to reduce the level of risk. Another stakeholder could be potential employees. Employees will want to see the business plan to understand the vision of the owner and how they will fit into the running of the business.

78. Cash-flow forecasts

1 An opening balance is the cash position that a business carries forward from one period (e.g. month) to the next.
2 A cash-flow forecast might be used to plan for when a business is able to make significant purchases.
3 A cash-flow forecast is calculated by (cash inflows – cash outflows = net cash flow) + opening balance = closing balance.
4 Net cash flow is the difference between cash inflows and cash outflows in a given financial period.

79. Using cash-flow forecasts and improving cash flow

1 Two ways a business could increase cash inflows would be to sell off excess stock at a discount or collect any outstanding debts from debtors.
2 A business could reduce cash outflows by agreeing trade credit with suppliers and delaying payments to creditors.

2.2.1

82. Sales forecasting

1 A business might conduct a sales forecast by using past sales data and extrapolating a trend line using time series analysis. They may also simply carry out a sales forecast based on past experience and the opinions and intuition of experts.
2 Some of the limitations of sales forecasting are that the forecast is only as reliable as the quality of the information being used. Sales forecasts are also subject to unforeseen fluctuations such as economic factors or changes in consumer tastes.

2.2.2

83. Sales, revenue and costs

1 Profit = total revenue – total costs
2 Variable costs are linked to the product and increase with output. In the short term, fixed costs do not change with the output.
3 A business could increase its revenue by promoting its products to make them more desirable. A business could also reduce the price in order to make its products and services more competitive.

2.2.3

85. Break-even 1

1 Break-even point = fixed costs / contribution per unit
2 A break-even chart will include fixed costs, total revenue and total costs.
3 A business might use break-even analysis to identify the break-even point, make decisions on price and answer 'what if' questions about different levels of production.

86. Break-even 2

1 A business could lower its break-even point by reducing variable costs or increasing its price.
2 The margin of safety is the difference in units between the level of output and the break-even point. It identifies the level that output could drop to before a loss is made.
3 One limitation of break-even analysis is that it simplifies the nature of costs and revenue at different levels of output. Break-even analysis is also very difficult to calculate when a business produces multiple varieties of products.

2.2.4

87. Budgets

1 Two examples of expenditure budgets are the salaries budget and materials budget.
2 An adverse variance is one that is worse than budgeted. This would be lower on a sales budget and greater on an expenditure budget.

3 Budgets are hard to forecast because a business will often experience unforeseen costs and factors that can impact its sales revenue.

2.3.1

92. Calculation of profit

1 Profit for the year is the net profit generated by a business. This is the profit that can be returned to the owners or reinvested into the business.
2 Financial ratios are important because they allow managers to compare different financial variables and compare financial performance over time.

93. The statement of comprehensive income

1 A statement of comprehensive income shows the revenue generated by a business, the costs it incurs and any profit generated, typically over the period of a year.
2 Gross profit is the profit that a business makes on its trading activity, taking into account the direct cost of goods sold, whereas operating profit takes into account other operating expenses.
3 Other operating expenses are expenditures such as salaries and rent.

94. Improving profitability

1 Three costs a business could reduce to improve profit are: the cost of goods sold, salaries and business insurance fees.
2 Price is important to the profitability of a business because it directly affects the demand for a product and the revenue received on each item sold.
3 When trying to improve profitability a business might face problems such as a fall in quality due to cost-cutting, an inability to increase prices due to lack of value added and unforeseen costs that will directly affect forecast profits.

2.3.2

96. Statement of financial position (balance sheet)

1 A balance sheet is a snapshot of a business on a given day and indicates the assets and liabilities of a business. A balance sheet is an indicator of the value of a business.
2 A current asset is an item of value that the business expects to sell or use within the year.
3 Net assets are the difference between the total assets and the current liabilities.

97. Liquidity

1 Liquidity refers to the ability of a business to pay its short-term liabilities.
2 A current ratio of 0.8 : 1 means that for every pound of liabilities the business has 80p worth of current assets.

2.3.3

98. Business failure

1 A deficit in leadership skills might lead to the failure of a business.
2 Ineffective marketing could lead to customers receiving the wrong message or not receiving the message at all. If customers do not connect with the marketing of a business they will not be attracted to purchase its products.

2.4.1

102. Methods of production

1 The benefits of job production are that the product will be bespoke and can be designed to meet the exact needs of the customer.
2 A business might adopt cell production in order to boost employee motivation and productivity. Cell workers support one another and can form strong team bonds.

103. Productivity

1 A business could increase labour productivity by finding ways to motivate the workforce, redesigning jobs to make them more efficient or training employees to improve their skills.
2 The potential drawback of increasing labour productivity is that it could lead to an overworked workforce. If this happens the business could experience high rates of labour turnover and dissatisfaction among employees.

104. Efficiency

1 Efficiency is important because it is linked to waste. The lower the level of waste in a business (anything that does not add value) the more profitable the business will be.
2 The seven types of waste are: motion, transport, inventory, defects, wait time, overprocessing and overproduction.

2.4.2

105. Capacity utilisation

1 Capacity utilisation is measured by existing output / maximum potential output × 100.
2 A business can increase its capacity utilisation by either removing unnecessary capacity or increasing output.

2.4.3

107. Stock control and lean production

1 Three pieces of information shown on an inventory control chart are: minimum stock level, re-order level and maximum stock level.
2 A business could increase flexibility when managing its inventory by moving to a just-in-time stock control system.

2.4.4

108. Quality 1

1 Quality is important because it is a key way that a business can add value to its products. Quality can help build a reputation of reliability and make a business more competitive at a given price point.
2 A business could improve quality by adopting quality management techniques such as quality control and quality assurance.
3 Quality is difficult to improve because it can be expensive to implement. It is also very difficult to interpret what quality means to many customers as it is very subjective and may depend on a wide number of variables.

109. Quality 2

1 Kaizen is a Japanese term that means continuous improvement. Kaizen is a quality management principle.
2 Three characteristics of TQM include: quality chains, controls and team work.

2.5.1

113. The business cycle

1 Two features of an economic boom include high demand for products and services and pressure on inflation.
2 Two features of an economic slump include sustained low demand and less investment in business growth.
3 Two features of an economic recovery include businesses starting to take on new employees and increased consumer confidence.

114. Exchange rates and inflation

1 When a currency is strong this benefits importers as their currency will buy more of a foreign currency. In effect, this lowers the cost of products and materials being bought from abroad. However, when the currency is weak, this has the opposite effect. A strong currency has a negative impact on exporters as this increases the price of their products in foreign markets. Unless the exporter is able to reduce their prices, demand is likely to fall. On the other hand, when the currency is weak exporters normally experience high demand due to their products being cheaper in foreign markets.
2 Businesses want a steady rate of inflation in order to manage the steady rise in costs without having to increase their prices sharply, which could have a negative impact on demand. A high rate of inflation may also mean cutbacks in households and similar falls in demand for non-essential items.

115. Government spending, taxation and interest rates

1 An interest rate is the cost of borrowing or the rewards for saving. An interest rate is calculated as a percentage on the balance of a loan or savings.
2 Government spending refers to the money a government will spend within the economy. This might include spending on education or public services. Government spending is part of fiscal policy.

2.5.2

117. Legislation

1 The drawback of legislation for a business is that it generally incurs a cost.
2 New legislation may create opportunities for a business to help customers or other businesses adhere to the new laws; for example, providing advice on new data protection legislation.
3 Legislation can make businesses internalise any negative externalities; for example, taxing a business based on the waste or pollution it produces.

2.5.3

118. The competitive environment

1 One factor that might determine the bargaining power of a customer is the level of competition in the market – the opportunity to switch to a rival.
2 The impact of operating in a market with a large number of competitors is that prices will be forced down. Businesses will also have to innovate and provide excellent customer service in order to be successful.

3.1.1

123. Corporate objectives

1 Businesses use mission statements to set out and clarify the purpose of the business and communicate this purpose to all stakeholder groups.
2 Whereas a mission statement will lay down the broad purpose of a business, the corporate objectives will set out clear targets that are specific and measurable.
3 Three areas that corporate objectives may focus on include market standing, shareholder value and growth.

3.1.2

124. Corporate strategy: Ansoff 1

1 The four strategic options outlined by the Ansoff matrix are market penetration, market development, product development and diversification.
2 Market penetration is low risk because it involves a business dealing with customers and a market with which they are familiar without the need for expensive investment in new products that might not be successful.

125. Corporate strategy: Ansoff 2

1 Diversification might be a suitable strategic option for a business when its current market is saturated and there is potential growth in a new industry/market.
2 Three factors that a business may consider when choosing a strategic option is their internal strengths, the relative strengths/competencies of competitors and the growth of the market/segment.

126. Corporate strategy: Porter

1 A business can achieve cost leadership by being the lowest cost operator. This means that it is able to produce its products at a lower cost than any other rival. This means that it can charge a lower price than its rivals or maintain price parity and achieve higher profit margins.
2 A business could differentiate its product in a number of ways. These might include its design, features, brand image, quality or the services that come with the product, such as after-sales service.
3 A niche market is a market with a relatively small number of potential customers with specific needs that separate them from the mass market.

127. Competitive advantage

1 A business can achieve a sustainable competitive advantage through innovation, architecture or reputation. Innovation refers to a business's ability to create new ideas, products and processes that are better than those of competitors. Architecture refers to the internal relationships between stakeholders that build synergy, understanding, trust and effective working relationships; reputation refers to the brand image that the business builds over time.
2 When choosing a strategic direction a business will consider the cost of the strategy and the investment required to achieve its goal, the potential returns on the investment and how the business's core competencies may support the strategy.

128. Impact of strategy and tactics

1 Strategic decisions are broad and long term and guide the overall direction of the business, whereas tactical decisions are day-to-day decisions made by managers within the business which lead to actions that support the business strategy.
2 An example of a functional objective is:
Marketing – to ensure 90% customer awareness of our brand.

3.1.3

130. SWOT analysis

1 SWOT stands for strengths, weaknesses, opportunities and threats.
2 A business might use SWOT analysis in order to identify its current position and form new objectives and business strategy.
3 The limitations of SWOT analysis are that often issues can be interpreted differently depending on your perspective. For example, something that is considered a strength to the business might also be a weakness.

3.1.4

131. Impact of external influences

1 A government will impose environmental legislation to protect the environment and ensure all businesses operate in a way that is environmentally sustainable.
2 An oligopoly is a market where four or five key competitors dominate.

132. Porter's Five Forces 1

1 Porter's five competitive forces are competitive rivalry within an industry, bargaining power of suppliers, bargaining power of buyers, threat of substitutes and threat of new entrants.
2 The rivalry within a market might be determined by the number of competitors, the degree of homogeneity between brands and the extent to which businesses within the market are willing to collaborate.
3 Where suppliers have a lot of bargaining power within a market, businesses may try to establish long-term supply contracts or look for alternative sources of a substitute product or material.

133. Porter's Five Forces 2

1 Two factors that may give buyers power in a market are the extent of their choice between rival businesses (or the availability of substitutes) and their access to information on the various competitors and their products.
2 A substitute product is one that is not the same, but could serve the same purpose or fulfil the same need for the consumer. For example, a skiing holiday might be a substitute for a cruise.
3 A business might compete with new entrants in a market by improving the quality of its products, lowering its prices to be more competitive or finding a way to differentiate itself from rival businesses. Each of these examples is a way to add value.

3.2.1

136. Reasons for growth

1 Organic growth is steady and gradual whereas inorganic growth is very sudden and can bring about significant change in an organisation.
2 Economies of scope refers to the benefits a business experiences by operating with a wide variety of products in a number of markets. These benefits include reduced costs shared across the different product lines and spreading the risk of any one product failing.
3 Financial economies of scale are experienced when a large business has more collateral and can therefore raise more capital through loans than a smaller business can.

137. Limitations of growth

1 Two diseconomies of scale a business might experience include communication problems and flexibility. Large businesses might find it more difficult to communicate with all stakeholders and guarantee the right message is received across the organisation. Large organisations also take longer to make decisions and implement them and this can reduce their ability to change quickly.
2 Overtrading refers to a business that grows too fast and overstretches its financial resources such as cash. Overtrading can lead to operational inefficiencies, such as lost orders, and cash-flow problems.

138. Mergers and takeovers

1 A business may choose to seek a merger instead of an acquisition because this model of growth will not require the capital investment required to buy the other company. Acquisitions can also result in resistance from internal stakeholders; this is less likely in a joint venture as growth involves partnership and not takeover.
2 A business might choose to take over a supplier so that it can guarantee and control the supply of materials or products. The cost of these resources is also reduced as there is no longer a mark-up added by the supplier.

3.2.3

140. Organic growth

1 A business can grow organically through attracting new customers, entering new markets or developing and selling a new range of products.
2 A limitation of organic growth is that it is relatively slow paced compared to external growth. For this reason a business growing organically might be overtaken by other competitors that use inorganic (external) growth to dominate the market.

3.2.4

141. Reasons for staying small

1 A small business might be more efficient than a large company because a small business might find it easier to manage business costs and control waste.
2 A small business might be able to provide better customer service than a large company because it is more equipped to know and understand the needs of each customer. Smaller businesses will find it easier to make decisions quickly and can easily adapt their product and service to a customer's preference.

3.3.1

144. Quantitative sales forecasting 1

1 A moving average is calculated by taking either a three- or four-point set of data and finding the average. This then becomes the centre point for a trend line. The first period's data drops out and the next period is added to calculate the next average which becomes the next point on the trend line.
2 Quantitative sales forecasting is limited because it assumes that all other factors will remain constant. However, there is no way for a business to predict all eventualities in the external competitive environment. Quantitative sales forecasting is also limited by the quality of the research on which it is based.

145. Quantitative sales forecasting 2

1 A business might calculate a seasonal variation so that it can predict future sales figures more accurately than simply using an extrapolated trend line.

2 If there is no correlation between two sets of data then there is no relationship between them. As one rises or falls the other is not influenced.

3.3.2

146. Investment appraisal 1

1 Investment appraisal might be used by a business to compare alternative investments in terms of the financial and non-financial return they may bring.

2 A business might calculate payback because this will indicate how quickly a firm is able to recoup its initial investment. This is important for businesses that may have cash-flow problems or need to repay a lender quickly.

3 The average rate of return (ARR) is useful when making investment decisions as it allows a business to directly compare potential investments in terms of the average profit it will generate over the life of the project or asset.

147. Investment appraisal 2

1 Two non-financial factors that a business may take into consideration when comparing potential investment decisions are the level of risk associated with each investment and the impact each investment may have on the Corporate Social Responsibility of the organisation.

2 Two factors that may determine the risk associated with an investment include the length of time it takes to pay back the initial investment and the experience the business has with that particular investment. The longer the payback period, the more chance there is for conditions to change and the likelihood that the investment will lose value. The experience of managers may also be a factor in determining risk as inexperienced managers may not see potential problems or issues that could disrupt the success of any investment.

3 A business might use sensitivity analysis to identify variations in forecasts to allow for a range of outcomes. This will allow it to ask 'what if' questions and put in place contingency plans to deal with various scenarios.

3.3.3

149. Decision trees 1

1 A manager might use a decision tree to calculate the probable outcomes of a range of decisions. Decision trees are used to calculate the financial impact of various decisions.

2 The expected value in a decision tree is the average financial result from the various outcomes anticipated by taking a course of action.

150. Decision trees 2

1 Decision trees require a probability to be attached to various outcomes. These probabilities can be inaccurate and extremely subjective. For this reason, the usefulness of a decision tree could be limited where this is the case.

2 Other decision-making tools that might be used alongside a decision tree include market maps, stakeholder maps and the product life cycle.

3 Student answer

3.3.4

152. Critical Path Analysis 1

1 On a network diagram the EST refers to the earliest start time of a task or stage of a project. The LFT refers to the latest finish time of a particular task or project so that it does not delay other stages of the project.

2 The 'float' on an activity refers to the amount of additional time (hours, days or weeks) that a task can take without having an impact on the preceding task. The float is useful to know as it helps managers identify those tasks that are flexible versus those that are critical to meeting the project deadline.

3 The 'critical path' refers to those activities or tasks within a project where there is no flexibility in terms of float time, and therefore, are critical to the projected finish time of the whole project.

153. Critical Path Analysis 2

1 The benefits of using Critical Path Analysis when implementing a strategy are that it helps managers to meet a deadline, identify critical tasks in the implementation of a strategy and effectively manage all resources involved in implementing the strategy.

2 The limitations of Critical Path Analysis are that often the duration of a task within a project is difficult to predict and durations are often estimates. Furthermore, Critical Path Analysis does not guarantee the project will be a success; all tasks still have to be managed effectively.

3.4.1

156. Corporate influences

1 The causes of short-termism might include the pressures on managers to achieve short-term targets. When employees are in a role for a short term (e.g. three years) they may set targets based on the performance in this time-frame to ensure they can demonstrate their impact and success on the organisation.

2 Intuition is important when the reliability of data is questionable or there is little evidence on which to base a decision. Intuition is valuable where managers have experience in a particular aspect of business or a situation.

3.4.2

157. Corporate culture

1 Factors that may influence the culture of a business include the leaders within the organisation, the values and beliefs, the structure of the business and the norms and traditions.

2 A power culture is a culture that is formed and dominated by one individual. This leader will dictate the tone and approach that the organisation takes. The existence of power cultures is more common in small organisations where the leader has more influence on all employees.

158. Managing corporate culture

1 A business might choose to change its culture if the managers believe that it is not effective and could lead to failure. For example, if the organisation has a culture of making key decisions slowly, the managers may try to change this if they believe it will help make the business more responsive to customer needs, and therefore more competitive.

2 Changing organisational culture is very difficult because many factors that contribute to an organisation's culture, such as the values and beliefs of employees, are not always obvious or 'visible'. People are also often resistant to any form of change because it brings with it uncertainty and many people will see this as risk.

3.4.3

160. Stakeholders 1

1 Customers, employees, shareholders.
2 The local community will want a business to provide trade and employment opportunities, while at the same time reducing negative externalities such as pollution and congestion.

161. Stakeholders 2

1 The factors that may determine the interests of a stakeholder group are the extent to which the activities of a business directly impact on the lives or fortunes of that stakeholder group.
2 Some people may consider shareholders to be the most important stakeholder group in a business because they finance the business activities and can influence decisions within the company. Other people may consider other stakeholders as being the most important to the long-term success of a business.

3.4.4

162. Ethics

1 Three examples of ethical practice by a business might include paying employees a fair wage and providing good working conditions; using sustainable resources and minimising the carbon footprint of the business; and avoiding trading with any country or organisation that is known to be corrupt.
2 The role of pressure groups is to expose the practices of unethical businesses and to convince them to operate in a socially responsible way.

163. Corporate social responsibility

1 Corporate social responsibility (CSR) is the belief that a business should act responsibly and protect the interests of its stakeholders.
2 CSR is important for all businesses as it promotes long-term sustainability. By focusing on the triple bottom line a business will ensure that it does not have a negative impact on the environment or society and this helps ensure that the conditions for businesses to operate in are maintained in the long term.

3.5.1

167. Interpreting financial statements 1

1 Employees will be interested in the statement of comprehensive income because it gives an indication of profitability – this determines the success of the business and future potential for growth, bonuses and job security.
2 Quality of profit refers to the extent that profit is sustainable and not based on exceptional items, such as the sale of a large asset.

168. Interpreting financial statements 2

1 Receivables are debts from debtors that a business expects to be paid within the next 12 months.
2 An intangible asset may refer to a brand, patent or some other asset that is not physical, but of value to the business.

3.5.2

169. Ratio analysis

1 A highly geared business is one that has a significant proportion of its capital employed provided through long-term borrowing. This business might face problems repaying its debts if performance falls.
2 One limitation of financial ratios is that they do not take into account qualitative factors such as a business's reputation, brand image or the motivation of the workforce.

3.5.3

171. Human resources

1 Labour productivity is important because increasing it can help a business reduce average costs.
2 High labour turnover can increase business costs and lead to demotivation where there is an unstable workforce. Labour turnover also has a direct impact on productivity.

172. Human resources strategies

1 A company could reduce absenteeism by introducing reward schemes linked to attendance and allowing flexible working practices that encourage employees not to take time off from work.
2 Employee consultation is important because employees need to feel as though they have some influence over their work and are not just controlled by the decisions of the company. When this happens, employees are more likely to want to stay and will be happier at work.

3.6.1

174. The causes of business change

1 As a business grows, its organisational structure will change to accommodate the different roles and responsibilities. New working practices may also be adopted, such as increased automation of production leading to economies of scale.
2 Poor performance will lead to business change in order to address the issues that lead to the poor performance. This might include the replacement of key personnel, adapting marketing or improvements made to the products.

3.6.2

175. Key factors in change

1 One factor that may change within a business is its workforce. Over time employees will leave and retire. A business must plan for the future needs of its workforce and put in place measures to ensure employees are replaced and trained. Furthermore, when managing workforce change a business must also plan for growth or the downsizing of the organisation. This could involve creating new jobs or, in the latter example, redundancies.

2 Two reasons why employees might resist change include: a focus on how their self-interests might be affected by the change, or a lack of understanding of the change, the need for it and how it might affect them.

3.6.3

176. Scenario planning

1 Risk is the likelihood of a negative event occurring multiplied by the impact that the event would have on the business.

2 A business can mitigate against risk by planning for any negative events occurring and having specific steps they take in order to minimise the impact. For example, this might include having sufficient insurance and developing the skills of employees.

4.1.1

181. Growing economies

1 BRICS and MINT are acronyms for the world's fastest developing countries. BRICS: Brazil, Russia, India, China and South Africa. MINT: Mexico, Indonesia, Nigeria and Turkey.

2 Emerging economies create opportunities for international businesses because trade becomes easier with these nations due to the development of supporting industries and national infrastructure, as well as an increase in average incomes leading to an increase in imports.

182. Indicators of growth

1 Health is an indicator of economic development because people have better health and live longer in wealthier countries. Measures associated with health include life expectancy and access to clean water.

2 Literacy rates are an important indicator of a developing economy because a higher literacy rate is an indication of educational achievement and the level of skills in the workforce.

4.1.2

184. International trade

1 FDI is Foreign Direct Investment – this involves investing in production facilities, local businesses or foreign assets. FDI leads to multinational corporations.

2 Exporting is less risky than setting up production in a foreign country because the business does not need to invest capital into a foreign market where it may have little knowledge and control.

4.1.3

185. Globalisation

1 The benefits of migration are that it offers many businesses cheap labour or, in the case of skilled professions (such as doctors), helps fill skills gaps. Migration also creates demand as net migration increases the population size of a country.

2 Political stability has created global business opportunities because countries that were previously politically unstable are now open to international trade and are safer places to do business. These countries, such as those in the former Soviet Union, create a large potential market for international businesses to trade with.

4.1.4

187. Protectionism

1 A government might impose protectionist strategies to protect domestic industries from international competition.

2 Three protectionist strategies might include: tariffs, quotas and subsidies for domestic businesses.

4.1.5

188. Trading blocs

1 A single market refers to an arrangement where there are no trade barriers or restrictions between countries. This includes the free movement of labour and common laws. A customs union involves a trade agreement between member states.

2 The benefits for member states of a trading bloc are harmonised trade agreements and openness to free trade.

4.2.1

190. Conditions that prompt trade

1 One push factor that may lead to a business trading internationally is the saturation of a domestic market. If there is very little opportunity for growth, or the market is shrinking, then many businesses may look for growth opportunities in foreign markets.

2 Outsourcing allows a business to use a third party to supply a specific business function, such as customer services or production. Outsourcing allows a business to benefit from cheaper specialists, who can be more efficient than if the business fulfilled the function itself, and means the business can focus on its core competencies.

4.2.2

192. Assessment of a country as a market

1 Student answer

2 Infrastructure is important when considering a country to trade with as without infrastructure it will be difficult for the business to transport its goods, access raw materials and communicate effectively. It may also find it difficult to find suppliers that have the necessary knowledge and capacity to provide goods and services to it.

3 Political stability is important because extreme political unrest, such as civil wars and opposition to the government, means that customers stop buying products because they are uncertain about the future. Political unrest also brings volatility to markets as there is uncertainty around the laws and regulations governing trade within the country and with international partners.

4.2.3

193. Assessment of a country as a production location 1

1 One incentive that a government might give to an MNC is lower business rates and subsidies when setting up.

2 An MNC might have production facilities across multiple countries in order to access those markets more easily – reduced shipping costs and barriers to trade.

194. Assessment of a country as a production location 2

1 Student answer.
2 Off-shoring is often cheaper than exporting because production costs are lower in developing countries and additional shipping or taxes can be avoided.
3 The level of unemployment might influence an MNC's decision to set up production in a foreign country because high rates of unemployment may affect potential demand and also the availability and cost of labour in that country.

4.2.4

196. Reasons for global mergers and joint ventures

1 An international patent gives a company the sole right to produce or use an invention for a specific period of time. By acquiring the patent a company may own this asset and gain the competitive advantage from being able to produce or use the invention in its own production processes.
2 If a company merges with an international firm that has a strong brand image and knowledge of its domestic market, then the business will be able to use these assets to enter the market without having to slowly develop the knowledge and brand image over time.

4.2.5

197. Global competitiveness

1 A company might protect itself from exchange rate fluctuations by agreeing fixed contracts with customers and suppliers to guarantee a set rate on all future transactions.
2 Global businesses can achieve cost leadership by achieving economies of scale. The scale of operation means large businesses can keep costs low and control the whole production chain.

4.3.1

201. Global marketing

1 The difference between ethnocentric and geocentric is that an ethnocentric strategy involves a standardised global product whereas geocentric dictates that there will be alterations and modifications made to suit the context of the local area – a 'glocal' strategy.
2 A business might adapt its marketing mix to an international market by ensuring its brand and advertising translate into a foreign language and that there are no alternative meanings or connotations in international markets.

4.3.2

203. Niche markets

1 A niche market exists where a small group of customers have a specific need or interest. Across international borders, niche markets exist because people have cultural differences and tastes that might not exist in the UK.
2 A niche market will affect the marketing mix because any niche marketer must have an excellent understanding of their customer, communication is more likely to be personalised and bespoke channels of communication will be used.

4.3.3

204. Cultural/social factors

1 Cultural barriers can cause problems when dealing in international markets because people have different social norms and expectations in different countries. For example, Eastern countries might expect to engage in socialising and pleasantries before engaging in business negotiations, whereas some cultures may prefer to get 'straight to business'.
2 Businesses need to be careful when translating marketing material because words might have different meaning and associations in different countries. There are many examples of marketing failures where brand names have been translated with an unfortunate meaning.

4.4.1

206. The impact of MNCs (local context)

1 An MNC setting up a factory in a local community can bring investment to the area (e.g. new parks, roads) and the creation of local jobs.
2 One drawback of MNCs is that the profits they earn may not always be reinvested into the country or local area. Often profits will go back to the holding company.

207. The impact of MNCs (national context)

1 MNCs will bring new technologies and experienced managers and technicians into a local community. This creates technology and skills transfer as the expertise and knowledge are passed on to workers in the local context.
2 An MNC will support the balance of payments for the national government in the country it operates from. This is because it will add to the country's net exports.

4.4.2

209. Global ethics

1 There is scope for unethical practices in MNCs because they are important to economic growth in developing countries. This means that international governments may 'turn a blind eye' to unethical practices if they believe the presence of the MNC will create jobs and prosperity.
2 MNCs may indirectly exploit workers through the trade they have with local or international suppliers who might not apply the same working conditions or care for their workers. All MNCs should carry out audits of their suppliers to ensure human rights are upheld and pay and working conditions are appropriate.

4.4.3

210. Controlling MNCs

1 Pressure groups are important because they lobby for change and expose unethical business practices. This exposure can lead to bad publicity for MNCs, meaning they are more likely to act in an ethical way.
2 Low tax levels might be applied to encourage FDI from MNCs. Taxes can also be applied to ensure any negative externalities brought about by MNCs are internalised (i.e. they are paid for by the MNC).

Exam-style practice answers

Unit 1.1

1. (a) The proportion of a particular market that a product or business holds.
   (b) Unique features of a company and its products that give it an advantage over competitors.

2. A dynamic market is one where there is a high level of change. For example, new entrants entering the market, continuous development of new products and fluctuations in prices. The UK music market is dynamic because music trends are constantly changing and this means that consumers are constantly buying new music. The nature of the market has changed too, with vinyl record sales having grown by over 450% over a four-year period. The way consumers purchase music has also changed with the majority now purchasing music via streaming sources.

3. The research that Rick has carried out is mainly secondary research. This involves accessing information that already exists and has been conducted by a third party. The limitations of secondary research are that it might not be specific to the target market or the needs of the business. Furthermore, secondary research can also become out of date quickly. In addition to this, Rick's research is statistical and does not provide him with any qualitative information on his customers' opinions or attitudes towards his record store. The research only provides information on the growth of the UK music industry and, in particular, vinyl record sales.

4. A market map is a business decision-making tool that allows a business to position itself in a market against rival firms based on two variables, for example price and quality. Rick could use a market map to compare his record store against other music outlets in the local area. This means that Rick will be able to differentiate his business to ensure he is not competing directly with other record stores. For example, the fact that Rick sells memorabilia and has a coffee shop in his store might mean that his business adds more value than other record stores in the area.
   One limitation of using a market map is that it only considers two variables and, as the product that Rick sells is generic, it might be difficult to identify how his business is different from any other. Furthermore, the market map will be based on Rick's opinions. As he has only conducted secondary market research, then it is unlikely to be representative of his customers' perspective. Overall, a market map would be useful because it would allow Rick to reflect on his business strategy, but it would only be useful when built on comprehensive market research.

5. If Rick was to modernise the interior of his record store it might help differentiate his business from any other stores in the local area. As a result, customers may choose to visit and browse the store instead of purchasing records online. Furthermore, as customers come to browse and meet other music enthusiasts, they may enjoy meeting in a renovated store and spending time in his café. However, renovating the store may simply make it a more attractive place to be; it will not add value to the actual product – the records. Investing heavily in renovating his record store may not actually attract more customers or help him increase his profits.
   Offering a record repair service will add value, as customers can not only buy records, but have their record players repaired too. As customers drop off their record players for repair, they are also likely to buy new records. However, record players rarely need servicing and offering this type of service may add little to store revenues.
   Overall, renovating the store might be the best option. This is because most of his customers enjoy browsing the store and meeting other people; customers are more likely to spend time and money in his record store if the environment is appealing. Overall, the best option may also depend on the cost of the renovation or the profit margin Rick could get on an average record player repair. In order to identify the most profitable option, Rick could carry out investment appraisal to compare the return on investment of each option.

Unit 1.2

1. One factor that could lead to a fall in demand for houses in the UK is house prices. National statistics show that prices rose by 5.8% to February, thus mortgage rates will also increase and this will mean that new house buyers may struggle to afford the higher payments. Furthermore, as house prices rise, some customers may put off moving house; this too means that fewer houses will be sold throughout the period.

2. A government subsidy for housing developers would help increase the level of supply in the market. This is because builders such as Taylor Wimpey will be able to purchase plots of land with support from the subsidy and this will make it easier for them to build houses profitably, such as those being built in Battersea. As supply increases in the market, house prices may fall. Consequently, more people will be able to get onto the 'housing ladder' and reduce the need for social housing.

3. One factor that may affect the price elasticity of a Taylor Wimpey home is the number of similar housing estates in the local area. For example, if another housebuilder were to build a large estate close by, customers would have more choice when buying a new home. In this instance, should Taylor Wimpey increase their prices, potential customers are more likely to switch to an alternative house builder. Another factor that could affect the price elasticity of a Taylor Wimpey home is the unique features of a Taylor Wimpey home. For example, the new estate will also have close access to leisure and retail outlets. Such a USP may mean customers are willing to pay a premium for a Taylor Wimpey house. Overall, the presence of other new homes in the area is the biggest factor affecting price elasticity of a Taylor Wimpey home; this is because there is a severe shortage of homes in the UK.

4. The graph shows an increase in supply within the housing market from S1 to S2. The increased quantity of houses from Q1 to Q2 has the impact of lowering the average price of a home in the UK from P1 to P2.
   As average prices fall, it is likely that Taylor Wimpey will make a lower profit on each house it builds and sells. Thus, shareholders will receive lower dividends and share prices may fall. However, the profit margin per house may depend on the costs of building a house. If market prices are falling, Taylor Wimpey may try to find ways to maintain its profit. This might involve lowering wages, sourcing cheaper building materials or finding ways to increase the price, such as selling the leasehold rights on its properties. Overall, an increase in supply is not good for a house builder because it means there is more competition in the market and customers have more bargaining power when buying a house.

Unit 1.3

1. NETGEAR prides itself on 'form as well as function'. Therefore it is important that its products look good and are aesthetically pleasing. Without design, it is unlikely that NETGEAR would win any of its design awards, which contribute to lots of positive publicity that can lead to a stronger brand image and increased sales for its Arlo security cameras.

2   Price skimming involves setting a high price when a new product is launched and then lowering the price over time. The benefit of price skimming is that profits are maximised through the early adopters who are keen to purchase the latest technology. Price skimming is also appropriate in the technology market because new versions of products are launched each year and many customers want to have the most technologically advanced products, especially when it comes to home security.

Furthermore, by winning the Red Dot award, the Arlo range will be in high demand over the coming year. People will be happy to pay a premium for an award-winning product and NETGEAR must capitalise on this. Nevertheless, no matter how many awards NETGEAR has won, if their products are considerably more expensive than others on the market, then customers will be deterred and may choose to buy cheaper options. Overall, providing prices are aligned to the market, NETGEAR can afford to use price skimming whilst its products are in high demand.

3   Using a wide variety of promotional methods to promote its products is important for NETGEAR as different promotional techniques have relative benefits and will help the company reach a wider target market. For example, sales promotions may help the company clear lines of old stock when they are ready to launch a new product line, such as an update to the Arlo surveillance camera. Furthermore, extensive advertising in technology magazines and trade shows will help NETGEAR create awareness and interest in new products. On the other hand, NETGEAR are currently market leaders so its brand image will be well-established. This might reduce the need for expensive advertising, direct marketing or sales promotions because many customer will naturally be attracted to new products when they are launched. Indeed, it is likely that NETGEAR has a loyal customer base. Furthermore, achieving awards such as the Red Dot award for quality design will create extensive exposure of its products and this too may limit the need for NETGEAR to spend heavily on a range of promotional tools.

4   Innovation is key in the home technology market. As technology advances firms will bring out new products each year. In order for NETGEAR to become a market leader, it must keep up with the trends in the market and ensure its products are the 'best sellers' in every category. NETGEAR has a good track record for innovation, as has been demonstrated by its recent technology awards; as a result, this might not be a priority for it.

Alternatively, NETGEAR could focus on customer service. If customers are given excellent customer service they are more likely to return and stay loyal. NETGEAR will sell most of its products online or through technology retailers such as Curry's or John Lewis. As a result, customer service might not be as important to the long-term success of the brand as customer service is in the hands of the retailer. Nevertheless, after-sales service such as product help and returns of faulty products is very important and, if NETGEAR get this wrong, customers will soon switch to a rival brand.

Overall, innovation is the most important strategy to pursue. NETGEAR has a reputation for innovation in the industry and this is what gives it a competitive advantage over rivals. The problem with innovation is that it has to be maintained and, if NETGEAR starts to focus on customer service, other rival tech firms could develop new products that supersede NETGEAR's. Ultimately, the importance of innovation will depend on the product life cycle of current products such as the Arlo security camera. With its awards this product may maintain its position as market leader for one to two years and this will give NETGEAR time to focus on other priorities.

Unit 1.4

1   Induction training is the training employees receive when they first join a company. The purpose of induction training is to ensure they understand the company policies, procedures and ways of working. This might also include health and safety training.

2   A suitable human resources objective that Louise could set would be to reduce labour turnover and retain the best employees. This would seem to be an appropriate objective considering the labour turnover for the first 18 months. Setting this objective will help boost morale within the tea room as the team become settled and established. As a result, the settled employees will start to work as a team and productivity will rise.

3   Qtr 1: £12 000 / £20 000 × 100 = 60%
Qtr 4: £35 000 / £72 000 × 100 = 49%
Change in labour costs as a percentage of revenue fell by 11% between Qtr 1 and Qtr 4.

4   Job design refers to the contents of a job in terms of its duties and responsibilities. One way that Paul could improve job design would be to introduce job rotation across the workforce. For example, this might involve factory workers joining the delivery team for a day or carpenters working with the upholsterers. This would add more variety to the work of Paul's employees and help them to appreciate how other areas of the business function. As a result, employee motivation may rise as they appreciate that they are part of a bigger team. Another aspect of job design is the extent to which decisions and tasks are delegated to Paul's subordinates. Paul could delegate some of his tasks to the factory managers in order to develop their skills and give them more autonomy over their jobs. This is a form of job enrichment and could help the managers achieve their self-esteem needs along with the opportunity for career progression.

5   Paul has introduced two new fringe benefits for employees that are types of financial rewards in the form of a staff discount and two more days' holiday, which is part of the employees' contract and working conditions. This will help motivate employees because it shows that Paul cares for his staff. It may also help retain employees because they have an extra incentive to work for Retro Homes. In terms of motivation these additions may help employees achieve some of their basic needs as outlined by Maslow, in particular, their physiological needs. On the other hand, Herzberg would consider holiday entitlement and staff discounts as 'hygiene factors' that will only prevent demotivation and not increase motivation of the workforce. Furthermore, neither of these initiatives will help employees achieve the 'higher order needs' or support the social aspects of work life. In order for Paul to truly motivate his workforce, he must think beyond simply financial methods of motivation and consider non-financial methods linked to job design.

Overall, these initiatives will help motivate staff as they improve the overall working conditions at Retro Homes and reward staff with a discount on furniture. Nevertheless, if Paul wants a highly motivated workforce he must consider other factors such as ensuring work is meaningful, that employees have responsibility for their work and that they see the results of their work. The extent to which Paul develops a highly motivated workforce may depend on how he designs the job of his employees to maximise these factors.

6   The key change to Retro Homes' organisational structure is that Paul has brought in an extra level of management. This includes a production manager, a tea room manager and a showroom manager. The impact of this change is that Retro Homes now has a tall organisation structure. The benefit of this is that it will allow greater supervision and management of each team within the business. This could help improve

productivity as each manager will be able to focus on their own area of the business and ensure their team is performing to the best of their ability. The new managers will also increase specialisation within the company and will reduce the span of control beneath Paul. Consequently, Paul and Louise can focus on strategic decisions and growing the company. However, employing three new managers will not be cheap and it will add considerably to the wage bill of the company. Recently labour costs as a percentage of revenue has fallen but it is likely that this will rise again in the near future. Paul will have to be careful that some employees do not become demotivated by these changes. For example, both factory managers may lose some of the authority and autonomy to make their own decisions if the production manager is autocratic and wants to influence most of the decisions made in either factory. Nevertheless, with a longer chain of command come opportunities for promotion and this could motivate employees in the long-run. Overall, the key to success at Retro Homes may be how well the various areas of the business work together. As Paul and Louise have more time to focus on strategic decisions and not the day to day management of the business, this might be easier to achieve in the new organisation structure. Nevertheless, performance in terms of unit costs and labour productivity may fall in the short term, but if the new managers are effective each area of the business should improve over time through greater efficiencies and productivity. In order to encourage a high performing workforce, Paul and Louise must agree the job design in terms of enrichment, enlargement and delegation so that all employees are motivated to work hard under the new organisation structure.

Unit 1.5

1   One entrepreneurial skill that may help Marley become a successful business owner is her willingness and confidence in taking risks. Running a business requires owners to invest their own time and capital into a venture that may fail and not all people are willing to do this. As Well-Mate is a high-tech smartphone app it will require lots of investment. It is also a very competitive market so Marley will be taking a big risk.

2   One reason why Benedick may choose to run his business as a sole trader is because it is far easier to run a business as a sole trader. A sole trader does not have to be registered with Companies House and the business accounts do not have to be made available to the public. Benedick set up his business for his love of art and bringing artists together. Therefore, he may want to keep the business small and simple in order to focus on his passion.

3   As Soul grows it will start to employ more people. If Benedick becomes an employer he may feel responsible for the incomes of these employees and this may influence his business objectives. For example, generating revenue may be more important in order to ensure he can pay his staffing costs. However, paying wages is not usually an appropriate business objective – breaking even may be more appropriate. Another factor that may influence his business objectives as the business grows is the need to reinvest in maintenance of the gallery and other facilities. A large business will need to reinvest more capital in order to remain sustainable. For example, artwork will need replacing and the facilities will need repairing. These costs will grow along with the business. It might be important for Benedick to set objectives around profit maximisation so that this can be reinvested back into the gallery. Nevertheless, Benedick may choose to run his business as a social enterprise. If so, there will not be a profit motive.

4   Opportunity cost refers to the opportunity forgone when a business decision has been made. It is the next best alternative. Should Marley accept the £800 000 for the business she would be able to reinvest this capital into an alternative business venture or perhaps retire. This money may be sufficient reward for the effort and energy that Marley had invested into the company and seen as an appropriate reward for her efforts. However, Marley has invested a lot of time and energy in the company and £800 000 may be poor compensation for the value of the company and future growth potential. If Marley accepts the money and sells Well-Mate she will lose the opportunity to grow the business and maximise the long-term profitability of the app. For example, in two years' time the business might be worth £5 million. By selling at £800 000 Marley loses the opportunity to earn profit in the future. Overall, Marley should not accept the offer. If another company values the brand they may be willing to pay more and by selling Well-Mate now she will lose the opportunity to gain further returns on her investment. However, the choice may depend on whether the buying company is a considerable competitor in the market and the projected growth of the app. Although Marley will be selling the business, it might be worth it if her research suggests limited future growth. Furthermore, Marley could invest the £800 000 into a new venture or even offer to work for the buy-out company. This would significantly reduce future risk.

Unit 2.1

1   Limited liability refers to a limited company that is a separate legal entity. The ownership and liability of the owners are separate from that of the company.

2   Crowd funding refers to the process of raising capital for a project or new business venture through an online crowd funding website. The general public can invest in a new idea for a share of the company or some other benefit, such as free products.

3   Harmeet could improve her cash-flow position at the start of the year by trying to secure better trade credit arrangements with her suppliers. This would then free up funds in January which could be used to pay other bills such as the rent of her premises. Harmeet is currently forecast to pay £450 for materials and if this could be postponed until February or March it could help avoid the net cash flow of (£215) she forecasts in January. However, she might only be able to do this if she has a good relationship with her suppliers. As she has not been trading for very long, this might be difficult as she is unlikely to have built up trust. Another option might be to give customers a special offer in January to help boost sales. January sales are the lowest at £400 and a special offer could help attract new customers in this period of low demand. Although this will reduce Harmeet's profit margins, in January it might be more important to boost short-term sales revenue to cover the negative cash flow. Overall, it might be better for Harmeet to delay some payments through trade credit putting off payment to creditors as there is no guarantee that sales can be increased in the short term, especially as the business is relatively new.

4   A financial objective is one that sets out the financial performance of the company and may flow from the corporate objectives. One objective that the owners of Hands On Puzzles Plc might set is to balance the capital structure of the company so that it is evenly proportioned between share capital and long-term borrowing. At the moment the gearing ratio has fallen over recent years from 60% to 30%. This suggests that the business has paid off long-term debt. As the business is looking to expand further with a new line of products, one option may be to finance the expansion through a long-term loan instead of issuing new shares. Another objective for Hands On Puzzles Plc might be to improve profitability. The data suggests that the company is effective at generating gross profit through

its direct trading activity, but since 2013 operating profit has fallen slightly. Although this may not be a worry for the company it could suggest it is struggling to manage operating costs. As a result, operating profit and profit for the year might be a suitable area to focus on in order to stop the declining trend. However, there may be a good reason for the overall fall in operating profit, such as the investment in new machinery or growth in the workforce. As Hands On Puzzles Plc is also looking to launch a new product line a suitable financial objective could be to set targets for the return on investment. The directors might set this target based on the return on investment of previous toy lines. However, the return on investment may be a long-term objective if they expect the payback to be over a number of years.

Overall, the key issue is that Hands On Puzzles Plc is a growing business that exports to the USA and Western Europe. Therefore, appropriate financial objectives might be based around growth. For this reason, the most appropriate financial objectives might be based around sales revenue growth and gross profit and, in the long term, operating profit and net profit once expansion has taken place. In order to hit these targets Hands On Puzzles Plc should invest in marketing to promote its products to a wider customer base and establish export links with new agents. If it is able to do this it is likely that sales will grow and directly impact the overall profitability of the company.

Unit 2.2

1 Break-even = fixed costs / contribution per unit
£900 / (£45 − 16) = **31.03 cakes**

2 75 − 45 = 30 parties (growth between Qtr1 and Qtr 4)
30 / 45 × 100 = **66% growth in forecasted sales**

3 Revenue is the income generated through sales of Jaume's hoodies. In order to increase revenue, one option is for Jaume to lower the price of his hoodies. If the product is relatively elastic then reducing price could help increase the volume of sales even though the contribution per hoodie would have fallen. This would be an effective strategy in a competitive market such as personalised hoodies.

4 Cash-flow forecasting involves forecasting future cash inflows and outflows from a business. Cash-flow forecasting is a valuable management tool for all businesses, but especially start-up businesses which may have more cash-flow problems as they establish a customer base. Jaume will be able to use cash-flow forecasting to identify periods within his first year when he may need extra capital or have a dip in sales. If he can identify any potential periods of negative cash flow, such as during the autumn when schools are not looking to purchase hoodies, then he can make arrangements to access extra cash, such as taking out a bank overdraft. However, cash flow can be very difficult to predict and without experience his forecasts are likely to be inaccurate.

Other factors that may be important for Jaume include the budgets he sets. Jaume must have a clear understanding of his revenue and expenditure budgets as without these he will not be able to construct an accurate cash-flow forecast. His budgets will also act as financial targets that he can set his objectives against.

Overall, cash-flow forecasting is very important to Jaume as many small businesses fail because they are unable to effectively manage this area of the business. However, Jaume must also put in place realistic budgets if he is going to manage his cash flow effectively. The accuracy of his cash-flow forecasts may also depend on the accuracy and extent of his market research.

5 Hands On Puzzles Plc could lower the average costs of its new sustainable bamboo products by purchasing bamboo in bulk. By purchasing bamboo in larger quantities, it will be able to negotiate lower prices. This will lead to economies of scale as the variable price per toy will be lowered. Even with the fixed costs of operating the factory in China the average cost per unit will be lowered.

6 Break-even analysis is an effective business decision-making tool as it allows a business to calculate how many products it will need to produce and sell in order to make a profit. As Hands On Puzzles Plc is a manufacturer it will know how many products it can produce in a given period within its factory. By calculating the break-even point the directors will know the margin of safety and be able to estimate profit at different levels of output. This is particularly important as the company will want to calculate its return on investment. As the company produces over two million puzzles each year, it will have a wide range of product lines. This can make it difficult to accurately calculate the break-even point, if many of the operating costs are being absorbed into other products.

Overall, break-even analysis is an effective business decision-making tool. Hands On Puzzles Plc can use break-even analysis along with its market research to forecast the success of its new bamboo products. However, break-even analysis is most effective when it is used alongside other financial planning tools such as sales forecasting and investment appraisal.

7 Issuing capital through the sale of new shares is an appropriate form of financing the business, considering that it is looking to expand. Issuing new shares through a stock market might attract lots of interest, especially as the company is already floated on the stock market and is profitable. As the business has plans for expansion, potential shareholders will see this as an opportunity to invest in a growing company and demand for the shares could be high. The benefit of raising finance through issuing new shares is that Hands On Puzzles Plc will not be subject to high interest loan repayments.

On the other hand, issuing new shares could dilute the directors' control of the company further. In the long term this could hinder business decision-making, make the company vulnerable to takeover and limit the extent to which profits can be reinvested back into the business because shareholders will expect dividends from the annual profits.

Raising finance through issuing new shares is a relatively safe option for Hands On Puzzles Plc, considering it is are a profitable and growing business. However, gearing has fallen over recent years and this suggests that a lower percentage of the capital in the business has come from borrowing.

In order to balance the capital structure of the business, Hands On Puzzles Plc could choose to borrow the money for the new product line from a bank. However, this may depend on the economic context and how willing the banks are to lend.

Unit 2.3

1 Ratio analysis, such as the gearing ratio, could be used by Sartorial to analyse performance. As the business has ambitions to become market leader it will have to expand over the next five years. The gearing ratio will allow the directors to assess the proportion of the company that is financed through loan capital. By knowing this, the directors will be able to ensure the company's financial position is stable and working capital is not subject to high loan repayments.

2 A business can improve profitability by either lowering its costs or increasing revenue. In 2017 Sartorial's gross profit increased slightly, which suggests that it is making more money on the suits that it sells. However, operating profit fell sharply in 2017 from 33% to 14%. This may be due to capital investment and expansion of the company. If the expansion is successful it is likely that operating profit margins may rise again in 2018 and beyond.

Furthermore, expansion could lead to economies of scale and a fall in cost of sales. If this happens, Sartorial might be able to increase the margins on each suit and this could support growth in gross profit. However, if the plans go ahead to move production to the UK, lead times may fall, but there is a chance that operating costs will continue to rise as running a manufacturing business in the UK is likely to be much more expensive than in the Czech Republic. Overall, the extent to which Sartorial will improve its profitability in the future depends on the success of the brand and its ability to own a larger market share. Nevertheless, gross profit margins are increasing and this demonstrates that its suits are popular. If the company is able to manage its operating costs effectively over the next few years, it is likely that net profit will start to rise again.

3   One internal factor that could lead to the failure of Sartorial is the skills of its employees. As Sartorial offers a bespoke suit service, its employees must be highly skilled. If at any point there is a shortage of highly skilled tailors then customer service and quality could easily fall.
Another factor is the relocation of the manufacturing facility to the UK. Although this will improve operational efficiency, it is highly likely that the new factory will be more expensive to operate. Sartorial is in a competitive market and, if it is unable to pass the additional cost on to its customers through higher prices, then profit margins will start to fall.
Ultimately, the main factor that might lead to business failure within Sartorial is its ability to charge a premium price. Bespoke suits are expensive and each unit must generate sufficient contribution in order to make a profit. The skills of the 'Sartorial Experts' are a key factor in adding value and if the tailors don't have the necessary technical skills and customer service training, customers could easily choose to purchase a suit from a popular high street chain.

4   Quality refers to how well a product is 'fit for purpose' and meets the specification. Quality is also very subjective and can mean different things to different people. This makes it difficult to measure. However, Sartorial Ltd has set a target of 'zero defects or complaints' and this might be one way to measure quality of its suits. If no one complains then this would suggest that they are happy with their purchase and this might mean that Sartorial Ltd is achieving its mission of giving customers a 'suit they are proud to wear'. On the other hand, quality can be difficult to measure. This is because it is subjective and can mean different things to different people. It is also very difficult to determine when providing customers with a service, as is the case when making bespoke suits. Furthermore, as the suits are bespoke it could be very difficult to standardise the product and set a benchmark for the desired quality. As a result, the quality of each suit and customer experience might be difficult to measure.

5   Financial performance can be measured by revenue or profitability. It can also be measured in terms of return on investment and liquidity. The gross profit margin is important for Sartorial Ltd because it gives an indication of the profitability of its main trading activity – selling suits. As the gross profit margin has fallen by 6 percentage points between 2014 and 2015, this could indicate that Sartorial Ltd's direct costs have increased, or that it is not generating as much revenue per sale. Although other profitability measures need to be considered, such as the operating profit and profit for the year, the gross profit margin gives a good indication of the performance before indirect costs have been deducted.
However, financial performance indicators need to be viewed alongside other indicators of long-term success, for example, social responsibility, sustainability, customer satisfaction and product innovation. These concepts take into account other factors such as the environment, learning and growth and the impact on stakeholders, to name but a few.
Without considering these factors when analysing performance, it is unlikely that a business will have sustainable success if it is only focusing on the bottom line. For example, without considering the engagement and motivation of the workforce Sartorial Ltd could lose a key asset in its highly trained tailors, which will have a knock-on effect on profitability.
Overall, Sartorial Ltd must measure profitability because without it the business will struggle to grow and become the UK market leader for bespoke suits. Nevertheless, measuring profitability alone is likely to result in a detrimental effect on long-term performance. The importance of profitability may also depend on the current situation, both internally and externally. For example, a business looking to expand may sacrifice profitability as it reinvests profit into expansion. Profits may also be less important in a recession, where many businesses will be focusing on survival.

Unit 2.4

1   Batch production refers to a technique where products are made in small to medium quantities. Batch production is semi-flexible and involves some automation.

2   £12 000 + £7000 + £5750 = £24 750 / 1300 = £19.04

3   The introduction of new ovens will increase the efficiency of the business by reducing the cooking times and increasing the quantity of food that can be cooked in a given time period. At the moment the capacity of the Cleethorpes restaurant is 65 tables per evening. With the new ovens this could increase the capacity of each restaurant and allow the waiters to serve a greater number of tables. As the hours worked will not increase, labour productivity will rise.

4   Capacity utilisation is the percentage of the total capacity that a business is operating at. If Tasty Tapas is able to maximise capacity utilisation it will reduce the average cost of each meal. This is because waiters will be paid the same for working a shift but will have turned over more tables, generating higher revenues for the business.

5   Outsourcing involves contracting out certain tasks or processes to another business. If Tasty Tapas outsources aspects of food preparation it may allow it to speed up the production of meals and serve more tables if the food is prepared quicker. Not only will this help combat the problem of complaints about slow service, it will also serve more tables. This will increase capacity and the potential to generate higher revenue from serving more customers. Indeed, the maximum capacity of the restaurant may rise from 65 tables per evening.
On the other hand, outsourcing production to another business could reduce the authenticity of the Spanish cuisine. There is also no guarantee that outsourcing food preparation will make the process faster and it could lower the overall quality of food. As a result, the reputation of Tasty Tapas could be damaged.
Overall, the pressure on capacity seems to be an issue with the waiters and not the preparation of food and the new ovens may also alleviate some of the pressure in the kitchens. I do not feel that outsourcing food preparation will 'ease pressure on the kitchens' because it will no longer be in the control of the chefs; therefore more mistakes or faults could be incurred. Nevertheless, outsourcing can help improve efficiency by allowing workers to specialise and outsourcing basic food preparation could reduce costs.

6   One way that Tasty Tapas could improve efficiency is through the installation of its new ovens. The new ovens could reduce cooking time and allow the restaurant to turn over a greater number of tables each evening. This means

that more customers will be coming through the door and the number of meals sold rises. If each restaurant can take more customers this could lead to a competitive advantage because Tasty Tapas could attract customers away from rival restaurants if they know that they will receive a quick service.

Another way that Tasty Tapas could improve efficiency is through a highly trained workforce. A highly trained workforce is less likely to make mistakes, which could cost the business money. Furthermore, a skilled workforce will keep customers happy as customer service is likely to improve too.

Overall, efficiency is closely linked to competitive advantage because efficient businesses are more profitable. However, other factors such as the quality of the food, a unique location and affordable prices are also as important. A competitive advantage cannot easily be copied, so selling unique dishes and excellent food is more likely to lead to a competitive advantage as rivals will find these things hard to replicate. Any business can be efficient in terms of service and turnover of tables.

Unit 2.5

1   One factor that could determine the level of competitiveness in the UK automobile industry is Brexit. If the UK has a trade deal with Europe then it is likely that competitiveness will remain high due to few barriers to trade – exporting to the UK for car manufacturers such as BMW and Mercedes. This is because there will be no trade tariffs and the price to buy a foreign car will not be inflated.

2   The data indicates that some public transport costs, such as rail fares, have trebled in the period between 1987 and 2013, with a sharp rise between 2009 and 2013. This increase may make it less accessible for some parts of the population to access public transport, lowering their mobility and access to jobs. As a result the standard of living in the UK will also fall. As motoring costs have not risen as sharply, this may mean more people opt to use cars instead of public transport. As a result, this will contribute to congestion and pollution, particularly in large cities.

3   The data suggests that government public sector spending increased considerably between 2006 and 2010. However, cutbacks were made between 2010 and 2013. The growth in spending may have included spending on infrastructure and subsidising public transport. This may have removed barriers to entry and made it easier for new public transport companies to enter the market. This may have increased consumer choice and improved the standard of public transport in the UK. If the government were investing in infrastructure, this would create a number of opportunities for contract firms to build and improve roads and rail networks. This would create more demand in the market and opportunities for growth in heavy construction and road maintenance. The competitive rivalry within the industry will be very high as these companies bid to win the government contracts to build new roads and rail links.

4   With the potential of in-car marketing it is likely that legislation will be introduced to ensure passengers are safe while travelling. As most legislation is in place to either protect consumers or employees, it is likely that there will be new legislation to govern in-car marketing. Furthermore, as cars become safer through active health monitoring and comprehensive vehicle tracking, legislation may be brought in to ensure that this information is shared with the highways agency or the police in order to track down criminals and erratic drivers. Technology advancement will benefit manufacturers as innovation leads to new cars and demand for the latest models. Nevertheless, legislation will often restrict some business practices and ensure technological advancement is safe for customers.

5   Sustained growth of 2% GDP between 2017 and 2020 will be good for UK businesses. A steady rate of growth means that the economy will steadily grow throughout this period. This will mean more products and services are being bought. As a result, this will encourage start-ups and employment will rise. Therefore, the overall standard of living will increase in the UK. Furthermore, as growth is fairly gradual at a rate of 2%, this will make it easier for the government to control inflation. Businesses and consumers can manage steady increase in RPI, leading to a stable economy.

Nevertheless, the economic forecast for other countries is not as hopeful. In particular, there is an expected slowdown in large economies, such as China and India, which have been growing fast over the past ten years. A slowdown in these countries could have a negative impact on the UK as many of our industries are linked, such as financial services and tourism.

Overall, forecast growth of 2% is good for the UK. However, forecasts change and can be inaccurate. During this period there could be any number of internal or external shocks that affect the UK economy and this means it is very hard to guarantee sustainable growth. Furthermore, growth may depend on other countries that the UK trades with and not all businesses may experience growth. For example, UK exporters may find it difficult if demand from China slows. In order to maintain growth of 2% the government will have to use a range of policies to help correct any fluctuations in the business cycle. This may include fiscal or monetary policy. International trade policy will also be very important if the UK is to maintain good trading relationships with other large economies.

Unit 3.1

1   One factor that may influence the strategy adopted by Right Plumbing Ltd is the political factors around renewable energy. Political factors refer to government policy and how this can affect markets and business activity. For example, it is possible that the government will want to encourage households to adopt renewable energy in the future and may therefore subsidise this technology. This could make the market more attractive for businesses like Right Plumbing Ltd by lowering the cost of the technology and boosting demand.

2   A SWOT analysis is a business decision-making tool that helps a business identify strengths, weaknesses, opportunities and threats. For example, the investment of £1 billion by the UK government into renewable energy should be considered a considerable opportunity. As Right Plumbing looks to enter the renewable energy market it can evaluate its own strengths in order to understand whether they are suited to the market. Furthermore, by understanding the opportunities and threats in the market it will be able to make a decision on whether it is likely to be successful.

3   Political factors will have a considerable influence on Right Plumbing as Jeremy looks to expand his business. The decision to invest £1 billion into renewable energy is a political decision aimed at influencing homeowners and businesses that work in the energy market. The investment could lead to subsidies for customers or businesses and this is likely to increase the demand but also the supply in the renewable energy market.

Economic factors will also be a considerable influence on Right Plumbing. No matter what fiscal policy the government employs to increase the use of renewable energy, if the economy is in a recession, people are unlikely to invest in green energy unless it will save them money in the short term. Renewable energy is a long-term investment so customers are more likely to put off investment. This would significantly reduce Right Plumbing's potential for success in this new market. Overall, political factors have a significant influence on businesses like Right Plumbing as the energy market is highly regulated.

4   Diversification involves entering a new market with a new product or service. At the moment Right Plumbing is considering two options, the second being diversification into the renewable energy market. The dangers of a diversification strategy are that it is high risk because Jeremy has little experience in this sector and Right Plumbing does not have a reputation for installing this technology.

Expanding the current range of business services across Lancashire is an example of market development. This is a much safer option, as Jeremy would not have to change his business model and the expansion would require little capital investment, simply the recruitment of additional contractors. Nevertheless, the renewable energy market has considerable growth potential as identified by Jeremy. With the UK government investing £1 billion over a ten-year period, the risks of diversification might be worth it if there is considerable opportunity for growth and profit.

5   A sustainable competitive advantage is one that is unique, not easily copied and may take a long time to achieve. One way that Right Plumbing Ltd could develop a sustainable competitive advantage is through innovation. Jeremy is looking to provide customers with renewable energy such as solar panels and wind turbines. Although his business has not developed this technology he may be able to find a unique way to bring this technology to households in an affordable way. Although his business may be one of the first companies to do this effectively, it will be difficult to protect unless he can develop a process that he is able to patent. Another factor that may lead to competitive advantage is the reputation that his business has for delivering excellent customer service. This reputation becomes the brand image associated with his business and a good reputation can take a long time for a business to develop. However, it can also be damaged very quickly. Customer service may also lead to a sustainable competitive advantage if customers associate his business with excellent service, but it does not mean that other companies cannot imitate this in the long term.

Overall, the reputation of Right Plumbing Ltd for excellent customer service is, perhaps, the most likely source of competitive advantage. However, it is very difficult for the business to protect this position as service is something that all businesses can develop. It does not depend on unique knowledge or skills. The sustainability of this competitive advantage may depend on Jeremy's ability to protect this position. One way to do this might be to achieve a quality mark for customer service. This may involve the business being assessed by an external body. This, along with the positive publicity, will reinforce its reputation and strengthen its strategic position.

Unit 3.2

1   A diseconomy of scale is a negative impact on a business that it might experience as it grows in scale, often leading to costs rising and inefficiencies. One diseconomy that Cloudburst Plc might experience is poor communication. As the company merges with Interact Gaming Ltd there will be far more employees to communicate with and this will make effective communication more difficult, leading to slower communication and miscommunication. This problem might be amplified due to the fact that Interact Gaming Ltd is a Chinese firm with a different language and culture.

2   Cloudburst Plc is a public limited company, which means that it has external shareholders who have invested in the company. These shareholders will expect a return on their investment and appreciation of the share price. Cloudburst must invest in new products and markets if it is to increase shareholder value as its current successful MMORPG game will not generate revenue forever – all products have a life cycle. Considering this game accounts for 70% of all revenue, it is important that Cloudburst looks for other areas of growth to satisfy shareholders in the long term.

3   One reason why Cloudburst may have chosen not to grow organically is that organic growth is slow. Cloudburst may be looking to find a replacement for its current MMORPG which accounts for 70% of revenue. If this product loses popularity, profits will soon start to fall. Another potential reason not to opt for organic growth is that Cloudburst wants to move into the smartphone app game market. It can take time to develop the expertise and build a reputation in a new market; instead, Cloudburst has the opportunity to merge with a business that already has the expertise and reputation. Considering that computer games have an 18-month life cycle, it is important that any move into a new market is successful quickly. Overall, the fact that Interact is a Chinese company might be the most significant reason for external growth. Merging with a Chinese company will make it much easier for Cloudburst to adopt a market development strategy and enter the Asian market for computer games.

4   The first option that Cloudburst Plc has considered is the merger with Interact Gaming Ltd. As Interact Gaming Ltd is a Chinese business, this will help Cloudburst Plc break into the Chinese market, and other Eastern markets, where there is a high rate of economic growth and demand for leisure products such as computer games. By merging with Interact, Cloudburst Plc will own the brand and this will make it easier for it to launch new products that are immediately accepted by Chinese consumers. Furthermore, Cloudburst Plc will have the intellectual capital of the company and the creative design skills of Interact's employees. However, both companies currently operate in very different markets and have significant differences in approach and culture. If the merger is to result in long-term success for Cloudburst Plc, the two businesses will have to be integrated effectively.

The second option of a partnership with a leading console manufacturer is very attractive as it will give Cloudburst Plc a USP and competitive advantage over its rivals. This is because its games will be promoted alongside the game console. As a result, Cloudburst Plc's reputation will be enhanced and potentially help it break into new markets where the console is sold. As games designers supply the games for console manufacturers, a close partnership is likely to benefit Cloudburst Plc and help it gain an advantage over other game designers. This is the 'architecture' that leads to a sustainable competitive advantage and refers to the relationships a business has with its stakeholders that are difficult to develop and copy. Overall, the strategy that is most likely to lead to long-term success is the merger with Interact Gaming Ltd. This is because the move will not only help Cloudburst Plc adopt a market development strategy, but it will also improve innovation across the company, which is of key importance to a business in an industry that is driven by creativity and technological advancement. The success of the merger will, however, depend on how well these two businesses can integrate – for example, how well the Chinese designers settle into the Cloudburst Plc way of doing things. In order for the long-term success to be guaranteed, it is important for the directors of Cloudburst Plc to have a clear vision and ensure this is understood and accepted by all areas of the company.

Unit 3.3

1

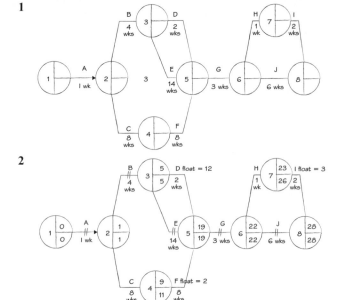

2

3 Quantitative sales forecasting involves using back data to extrapolate a sales trend line in order to estimate future sales figures. Cloudburst may want to use quantitative sales forecasting to forecast future sales revenue for its MMORPG. As 70% of sales come from this product Cloudburst will be very interested in future sales projections as it will require the revenue from this game to finance future projects, such as the merger with Interact Gaming.

4 Increasing advertising of current products: $(0.8 \times 25\,000 = £20\,000) + (0.2 \times 2000 = £400) = £20\,400 - £3\,000 = £17\,400$

Launch new product range: $(0.7 \times 50\,000 = £35\,000) + (0.3 \times 0 = 0) = £35\,000 - £5000 = £30\,000$

Launching a new product range is the best option.

5 Uber's partnership with Facebook may help it increase its competitiveness because it creates a barrier for other companies that want to enter the market. Should other companies wish to start up a taxi hailing app, the link with Facebook, a leading social media platform, limits the routes other firms can take to reach customers online. This move also gives Uber greater bargaining power. The partnership makes it even easier to use Uber's service, and therefore, reduces the bargaining power of customers because Uber is the easiest and most accessible option.

Nevertheless, the partnership with Facebook would mean sharing some revenue and Uber must compare this option to other investments. The ARR of 4% may be attractive, but this should be compared to other investments. A drawback of the partnership is the negative publicity the business has received. Uber will have to consider the impact the partnership may have on CSR and how this could affect the long-term success of the company. For example, Uber should consider Carroll's CSR pyramid and its 'legal' and 'philanthropic' responsibilities. It is possible that Uber may have to pay legal costs due to the pending lawsuits. For this reason, Uber may consider the payback of this investment and whether it may need these funds within the next five years in order to pay legal fees.

Overall, Uber is a private limited company driven by profit. The partnership with Facebook helps it protect its market share and improves competitiveness and is therefore the right choice. However, in the long term this may depend on the popularity of Facebook as a social media site and how the partnership is perceived and valued by Uber's customers. If few customers access Uber's services through Facebook the partnership may have little value.

Unit 3.4

1 One factor that may influence corporate culture at Cloudburst Plc is the routines and rituals within the company. This might simply involve how meetings are run or the process of developing a computer game. For example, the pace of game development might become a problem when the two companies merge because Cloudburst employees were used to taking their time to ensure everything was of the highest quality. As a result, the culture may be less amenable to quick turnaround of new games.

2 One factor that may lead to Cloudburst's stakeholders considering the business ethical is the way it treats its employees. Employers have a responsibility to care for the well-being of their employees. This might include fair pay, safe working conditions and flexible working. As Cloudburst merges with Interact, employees might fear for their jobs. In order to be considered an ethical business, Cloudburst should approach the merger and employee contracts/roles in an open and transparent way.

Other factors that could contribute towards a reputation for being an ethical business could include the way it markets its products. Cloudburst should market its games with the correct age rating and ensure the content of the games is appropriate for the target market, often young children and teenagers. Overall, the factors that contribute to Cloudburst being considered ethical may differ across stakeholder groups. Employees may have a very different perspective to the people playing the games or the companies that regulate the computer game industry. Overall, an ethical business is one that does its best not to create negative externalities in the market and to operate in an honest way.

3 One reason why the directors at Cloudburst Plc may find it difficult to integrate the two companies is that they are likely to have very different cultures. For example, at Cloudburst Plc big decisions are kept with project managers and this might represent a power. However, at Interact Gaming Ltd game designers have much more freedom, perhaps representative of a role culture. Culture can be very difficult to change as it is embedded in people's values and beliefs. Another factor that might make integration difficult is the fact that the employees of Interact Gaming Ltd are used to a different organisational structure. As Interact Gaming Ltd previously adopted a functional structure it may not be used to working in a product structure. This may cause problems because the employees may not know how their roles relate to those of other employees and the different ways of working required from a product-orientated approach instead of a functional approach, such as a dedicated marketing team supporting all areas of the business. Culture is a key factor in mergers failing; this is partly because it is not an obvious or tangible factor and secondly, changing culture is difficult because it is rooted in people's attitudes and beliefs.

4 As Cloudburst is a public limited company, the decisions of the directors will be considerably influenced by its shareholders. Shareholders want to see a return on their investment through appreciation of the share price and dividends. The merger with Interact led to share prices rising by 30p and this will satisfy shareholders. However, some companies fail following a merger and the shareholders will hope to see new product launches in the coming months.

Cloudburst may also be influenced by the stakeholder perspective. This perspective dictates that a business focuses on the interests of wider stakeholders and not simply the short-term profit motive of shareholders. There is little to suggest that Cloudburst would adopt this perspective; however, it has high standards of quality and there is no indication that employees have lost their jobs through the merger process. This gives us some idea that Cloudburst does consider the perspective of employees and customers. Overall, all Plcs are influenced by their shareholders because they would not exist without the capital from the owners.

Unit 3.5 and Unit 3.6

1 $8 / 62 \times 100 = 12.90\%$ absenteeism rate

2 $2m / (2.8m + 2m) \times 100 = 41.6\%$

3 Winstanley and Walker could use labour productivity to assess the performance of the company. The labour productivity ratio is output / total number of workers' hours for the period. The labour productivity ratio will allow the directors to calculate the efficiency and labour costs. This is important to know, considering that output has increased by 300%. Monitoring labour productivity will give an indication of the performance of the workforce.

4 Winstanley and Walker is going through a period of significant change. The company has grown significantly and is taking on new production processes to increase production of its chocolates. Scenario planning will help it identify possible scenarios in the future and this means that it can plan for such eventualities. For example, labour turnover is high and absenteeism has risen to 12%; scenario planning may help the company identify the issues should key chocolatiers leave and identify a strategy for how it could replace these key employees. Scenario planning may also help the company use its market research to plan ahead. As prices of cocoa continue to increase over the coming five years, Winstanley and Walker will need to put in place contingency plans to ensure it is able to absorb these costs into its operations and pricing strategies. No matter what scenario planning a company does, there will always be external factors and changes in the market that are hard to plan for. Scenario planning is a useful process for managers to use so long as it is part of risk management and succession planning.

5 A key change at Winstanley and Walker is the move towards automated production. Originally the company has based its heritage on luxury hand-made chocolates and this has now changed. Some employees may not be happy with these changes and this could be linked to the high labour turnover and absenteeism over the past few months. All employees will need to be trained in the new working practices. This brings uncertainty as many employees will know their current job very well. Furthermore, any sort of change to working practices could lead to a fall in productivity. Overall, the changes at Winstanley and Walker are likely to affect the culture of the business. The increased output of 300% and a focus on just a few lines is likely to make the company feel more corporate and less of a family-run enterprise.

6 Labour productivity is a measure of output per employee over a given period. At the end of August labour productivity in the factory was 800 boxes of chocolates per employee vs 363 boxes at the start of July. This shows a significant increase and possibly an indication that the workforce is more effective. However, as the company has been introducing aspects of automation in this period, it is unlikely that the two figures are representative considering production processes will have changed. Absenteeism has also increased from 3% to 2% in the same period. Absenteeism is perhaps the most significant issue at present because it is an indication that employees are not happy. Winstanley and Walker cannot afford to lose its highly skilled chocolatiers and this is why it would be more beneficial for the company to carry out an investigation into absenteeism rates and the reasons for it. If Winstanley and Walker understands these issues then it can do something to boost employee motivation and ensure it retains its best workers. An investigation into productivity at this point may be of little use to the managers until the new production techniques and ways of working have been embedded.

Unit 4.1 and Unit 4.2

1 CompTech Sports might use the HDI to help it choose an appropriate location for a new factory. HDI gives an indication of the standard of living in a country. CompTech could use this information to understand the sort of labour costs associated with operating in a country or the potential skills within the local workforce. As a result, it will be able to identify a country that has the characteristics to set up an additional factory for the production of its sports equipment.

2 Protectionism involves the political strategies a nation might use to influence international trade and protect domestic businesses from foreign competitors. CompTech Sports is known for good quality at reasonable prices. It also exports to a number of international markets, including the USA and Europe. If these countries put up trade barriers, such as tariffs and quotas, then the price of CompTech's products would rise. This would make it less competitive in international markets and demand could fall.

3 One factor that CompTech should consider when deciding which countries to develop trade links with is economic growth. If economic growth is high, then so will be incomes and demand for products. As nations become wealthier, citizens spend more time and money on leisure pursuits. As CompTech is a specialist sports manufacturer, this is a real indication of a profitable market. Another factor that CompTech should consider when choosing nations to trade with is the exchange rate. Political unrest or conflict is just one factor that could lead to an unstable exchange rate where the value of the currency fluctuates a lot. When this happens it is difficult to predict demand and sales. There is an even greater risk if trade deals are agreed at a fixed rate or payments made in the foreign currency. Overall, the main factor that CompTech Sports should consider when trading internationally is how easy it is to get its products to the end user. To understand this, CompTech Sports should investigate the trading laws and infrastructure of countries to ensure there are no obstacles or hidden costs that might make its products uncompetitive.

4 Some economic indicators suggest that Latvia might be a good country in which to set up a new factory. For example, the HDI trends for Latvia are higher than similar countries in the region. This would suggest that there is more economic growth. Furthermore, life expectancy and mean years of schooling have also been rising since 1990 and this is another indication that there is growth in the country. Economic growth is important because it suggests that there will be a skilled workforce to employ and improved infrastructure to support international trade. However, these figures tell us little as we would expect life expectancy to rise for all countries between 1990 and 2015. Apart from economic indicators suggesting that Latvia has a growing economy, it is also much closer to a number of international markets that CompTech may choose to trade with. Setting up a factory in Latvia would potentially make it easier to export to Eastern Europe and Asian markets. Despite these positives, CompTech has a skilled workforce and a 'made in the UK' brand that many international customers will respect. If a new factory is opened in Latvia it might be difficult to ensure its employees have the same level of skills and the UK brand could be tarnished. Before CompTech opens a factory abroad, it should carefully consider the impact this would have on branding and marketing. A factory in Latvia may help lower production costs, but this will create a trade-off against the reputation the company has in its current markets.

5   Merging with a small Californian company would give the company greater exposure in the US market, especially if production could be moved to California. Production in the USA would negate the impact of the exchange rate and shipping costs. The expertise of the US market gained from the smaller manufacturer may also help CompTech build trade links and find new suppliers. However, as the company is only small, it may not have the capacity to take on production of CompTech's sports equipment.

Another option to maximise sales in the USA would be to develop contracts with a range of US retailers. This might be a profitable move as it could ensure CompTech products are stocked nationwide. However, large retailers will often want substantial discounts and exclusivity and this could force prices down.

Overall, a merger with a local sports manufacturer in California is possibly the best option. The Californian manufacturer will have its own branding and CompTech could use this to gain trust from US customers. The exchange rate and shipping costs will be a key cost for any US customer purchasing a CompTech Sports product from the UK, so avoiding these costs could have a significant impact on the competitiveness of CompTech's products in the USA. The success of this strategy will very much depend on the potential to move production to the USA and the success of the merger between the two companies. Mergers often face difficulties when two business cultures come together and this is something that will need to be managed carefully.

Unit 4.3 and Unit 4.4

1   One way that CompTech Sports could improve government revenue in Latvia is by paying corporation tax. If CompTech Sports is successful then it will generate profit, a proportion of which should be paid to the Latvian government. The new factory will also employ Latvian workers and their earnings will be subject to income tax; again this will contribute to government tax revenue.

2   One cultural factor that CompTech will need to consider is uncertainty avoidance. Chinese businesses have a lower threshold for risk as identified by Hofstede's cultural dimensions. This means that when trading with Chinese firms, CompTech must be able to provide guarantees and certainty. This might involve guaranteeing future prices and shipping times.

3   Targeting the lacrosse market in China could be a profitable venture for CompTech. Lacrosse requires safety equipment and CompTech has considerable experience in developing this type of product. As a result, CompTech could target the Chinese market with a wide range of lacrosse equipment. Incomes are also rising fast in China and soon China will become the world's largest economy. If growth continues, the lacrosse market could become a profitable market for CompTech, providing it can develop a successful line of equipment. However, lacrosse is still a niche market in China and CompTech has limited experience trading in this country. Developing a new line of products will also be expensive and there is no guarantee of success. Overall, targeting the Chinese lacrosse market is a good idea. The market will continue to grow and has tripled in the last four years. At present competition may not be high and it will be easier to enter the market now than at a later point when the market is saturated.

4   A polycentric marketing strategy involves developing and marketing products differently, based on the needs of the local market. The limitations for CompTech of adopting a polycentric strategy is that this will incur additional costs in marketing and production. Evidence suggests that the Chinese market would require alterations in the size of sports equipment and a change to the way products are marketed (colours, etc). A polycentric strategy might help adapt to the needs of an international market, but it will limit the economies of scale required to compete on a global scale.

5   New legislation on product safety standards will generally lead to costs being incurred by manufacturers. Safety legislation means that products have to be redesigned and tested by safety regulators before they can be approved. In the case of sports equipment, safety standards are very important and considerable investment will be required to ensure standards are met. However, CompTech Sports operates in the UK and the USA where safety standards are very high. It is unlikely that new legislation imposed by the Latvian authorities will surpass these standards. Nevertheless, there will still be costs incurred.

Import tariffs may affect CompTech Sports if it purchases raw materials or components of its sports equipment outside of Latvia. As CompTech Sports trades internationally there is a significant chance that this will be the case. New import tariffs may therefore increase the costs of production at the Latvian factory. CompTech Sports could counteract the import tariff by switching to local suppliers. As Latvia has a growing infrastructure there is potential for CompTech to find an appropriate supplier in the local region.

Overall, import tariffs might be the biggest concern for CompTech. This is mainly because any protectionist actions by a government are usually met with similar actions abroad. If foreign countries increase protectionism it could lead to CompTech's products becoming less competitive if a tariff is placed on them. CompTech can either choose to absorb these costs by lowering their production costs or finding other ways to reduce costs further.